NATO AND THE CHANGING WORLD ORDER:

An Appraisal by Scholars and Policymakers

Edited by
Kenneth W. Thompson

Volume IV
In the Miller Center Series on
A New World Order
made possible through the generosity
of
Ambassador George C. McGhee

UNIVERSITY
PRESS OF
AMERICA

Lanham • New York • London

The Miller Center

University of Virginia

Copyright © 1996 by
University Press of America,® Inc.
4720 Boston Way
Lanham, Maryland 20706

3 Henrietta Street
London WC2E 8LU England

Copublished by arrangement with
The Miller Center of Public Affairs,
University of Virginia

The views expressed by the author(s) of this publication do not necessarily represent the opinions of the Miller Center. We hold to Jefferson's dictum that: "Truth is the proper and sufficient antagonist to error, and has nothing to fear from the conflict, unless by human interposition, disarmed of her natural weapons, free argument and debate."

Library of Congress Cataloging-in-Publication Data

NATO and the changing world order : an appraisal by scholars and policymakers / edited by Kenneth W. Thompson.
    p.   cm.
1. North Atlantic Treaty Organization. 2. Peaceful change (International relations) 3. Security, International. I. Thompson, Kenneth W.
JX 1393.N67N335   1996   355'.031--dc20   95-46219 CIP

ISBN: 0-7618-0202-9 (cloth: alk. ppr.)
ISBN: 0-7618-0203-7 (pbk: alk. ppr.)

S. Nelson Drew

Joseph J. Kruzel

In Memory of
Colonel S. Nelson Drew, USAF
and
Deputy Assistant Secretary of Defense Joseph J. Kruzel
who gave their lives
in the quest for peace
and in the pursuit
of national and international security

Contents

I. THE UNITED STATES, NATO, AND EUROPE

II. IS NATO OBSOLETE?

CONTENTS

III. THE ENLARGEMENT OF NATO: CHANGING FACES

IV. THE FUTURE OF NATO

Foreword

A NEW NATO FOR A NEW ERA*

To say that we are living in the best of times and the worst of times is undoubtedly an exaggeration. But it is a fact that we are confronted with two contradictory realities: on the one hand, the resurgence of democracy following the West's historic Cold War triumph, and on the other a reemergence of war in the heart of Europe as a seemingly acceptable instrument of policy. Thus, at the very moment we should be basking in the glow of success, we are confronted with nightmare images from Europe's past—images of "Sarajevo," of the "Balkan powder keg," and of man's inhumanity to man.

A gap is emerging between our vision of a new international order and these grim realities. We witness "peacekeepers" with no real peace to keep; "nonpartisan" sanctions that favor the aggressor; mass murder, the strangulation of cities and the expulsion of people from their homes.

And yet, I do not believe we should succumb to pessimism, any more than we should have been carried away with euphoria in 1989. The fact is that we are in a transitional period between the collapse of an old order and the establishment of a new one. Following a period in which international relationships were virtually frozen, the world has suddenly become full of possibilities, both good and bad. The question is whether we will demonstrate the vision, courage,

---

A speech made by former Secretary General Manfred Wörner at the National Press Club, Washington, D.C., 6 October 1993.

and leadership of the generation of Truman, Adenauer, and Monnet, or whether instead we will succumb to the risk avoidance and selfish nationalism which so disastrously characterized Western leadership following World War I. This is the task before us, and history will judge our generation by how we respond to it.

We enjoy a tremendous advantage over previous generations— namely, a structure of international institutions and an ingrained pattern of international cooperation which can enable us to build a better and more peaceful order in the era to come—*if* we use this advantage properly. That remains our challenge—the main challenge of our times. We cannot leave the world to the forces of disorder and limit ourselves to safeguarding our own borders. Neither we in Europe, nor you in the United States, can afford such passivity, not only because it goes against our principles but also because it goes against our national self-interests. In the world of today you simply cannot hope to live in security if you are surrounded by chaos.

We cannot meet this challenge without NATO; to master each and every major security task of our time you need NATO. To provide stability in a world that has become more unstable, you need NATO. To prevent, manage, and resolve major crises and conflicts in the wider Europe, you need NATO. To prevent Europe from sliding back into renationalization and fragmentation, you need NATO. To keep transatlantic relations working smoothly and effectively, you need NATO. To face the new kinds of risks emerging from the proliferation of weapons of mass destruction, from mass migration, and from extremism, you need NATO.

So this Alliance is not sustained merely by nostalgic memories or by purely philosophical reflections on common values and destinies. It survives, indeed prospers, because it serves the concrete requirements of its member nations in North America and Europe.

I am aware, however, that a different view has been expressed by some in this country, to whom the international community's failure to prevent or reverse the conflict in ex-Yugoslavia is a demonstration of NATO's irrelevance today. I reject this argument. As much as I am personally disappointed with the way this crisis has been handled, I think we have to recognize that the international community was unprepared for the different security environment with which we have been confronted in the post-Cold War era, just as the West was initially unprepared for the type of challenge Soviet power confronted us with in the years immediately following World War II. The argument that we should disband NATO because of Yugoslavia is masochistic in the extreme; it is as if we were to banish doctors for the persistence of illness, or abolish police for the persistence of crime. What we need to do, obviously, is to draw the lessons of Yugoslavia so that there will be no more Yugoslavias.

It goes without saying that one lesson is that NATO must be used differently, and indeed that NATO itself must continue to adapt to a wholly different set of challenges from those we faced during the Cold War. That is why we are holding an important NATO summit in January, upon the initiative of President Clinton. Today, I would like to point the way toward NATO's agenda for change by addressing three questions:

- Why NATO?
- Why the United States in NATO?
- What kind of NATO do we need for this new era?

I. *Why NATO*

First, in a world full of crises and conflicts, where history moves fast and is full of surprises, NATO still serves its main strategic purpose: to maintain the common defense and security of its member countries. Today it does so with fewer troops and at lower cost. NATO serves as the insurance policy against the remaining risks and new dangers. Once dissolved, an effective Alliance could not be recreated overnight.

Second, the transatlantic relationship is the most stable and valuable geopolitical asset on the globe today, bringing together the world's two largest trading zones and the two regions with the greatest global outreach and sense of global responsibilities. How could we seriously hope to achieve a more stable world without a strategic alliance of these two major power centers? Where else but in NATO could they coordinate their policies and pool their capabilities to deal with major security challenges, as was done so successfully in the Gulf War? Moreover, the countries of Central and Eastern Europe already rely upon the stabilizing influence that the Alliance exerts around its periphery. The end of NATO would increase the risk of conflict in Europe dramatically.

Third, one of the greatest achievements of the Atlantic Alliance has been to put an end to the bad habits of European power politics. There was simply no longer any need for secret pacts and cordial, or not so cordial, ententes. The American presence provided for a stable balance between former rivals and enemies. It even made possible the realization of German unification without a major crisis in West European politics. By contrast, the dissolution of NATO or the disengagement of the United States from Europe could and would undermine the European integration process. This would be damaging not only for Western Europe and the United States, but would also gravely affect the political and economic transition of the countries of Central and Eastern Europe, which are urgently looking for links to the political, economic, and security institutions of the West.

Fourth, NATO is the *only* organization that possesses the right package of political-military tools for effective crisis management. It provides the bedrock of "hard" security on which any new security order must be based. Only NATO has the means to turn political declarations into coherent action, a fact that the United Nations, after decades of viewing us with suspicion, has recognized in calling upon NATO to perform a range of peacekeeping functions in the former Yugoslavia. Which other instrument could you turn to in a crisis situation, assuming the political will was there to act? Which other institution could offer the integrated structure and the political/military consultation mechanism?

The Yugoslav crisis demonstrates not NATO's irrelevance but its vitality and its potential. For the first time in our history we are both acting out of area and, through our commitment to conduct air strikes, poised for actual combat operations. NATO has offered its support to the United Nations, and it has done everything the U.N. has asked; and the Alliance has done so efficiently. We are enforcing the embargo at sea and the no-fly zone in the air. We have supplied UNPROFOR with command and control equipment and we have coordinated our military planning with the United Nations. We have also offered the United Nations our protective air power in case of attack against UNPROFOR, and we are prepared to use air strikes, if necessary, to relieve strangulation of Sarajevo and other areas. All of these tasks are being performed with the professionalism and dedication you expect from this Alliance.

II. Why the United States in NATO

A strong NATO is not only important for Europe but is also critical to American security interests. The United States will not be able to pursue domestic renewal successfully without peace and stability in Europe, a region where your geopolitical stake remains paramount. Even excluding Russia, it embodies the largest collection of military power and potential. It is also a key geographical strategic and logistical link to the Middle East and Persian Gulf areas. NATO members, including the United States, hold six of the seven G7 seats, make up 16 of 22 members of the IMF, and hold three of the five permanent seats in the United Nations.

Moreover, America and Europe have never been more dependent on each other for their economic well-being, and that dependency is steadily growing. NATO Allies are collectively the United States's largest trading partners; two-way trade between the United States and the EC in goods and services was close to $400 billion last year alone. U.S. exports to Europe and European investments in the United States have created millions of American jobs.

Since it is obvious that the United States cannot prosper amid chaos and conflict, it needs the Alliance more than ever as the most important vehicle of U.S. influence in Europe and the main instrument of U.S. leadership. But it is important to understand that NATO helps protect America's manifold interests in Europe in return for a relatively small U.S. investment. NATO costs the United States proportionally little for great return, and the good news is that those costs are going down. Planned U.S. cuts in European-based forces are at least double the total reductions by all other NATO nations combined. By 1995 the burden of stationing U.S. forces in Europe will be cut by more than half from Cold War levels. By being part of an integrated military structure, the United States has secured major weapons contracts and multiplies its defense investment and capability. What the United States appears to "pay for NATO" is in fact a bargain for U.S. geostrategic interests that would require protection with or without the Alliance.

Indeed, America's most important stake in Europe is peace. Here, there is one simple lesson: whenever Europe and the United States go separate ways, they pay a terrible price. Twice in this century the United States has withdrawn from Europe at its peril. Twice this century the Atlantic democracies have been brutally reminded that their security is indivisible. These are lessons that we simply cannot afford to relearn.

So those voices are clearly wrong that advise Americans to declare victory, pack up, and go home. A superpower simply cannot take a sabbatical from history, not even a vacation. We need U.S. leadership. Without the leadership of the United States there will be no leadership at all, and most likely no meaningful action in crisis situations. Either you meet crises head-on, or they will jump you from behind. It is therefore infinitely better to remain in Europe and prevent wars (with reduced strength of course) than to leave Europe and have to return to fight again.

So what does the United States derive from the Atlantic Alliance? Security for economic growth, capabilities for multilateral coalition-building, and influence where it counts the most.

III. *The Way Ahead: A New NATO for a New Era*

Contrary to what some have argued, NATO has not stood still since the end of the Cold War. This Alliance has changed more than any other international institution in the last three years and remains a state-of-the-art model. We have had to accept two new missions to meet the demands of a vastly changed security environment: (a) projection of stability to the East, and (b) crisis management. We have adopted a new strategy and force posture. We have started to strengthen our European pillar. Most important, we have established close relations with our former adversaries by creating the North Atlantic Cooperation Council, and we have started participating in crisis management beyond our borders. So the slogan "out of area or out of business" is obviously out-of-date. We *are* acting out of area and we *are* very much in business.

Still, we need to continue to adapt the Alliance to play its role in stabilizing Europe. Let me list four main areas that shall be at the top of the Summit's agenda. The first and most important area where change must come is in further developing our ability *to project stability to the East.* Security is the oxygen of democracy; if we want our new democratic partners in the East to survive and to flourish, then we must seek to give concrete meaning to our 1991 Declaration in Rome that "our own security is inseparably linked to that of all the other States of Europe." This means that we must transform the North Atlantic Cooperation Council to address the real security needs of our partners through stepped-up consultations and joint action in peacekeeping.

Moreover, we should now open a concrete perspective for expanded NATO membership. This will be a lengthy road and we need to act gradually, carefully, and flexibly, but the important point now is to commit ourselves in principle to begin traveling down that road. Doing so, even if enlargement is not for today, would increase the stability of the whole of Europe, particularly if we are also willing to enhance fundamentally our security relationship with Russia. The same holds true for Ukraine and other cooperation partners. Nobody will be isolated. We intend to build bridges and not barricades.

Second, we must achieve a *more balanced sharing of burdens and responsibilities* between the two sides of the Atlantic. As Secretary of State Christopher has emphasized, the choice cannot be between unilateral American action and no action at all. Public opinion in the United States can rightly criticize Europeans for failing at times to defend adequately their own interests. The result could be a more reluctant U.S. leadership and less involvement of the United States at the very moment when crises and conflicts are multiplying. Hence, it is important for Western Europeans to clearly demonstrate their willingness and capacity to do more. This means that a further development of the WEU as the European pillar of the Alliance is not a threat to NATO's survival but rather the precondition for ensuring its long-term future.

Third, we must *further develop the Alliance's capabilities, forces, structures, and procedures for crisis management, peacekeeping, and peacemaking.* And we must achieve a more structured relationship with the United Nations in order to generate the conditions that are essential for future crisis management—namely, a clear-cut mandate, a better coordination between humanitarian and peacekeeping/peacemaking missions, and a unitary chain of command.

We must understand and take to heart the lessons of our collective failure in the former Yugoslavia:

- We must consult among ourselves far in advance about potential future conflicts and undertake the necessary planning for such contingencies.

- We must intervene with diplomacy backed by force, and the credible resolve to use it if necessary, at an *early* stage of crises so as not to be confronted, as we are today in ex-Yugoslavia, with a much higher cost of reversing aggression.

- We must be willing to contemplate limited military options for limited diplomatic objectives, so as not to be hamstrung as we are today, with an all-or-nothing mind-set.

- We must, if we are not willing to help the victim of aggression, enable him to defend himself.

- We must define the strategic objectives of our actions as early and clearly as possible.

- We must avoid situations in which our own troops become hostages, thereby preventing military action.

- Above all, we must possess the will to utilize the instruments available, amongst them our Alliance.

Fourth and finally, we must *maintain a significant level of well-trained and well-equipped armed forces.* The stabilization of defense budgets is now urgent if we are to avoid a kind of free-fall, structural disarmament that would rapidly deprive our member nations of meaningful military capabilities for many years to come and weaken seriously our conventional deterrence posture. In handling any crisis, what you have available very much determines what options you have: the fewer deployable forces, then the fewer options for decisionmakers and the less credibility accorded subsequent actions.

I firmly believe that our generation still has a better opportunity than any other generation ever had in the long and bloody history of this century: to build a peaceful Euro-Atlantic order. If we fail, this opportunity may never return. We can only succeed if we stay together and understand that our security is indivisible. Your great and still vital nation has an enormously important mission of historic dimensions. We need your presence and we need your leadership. But you also need Europe, for it is only by moving forward together that we can hope to shape a better world and a better future for our peoples.

Manfred Wörner
Secretary General of NATO, 1988-1994

Preface

In our planning for a volume on NATO and the changing world order, we conceived primarily of a study that would deal with the more controversial issues concerning the future of NATO. As we launched the study, I turned to a former graduate student who wrote his dissertation under my supervision, Colonel S. Nelson Drew. Characteristically, when Nelson addressed the subject, he was immediately helpful in suggesting the main themes and the authorities who would contribute most to the discussion.

Three of us had worked closely with Nelson: Professor Inis Claude of the Government Department and Professor Norman Graebner of the History Department. We all agreed he had taught us as much as we had taught him. He decided rather late in his graduate career to concentrate in international relations, after having completed most of his course work in American government. When I asked why he had shifted, he replied, "I think I can make a greater contribution," and he added words that too seldom are heard of late: "to my country." Could anything have been more prophetic? A native of Louisa County, he had an early association with the Miller Center and gave a series of Forums we shall always cherish for their clarity and cogency of thought and analysis. He was always at home at the Center, perhaps because of his deep concern for public policy and the national interest.

The second person who proved especially helpful in the organization of our study was Professor Joseph Kruzel. I had known him for his vital and effective teaching and penetrating scholarship. He entered the Clinton administration later than the early appointees but was promptly recognized as a strategic thinker. He became deputy assistant secretary of defense and was the logical official to whom we turned for the series on NATO. He was a graduate of the Air Force Academy who served in Vietnam and thereafter received an M.P.A. and Ph.D. from Harvard. He taught at Harvard, Duke, and Ohio State and at the latter was director of the Mershon Center. His *American Defense Annual* became for many a bible on national security issues.

With their many friends and family, we mourn the death of Nelson and Joe. They were killed in a fatal accident when the military vehicle in which they were riding plunged 300 feet over the rain-soaked shoulder of a road leading to Sarajevo. They were traveling to meet the Bosnian president and foreign minister. Their loss is unfathomable to their many friends. Both looked forward to long public service. They represent the type of creative and fearless young leaders to whom the country must turn if peace is to be preserved. Colonel Drew was the author of the Combined Joint Task Force concept within NATO, providing for a smaller collective defense unit in a larger collective security organization. Secretary Kruzel had won the Distinguished Service Medal for his role as a member of the U.S. delegation to SALT I.

In reading their insightful chapters in our NATO volume, a great sense of sadness comes over us. Two young men who were just coming into their own have been taken from us. No one can say what further service they might have rendered. All that we know is what they had already done for us all. Perhaps that is enough. As Nelson's brother wisely remarked, "How many have done more." As a nation we need to remember them when we are overwhelmed by stories of violence, crime, and greed. Tucked away in the hidden corners of society, often unheralded and unsung, young men and women like Nelson and Joe serve the republic. If we are to restore hope for the future, they are the ones to seek out. An aging population must recognize the commitment of its young. They deserve our trust. Recognition ought not be reserved for memorials. Colonial Drew and Secretary Kruzel's greatest legacy may be the reminder that there are young leaders among us who are willing and able to shoulder the burdens of leadership. We shall always remember them as colleagues carrying forward the mission of the Miller Center.

Introduction

NATO and the Changing World Order is divided into four main subjects: The United States, NATO, and Europe; Is NATO obsolete?; The Enlargement of NATO; and the Future of NATO. On 6 October 1993, the former secretary general, Manfred Wörner, delivered an address at the National Press Club that serves as a foreword to the volume.

In chapter 1, Colonel Nelson Drew, to whom the volume is dedicated, discusses "Post-Cold War American Leadership in NATO." Colonel Drew reports on the years from 1990-94 and in particular on American leadership. He chronicles the events that swept across Europe in a period of breathtaking change. In the Gulf War, NATO transported tanks and made possible the end run around the flanks of the Iraqi army, a story that the press failed to report. Drew writes about the contribution of another U.Va. alumnus who wrote his dissertation with me, Alberto Coll, now of the Naval War College. It is worth noting that Colonel Drew, although he claims no credit in his essay, was the author of the Combined Joint Task Force concept and Coll, then a deputy assistant secretary of defense, wrote the most significant paper on the culture of peacekeeping. As universities including Virginia are scaling down numbers of graduate students in international politics and foreign policy, we recognize the contributions of Drew and Coll. Drew's paper introduces policy changes of which he was the architect and conceptualizer.

Joseph Kruzel follows Colonel Drew in our volume. The deputy assistant secretary of defense, who also met his death in Bosnia, describes the various meetings that took place and the challenges to which the United States responded. These included demonstrating that we were in Europe to stay, supporting the success of democratic and economic reform in Central and Eastern Europe, and developing a new security system based on changing realities in Europe and beyond. He quotes Lord Ismay's statement on the three founding purposes of NATO: to keep the Russians out, keep the Americans in, and keep the Germans down. All have changed, at least from the standpoint of emphasis. His analysis of the Partnership for Peace is instructive both as to its purpose and its limitations. As with Nelson Drew's penetrating study, Kruzel helps us understand continuity and change in our ongoing participation and role in NATO.

The third chapter in part I is by a senior military leader of great stature, General John R. Galvin. I cannot help reflecting that Colonel Drew represented the rising leadership in the U.S. military, who were destined to play an ever more important part in U.S. military policy-making, whereas General Galvin can look back on a long career of responsibility in critical times of American policy. He comments on the effect of elections on attention to military problems, the changing responsibility of the United States, the rise of China, the complexity of the problem of the former Yugoslavia, the need for a global security architecture, and the persistence of conflicts—125 small wars since 1945. General Galvin's answers to some of the hard questions that are being asked about national security merit serious discussion.

The authors in part II debate the question, "Is NATO obsolete?" James Chace, who is Henry Luce Professor of International Relations at Bard College and editor of the *World Policy Journal*, answers yes, citing NATO's failure to deal effectively with the Bosnian War. Chace, who was formerly managing editor of *Foreign Affairs*, charges that NATO has become little more than an expensive fiction. Even if it decides to respond to crises like Bosnia, it must do so through a coalition of American, French, British, and Russian forces, not through NATO as such. Unless NATO is transformed, it will remain a forgotten and irrelevant relic of the past. The countries of Eastern and Western Europe must form themselves into a Pan-European collective security organization with NATO at its core in order to be relevant to the post-Cold War era. Such an organization would resemble the 19th century concert of Europe that prevailed from 1815 to 1853. Without changes of this magnitude, Chace concludes that NATO is and will remain irrelevant.

Richard Kugler, formerly of the RAND Corporation, has served as executive manager and adviser to the secretary and deputy secretary of defense and the chairman of the Joint Chiefs of Staff. He answers the question, "Is NATO Obsolete?" by arguing that NATO must take action outside of its area or it will have no function to perform. It must respond to the needs of the new era and reach beyond NATO's borders. These include taking action if needed in an arc-of-crisis zone stretching from Poland through Central Europe into the Balkans through Turkey and on into the Caucuses. The greatest dangers in the post-Cold War years are likely to crop up in the arc of crisis and across the rest of Europe. It is the site of a silent crisis created by five dangers that include the loss of cohesion and vision in some European international institutions, the spread of ethnic violence in the Balkans, a power vacuum in East Central Europe, turmoil in the former Soviet states, questions about Russia's transition to a market economy, and a possible conflict between Russia and Germany. NATO has a critical role to play, and the author delineates seven actions that it can take. Thus, Kugler's answer to the question, Is NATO Obsolete? is no, provided it focuses on the five dangers he outlines in his chapter.

John Duffield is the author of an important book, *Power Rules: The Evolution of NATO's Conventional Force Posture.* He organizes his answer to the question, Is NATO Obsolete? around the theme, "Why NATO Persists." He explains why NATO continues to enjoy strong support from its members, saying that it still performs a number of valuable security functions for them including both external and internal functions. The former are maintaining a strategic balance in Europe by neutralizing a residual military threat from Russia and managing ethnic, territorial, and national conflicts within states that threaten to spill over and affect other NATO countries. Internally, it must reassure its members that they have nothing to fear from one another. The great merit of Professor Duffield's paper is his success in placing the future of NATO in the context of what it has done and is doing for security within and beyond its historic region.

Part III directs attention to the question of the enlargement of NATO. Who should be the new faces in a transformed NATO? In this connection, what can be said about the Partnership for Peace and the potential membership of countries such as Russia and Japan? What are the conflicts and contradictions in the various designs for enlargement?

Douglas K. Bereuter is a conservative congressman from Nebraska with strong international interests that have come to focus on the North Atlantic community. The congressman addresses many of the same issues discussed in parts I and II. He identifies NATO's two traditional missions as first, serving as a forum for transatlantic consultation and defense planning, and second, providing for the mutual defense of member states. Beginning in 1993, commentators urged NATO to expand its mission to include crisis management and crisis prevention, out-of-area activities, and risk reduction in the former Warsaw Pact region. Members are reducing the size of their forces, including a reduction in U.S. forces from 330,000 to 100,000 military personnel. He reviews the functions of the North Atlantic Cooperation Council created in 1991 and the arguments of proponents and opponents of the enlargement of NATO. The congressman analyzes two relatively new bodies, the Partnership for Peace and the Combined Joint Task Forces. Congressman Bereuter's attention to the multitude of old and new institutions dealing with NATO's future is especially helpful.

Dr. Ira Straus is a brilliant young scholar who is to some extent a successor to Clarence Streit of Union Now. Since 1985, he has proposed at first hypothetically and more recently concrete plans for Eastern Europe and Russia joining NATO. Straus argues that NATO represents the third generation of the coming together in alliances of the Atlantic countries. The first occurred in World War I with the objective of resisting Germany and its allies. The second was the Grand Alliance in World War II. NATO in the Cold War was the third and the fourth has come to light in the post–Cold War debate over a transformed NATO. Straus's analysis is historically and institutionally the most wide-ranging and provocative in the book, defying a summary statement because of the range of its content.

Alan Tonelson of the Economic Strategy Institute adds another dimension to the volume through his discussion of NATO, East Asia, and Japan. Tonelson is critical of the view of a group he identified as "archetypical Atlanticists" and points to a pair of critical problems that plague U.S. alliance policies. First, American policymakers have attempted "to smother" the desire of allies to conduct independent foreign policies by affording military protection and favorable terms of trade and commerce. During the Cold War, the United States could pursue such policies with acceptable costs and risk because the same missions and force structure necessary for these purposes were used to contain the Soviet Union. In the post-Cold War era, the threats to stability in Europe and East Asia can no longer be addressed through military power. Instead, they include structural economic decline in Europe, continued economic stagnation in the newly independent countries of Eastern Europe and the former Soviet republics, and growing refugee flows into Western Europe. The military threats that exist are too local, and their implications for U.S. national security too uncertain, as in the case of China threatening to invade the Spratly Islands. Most local problems even within the NATO region are likely to be seen as local by the United States and NATO.

The second problem Tonelson discusses is the lack of a strategic view of foreign economic policy. American policymakers take note of the 6 to 8 to 10 percent annual growth rate in some of the countries in East Asia and the Pacific Rim. Responding, we have shifted our priorities and are giving major attention to Asia. We run the risk of ignoring the fact that trans-Pacific economic flows generally do not work to America's economic advantage. In most trade and technology transfers and investment activities producing massive trade imbalances, the United States is the clear loser. Economic flows between the United States and Europe are more balanced and militarily beneficial, but Tonelson is concerned that indiscriminate global multilateralism is drawing the United States away from Europe. He questions these changes from a strategic viewpoint.

Part IV on NATO and the future brings the volume to a close. David Acheson is president of the Atlantic Council, a highly respected and unique Washington institution that draws on policymakers, scholars, and journalists. After having explored and responded to the question, "Does NATO have a role in the post-Cold War Era?", Mr. Acheson discusses the difficult problems involved in expanding the membership of NATO. He asks if the former Soviet Union should be added to NATO and if so, which of the republics should be included. Acheson writes from firsthand experience with officials of NATO and especially SHAPE. He discusses the military budget of NATO, its transparency, and various uses of military forces. He examines the desire of states to join the Partnership for Peace and spells out what is required of new members. Acheson offers valuable insights on the future of the institutions and practice of NATO.

John Woodworth is a former deputy assistant secretary of defense. In fact, he was Joseph Kruzel's predecessor. From the vantage point of this important office, he discusses NATO's prospects. Woodworth reminds us that NATO has experienced crises throughout much of its history. He evaluates NATO as it relates to global trends and global economics. He deals with more specific world problems such as Asian economic strength, the rise of China, the gap between rich and poor, and Russia's future; in short, he places NATO in a global context. As he sees it, the major issues for NATO in the future are redefining its purpose and confronting problems in the Balkans, Islam, and nuclear proliferation. Not Russia, but NATO's success in maintaining a sense of direction for its future is NATO's greatest challenge. He completes his institutional and political evaluation with a summary discussion of the enlargement of NATO and, once again, the Russian factor.

Dr. Andrew Pierre is a longtime student of NATO and Europe and is a senior associate at the Carnegie Endowment for International Peace. The distinctive feature of his paper, which offers historical and institutional analysis, is its comprehensive character. He deals not only with NATO but associated institutions such as Western European Union, the Organization (formerly the Conference) for Security and Cooperation in Europe, the North

Atlantic Cooperation Council, the Combined Joint Task Forces, the Partnership for Peace, and the North Atlantic Council. Because of his long association with Europe and NATO, Dr. Pierre is well qualified to summarize the main themes in our study of NATO. He contributes the concluding observations on the subject.

I.

THE UNITED STATES, NATO, AND EUROPE

CHAPTER ONE

Post–Cold War American Leadership in NATO*

COLONEL S. NELSON DREW, USAF

NARRATOR: Colonel Nelson Drew is the type of young scholar and leader who makes his professors look good. He was a truly exceptional and brilliant graduate student in our Department of Government and Foreign Affairs. He studied the relation between policy formulation and the education of the public on public policy. He was a professor of national security policy at the National War College.

Colonel Drew received his bachelor's and master's degrees from the University of North Carolina. He received a Ph.D. at the University of Virginia. He was a Senior Service School graduate of the National Security Fellows Program at the Kennedy School at Harvard. His breadth and versatility are reflected in the way he has combined theory and practice throughout his career. He was a member of the faculty of the political science department at the U.S. Air Force Academy for six years and served as an operational intelligence officer for seven years. During two "on-loan" tours from

---

Presented in a Forum at the Miller Center of Public Affairs on 5 May 1994. The views expressed are those of the author and do not necessarily reflect the views or positions of the U.S. government, the U.S. Air Force, or the National War College.

the Air Force Academy, he was staff officer of the headquarters of U.S. European Command and a National Security Council staff officer. His next assignment was assistant for defense operations and policy of the Office of the Defense Adviser of the U.S. Mission to NATO. At NATO he was the primary architect of the NATO Combined Joint Task Force concept, which was designed to enable the alliance to conduct operations in support of peacekeeping and European security. He is the author of numerous articles and papers as well as co-author of a book entitled *The Future of NATO* and author of *Trans-Atlantic Security and the Development of a European Security and Defense Identity.* We welcome Colonel Drew on his return to the Miller Center.

COLONEL DREW: It is an honor to be invited back to speak here. I will begin by relating a story told by Ambassador Robert Hunter, the current U.S. ambassador to NATO, who served on the National Security Council (NSC) staff during the Carter administration and dealt with the State Department regarding some NATO issues. He said that the chief of the European branch at the State Department during that time used a custom-made rubber stamp on all papers dealing with NATO that crossed his desk. The stamp read: "NATO: At this time of unprecedented crisis in the alliance. . . ." It seemed as though every paper written about NATO talked about a crisis in the alliance. If what was happening to NATO during the Carter administration was a "crisis," I don't think there are any words in the English language to describe what has been going on in NATO over the last four years.

I first became associated with NATO in the fall of 1989 in a research capacity. In November I began to interview several dozen NATO staff officers from the U.S. mission, the international staff, the SHAPE staff, and the staff of the Military Command located in Mons, south of NATO headquarters. Of all the people I interviewed, I could find only two who were willing to even entertain the thought, as the Berlin Wall was coming down, that NATO would have to change its basic strategic concept to deal with the new world that was about to emerge. They believed that the existing strategic concept was flexible enough to adapt to any change they could foresee in the European landscape. They also believed

4

that a fundamental reorientation would be like opening Pandora's Box. By historical comparison, it had taken over seven years of intense deliberation within the alliance to craft MC 14-3—the secret strategy that governed NATO from the late 1960s through the early 1990s. Most NATO officers with whom I talked loathed the idea of repeating another seven-year process, especially since the cost of agreement on this strategic concept was the withdrawal of France from NATO's integrated military structure. They didn't want to risk sacrificing another ally to achieve a new strategic concept.

When I returned to NATO as a full-time staff officer the following summer, I brought with me the galley proofs of the results of the research I had been doing and circulated those proofs to all the people I had interviewed before. The comments I received were almost unanimous: "How could you have included so much old thinking in this document? It's certainly not visionary enough. It doesn't reflect a tenth of the dramatic changes that are going to take place in the alliance. The new strategy that you propose is still not forward-looking enough."

By November 1991, two years after my research, NATO adopted a totally new strategic concept at the Rome summit. Interestingly, that strategic concept was unclassified—the entire strategy of the alliance was laid out for public consumption and did not have the word *threat* anywhere in it. There were challenges but no threats. The Warsaw Pact countries were embraced as new partners in an organization called the North Atlantic Cooperation Council (NACC), which proposed a wide range of programs to enable the former Central and East European Soviet satellites to develop as free-market economies and democratic societies.

The first meeting of NACC occurred a month later in Brussels, perhaps one of the most telling moments in the history of the alliance. Near the end of that meeting, the representative who was sitting behind the placard that proclaimed "Soviet Union" was called from the room. About an hour later, he came back and asked for the floor. He then announced that the official record should not indicate that the Soviet Union had participated in this meeting, because as of that morning, the Soviet Union had officially ceased to exist. It had been succeeded by the Confederation of

Independent States (CIS), under the leadership of Russia, while the meeting was underway.

NATO found itself in somewhat of a quandary as a result, because NACC barely had been a workable idea with just the 16 NATO nations and the members of the old Warsaw Pact meeting together. With the breakup of the Soviet Union into a multitude of independent states, we had to decide whether or not our invitation to join NACC had been intended only for Moscow and the former Warsaw Pact states or for all of the successor states to the Soviet Union. We decided on the latter position, and suddenly NACC became the Conference of Security and Cooperation in Europe (CSCE) "on steroids"–that is, it included too many people for a workable consensus to be reached, but it was still indispensable as part of our outreach to the East. Since that time, the alliance has struggled to come to grips with how it should treat this polyglot of new associate states, all with vested interests in strengthening their ties with NATO.

During that same period of time, from 1989 to 1991, NATO members also became involved in the largest military operation in the history of NATO's existence: the Gulf War. Had it not been for NATO's contributions to moving military personnel and equipment from Europe to the Gulf and supplying equipment such as Patriot missiles to Turkey and Israel, the United States would have been unable to prosecute that war in the manner it did. As a matter of fact, the entire "end-run" strategy would have been impossible had it not been for NATO allies and the breakup of the Warsaw Pact. There weren't enough heavy lifters in the U.S. inventory to transport tanks at high speeds overland in the desert to carry out the end-run around the flanks of the Iraqi army. The German government responded favorably to our request for such vehicles, but it was a matter of serendipity that they had just acquired the military inventory of the former East Germany, including an abundance of tank-transport vehicles.

All of those things coming together at one time and the tremendous support from NATO did not receive due attention in the American press. During the remaining two years that I worked in the alliance, I was surprised by the opinions expressed by a number of members of Congress that visited NATO. We would brief them on what NATO was doing and how it was advancing, or attempting to advance, U.S. policy goals. But when we mentioned NATO's role in the Gulf War, they would say, "Wait a second, NATO wasn't a player in the Gulf War." We would then itemize the examples of cooperation we had received through the alliance; the number of times we made a request and got 15 positive answers from our allies; the massive transfer of the Germans' transportation network that enabled us to move a corps out of Europe and into Saudi Arabia; and the deployment of air elements from the ACE (Allied Command-Europe) mobile force from Central Europe–where everyone had assumed it would be used–to Turkey, in order to deter a potential Iraqi attack in Turkish air space.

True, we had a tremendous fight within the alliance to make all that happen, because it shook the belief of most NATO experts about how the alliance might be used in the future. It especially shook the Germans, who had looked forward to a new NATO but had not really contemplated what that might mean. To them, NATO had always been a security blanket: If they were attacked, they knew NATO would be there to come to their defense. It never dawned on them that the first country threatened with imminent attack might be Turkey and that Germans might have to go to the defense of Turkey. That took a dramatic revolution in thinking on the part of their government. George Bush had to make several phone calls to Helmut Kohl in order to smooth things over, because of German constitutional concerns over out-of-area deployments. Some Germans worried that if they actually had to go into Iraq as part of the missions, they would be violating their constitution. They weren't the only ones. Most of the allies had problems early on (the United States included) in figuring out what role NATO might play in something like the Gulf War.

The alliance had no sooner recovered from trying to come to grips with the Gulf crisis and the new world situation than it also had to come to grips with the consequences of the Rome Declaration on Freedom and Cooperation. This pledge stated that the alliance would take steps to promote stability throughout "the Euro-Atlantic Community"–loosely defined to mean from Vancouver to Vladivostok, going the long way.

7

Unfortunately for the alliance, while those words needed to be spoken, there were no mechanisms in place to put substance behind them. The Rome Summit Declaration was designed to provide a road map so the alliance could develop the capabilities to promote stability throughout this region in the future. No one at that time dreamt that less than a year later Yugoslavia would break apart and that NATO would be under increasing pressure to do something about it. The record of the alliance in dealing with the former Yugoslavia is no better and no worse than the record of any of its 16 member states, and no better and no worse than the United Nations in dealing with the crisis. There was simply no organization that was prepared for the shock the events in Yugoslavia sent through the Western political system. In fact, at the outset of the Yugoslav crisis, the European Community was assuring us that the United States could indeed draw down its NATO presence; some even suggested that NATO perhaps no longer had a mission because the Europeans had advanced beyond the point of ever using force to settle their disputes.

The events in Slovenia and Croatia and then in Bosnia shook the European Community to its foundations, and NATO, as part of the Trans-Atlantic American-European Community, was equally shaken.

It also shook the United Nations. Just a few weeks ago, Alberto Coll, who is another graduate of this school, did a fine analysis of the change in the culture of peacekeeping that was required after the end of the Cold War. He pointed out that for 40-odd years, U.N. peacekeeping efforts had been geared toward making sure that no conflicts spread to the point that superpowers would become involved. That effort dictated a culture that said, "You are strictly neutral, and you do everything in your power to avoid the use of force, because if force comes into play, it is likely that one or the other of the superpowers will see its interests threatened and will become involved." This entire culture of peacekeeping was designed to deal with a set of circumstances that have ceased to exist.

In that culture, NATO was seen as one of the two sides designed to be kept out, since it represented superpower confrontation. At the outset, when the United Nations was looking for forces that could be deployed to Bosnia, they turned not to NATO but to the CSCE, which happens not to have any forces. In fact, it was only within the last two years that it even developed its own permanent staff with a secretary general to head it. As a result, when the United Nations solicited action by CSCE in July 1992, CSCE turned to NATO. The United Nations at least had the foresight to send to NATO a carbon copy of the request it made to CSCE, since the CSCE didn't meet during the summer.

The previous month, NATO had a ministerial meeting in Oslo and for the first time in its history agreed that NATO forces could be used for peacekeeping missions on behalf of CSCE. The United Nations originally was not considered as a vehicle to authorize such missions because it had global responsibilities, and NATO was still struggling to decide where its forces might or might not be used.

Less than a month after the ink had dried on that commitment, we found ourselves called upon to move into the peacekeeping arena. Yet we had never run an exercise with NATO forces for the purpose of peacekeeping and had never even drafted a contingency plan for peacekeeping operations. All we had was the fact that NATO standing forces existed, and it looked like the most logical place to use such forces in the future would be in trying to promote stability; that involved peacekeeping as an outgrowth of the Rome summit.

In the summer of 1992, the call for help came down first from the United Nations through CSCE and later directly from the United Nations to NATO. They needed help in planning how many forces it would take to guarantee the delivery of humanitarian assistance from the Adriatic coast to Sarajevo. We "tossed" that plan over to the NATO staff and said, "See what you can do."

It wasn't easy to get approval to send it to the NATO staff because NATO is an organization that requires consensus to act. During this transformation NATO has been forced to move away from a reactive posture in which the alliance would act only if attacked by other countries. It is fairly easy to generate consensus when you see hundreds and thousands of tanks pouring through the Fulda Gap. From that reactive posture, the alliance has suddenly found itself thrust into trying to be "proactive" in its policies. It has had to go into areas where war does not yet exist, or at least to plan to go into such areas, for the purpose of ensuring that war does not break out. It is tremendously difficult to generate consensus within one government, much less 16 governments, to commit forces that might wind up in harm's way, where your nation's troops may be killed while trying to prevent other nations' troops from killing each other or civilians. Trying to get consensus in an organization like NATO is no mean feat. Trying to get consensus at the same time you are talking about expanding the organization to invite more nations with even more diverse backgrounds is an even greater challenge. After debating throughout most of the summer, NATO agreed that its military staff could take on this first planning requirement. The staff estimated that roughly 75,000 troops would be needed. We passed that figure to the United Nations, and the U.N. Peacekeeping Organization (UNPKO), and their response was one of shock. They had envisioned a force of about 2,000 personnel, not 75,000. They came back to NATO and said, in effect, "You have given us the wrong answer. The answer is 2,000. Redefine the question so that 2,000 is the answer." The planning staff at SHAPE responded that the only way 2,000 troops would have any impact is if there were a totally permissive environment in which all the parties have agreed to stick by their agreement that they want these forces there and that they will assist in the delivery of humanitarian aid, that these forces are merely there to drive trucks and to assist. The U.N. deployed forces under that scenario, even though it was a myth at the time. A permissive environment did not exist when the United Nations first asked us for help; it has not existed since then, and I see no signs that it will exist in the foreseeable future.

The forces have grown since that time, but the mission for which those forces were deployed could never be attained without either the cooperation of all the parties or a change in rules of engagement and a massive deployment of forces equipped to fight their way through if they were blocked. That is something the United Nations has never done in its peacekeeping operations, however. It is totally alien to the entire culture of the UNPKO. Such a situation would cause many of those organizations outside the United Nations that are engaged in humanitarian assistance to stop their operations, because they would feel that there would be no way their organizational outpost could be protected under those circumstances. Thus, NATO has been put in a position of great tension as it contemplates what it hopes to accomplish by application of force. What I would like to see in the future is the application of deterrence theory to peacekeeping so that we don't have to actually use the force. We could threaten the use of force in a credible manner by having done so once or twice to get the attention of those who are engaged in the fighting, but there is a tension between the policies that would be required to do that and the policies required to actually deliver the humanitarian assistance.

In early May 1994, Danish forces fired on the Serbs after the Serbs had been shelling the Danes for some 12 hours, first at an outpost and then at the relief column the Danes sent to that outpost. Several organizations then declared they couldn't operate in this environment since it was turning into a shooting war. The Serbs started crying that the United Nations was no longer neutral since it had fired on Serb troops. In the *Washington Post* today, there is a fine account of that incident and the rules of engagement that require the Danes to spotlight their own vehicles in night operations (making them easy targets) to send a signal so they would not be fired upon. This complication poses real problems for both military planners and political planners in generating consensus. Among the 16 NATO nations, there are some that are committed to the classical concept of peacekeeping, some that are committed to returning fire whenever they are fired upon, and some that are firmly of two minds. I must say that more often than not, the United States falls into the category of being firmly of two minds on the subject.

NATO has taken on this peacekeeping role, but it hasn't yet resolved how it is going to accomplish its objective. At the summit in January 1994, it began to clarify a cluttered situation by taking a number of initiatives designed to create the capabilities of carrying out peacekeeping operations and provide stability. One of them was the creation of a Combined Joint Task Force concept that is based on the way in which the United States deployed forces in the Persian Gulf. It restructures NATO forces so that interchangeable modules of forces can train together in various configurations. When a contingency arises for which force is required, NATO can join various modules together under a unified command that has worked together in the past and deploy the specifically tailored multinational force-module to the field as necessary.

I am convinced that had such a force existed at the time Slovenia and Croatia first declared their independence and had the requisite political will existed in the nations that make up the alliance to deploy it, they might have been able to bring this concept of deterrence in peacekeeping to bear. Quite possibly, shots would never have been fired. If forces had been deployed, say, along the Croatian border with Serbia, that action may have sent a much sharper signal than was actually done at the time. Making such an assumption may be a way of trying to look backwards and rewrite history, and there is no way of saying that this is what would have happened. We might have been dragged into a prolonged peacekeeping operation with forces almost permanently deployed along borders, in much the same way they are in Korea or Cyprus right now, simply in order to maintain a fiction of peace.

I would like to think that we could have avoided what happened in Bosnia, but, as someone who at one time in my career was labeled a "Yugoslav expert," I don't think a multi-ethnic Bosnia was ever viable apart from a multi-ethnic Yugoslavia. Once Milosevic orchestrated events in Yugoslavia by playing on Serbian nationalism as a vehicle toward national power, he made it impossible for Croatia and Slovenia to seek greater autonomy within Yugoslavia, forcing them to seek full independence. I cannot envision any scenario where "they all live happily ever after." It has become what can only be described as a "test case from hell" for peacekeeping, because there seems to be no logical resolution for it.

It is difficult to determine how all the pieces will come together in the future in Bosnia because public support for peacekeeping is liable to dry up. Because of the commitment it made in Rome to promote stability, NATO is going to be judged on how well it actually deals with the situation in Bosnia, whether it wants to be or not—and whether or not the problem is soluble by the application of outside force. NATO has created that situation itself. The question is thus legitimately asked: If they cannot promote stability in their own back yard, how are they going to promote stability in the Asian republics of the former Soviet Union? How are they going to promote stability in Nagorno-Karabakh, where they have not even picked up the gauntlet yet? What if they are called on to promote stability outside of the European area? What if the U.S. Congress decides that if NATO cannot get involved in places like Somalia or Rwanda, then it is no longer furthering U.S. interests, thus leading the United States to present the alliance with an ultimatum—either move out or we'll pull out? That scenario is no longer totally implausible as it was during the Cold War. I would like to think it is not probable.

The Combined Joint Task Force is designed to be used not just within the alliance but also to be used with non-allies, such as the members of the newly created Partnership for Peace. That organization received perhaps the most attention of anything the alliance did at the summit. In effect, it reaches out to the NACC members and the neutral states in Europe and says, "If you would like to participate with the NATO alliance in peacekeeping operations, here is a vehicle that will allow us to train together, to develop a common doctrine for peacekeeping, and to jointly plan our own respective force structures so that we can put them together for peacekeeping." That is no mean accomplishment if you can persuade many of the former Eastern and Central European states to have transparent force planning. This action would go a long way toward promoting the sort of security they are seeking through NATO membership. The loudest voices we often hear are those that clamor, "We need NATO membership to protect us from a potentially resurgent Russia." Yet when we talk to many of the representatives of these countries in private, they say, "We also need NATO membership to protect us from each other." One of the things communism did was to put a lid on nationalist aspirations, and Bosnia is not the only place that is potentially explosive in that regard.

When most Eastern Europeans talked with me about their desire for NATO membership as protection against a resurgent Russia, they mention in almost the same breath the need not to renationalize their defense. They want a cooperative defense structure that makes it impossible for them to go to war with one another because the "parts" don't function properly if you start

13

pulling military units out and using them against each other. That is one of the things NATO has been fairly successful in doing among its members, and it is critical to the future of the alliance.

It is clear that the old mission of the alliance, drawing a line in the sand through Europe and saying, "This far, no further," is no longer a legitimate justification for its continued existence. Members of the alliance see that as well. The following Greek poem about ancient Alexandria entitled "The Barbarians" is cited frequently by NATO spokesmen and will illustrate this situation:

> Why this sudden bewilderment, this confusion?
> Why are the streets and squares emptying so rapidly, everyone going home, lost in thought?
> Because night has fallen and the barbarians have not come.
> And some of our men just in from the border say there are no barbarians any longer.
> Now what's going to happen to us without the barbarians?
> They were, those people, after all, a kind of solution.*

NATO had its own "barbarians" as a reliable adversary for a long time. I would suggest that the "barbarians" have not disappeared, but they are not the "barbarians" we thought they were. NATO may or may not be in a time of crisis right now, but it is certainly facing a situation where, as I look back over the last four years, events have been changing at a pace far more rapid than bureaucratic institutions are capable of matching. Nevertheless, in order to maintain the justification for the existence of an organization that is critically needed for a number of reasons other than facing the "barbarians" in a line across Europe, NATO has had to take on commitments for which the Allies are not yet ready. It will be judged accordingly, which is going to create problems.

Rapid change has created problems for two administrations because neither has ever had to deal with NATO in a situation where American leadership was not simply taken for granted. The

---

*Attributed to Constantinos Kavafis, as cited in presentations by several NATO officials, 1992-93.

only time the subject of NATO came to our attention was during the annual budget hearings in which Congress bashed the allies for failing to meet their share of the defense burden.

NATO also has been taken for granted by the allies. The French have at times been resentful of NATO. The Germans have taken it for granted as the cost of doing business as a major power in a world that had no reason to trust them. The British have used American leadership as a tool to maintain their own leadership via the "special relationship." Most of the smaller members of the alliance use American leadership because they look at America as the one honest broker with no territorial ambitions anywhere in Europe as a check on the other members of the alliance. The thought, for example, that the American nuclear umbrella could be withdrawn from NATO, leading a future generation of German politicians to feel the need to develop their own nuclear capability, concerns many of the other NATO allies—especially the French, who are trying to develop a special relationship with the Germans.

Except for Moscow, the vision of what the future was going to look like was nowhere more shattered by the collapse of communism and the Warsaw Pact than in Paris. The French had a vision of an EC (rather than American) -led unified Europe bound together by the massive enemy on the outside. When the massive enemy on the outside went away, the French vision of the future of Europe was absolutely devastated. They did not have a vision to replace it, and they are still struggling. Much of what has been seen as French-American rivalry within the alliance could more accurately be depicted as two allies trying to figure out what it is they want, what their policies will be, and how to manage their relationship in NATO.

There are problems facing the alliance, and questions about what purpose the alliance serves. I would conclude by suggesting that the answer to that question can be found by going back to a somewhat waggish statement made by Lord Ismay, the first secretary general of the alliance. He said, "NATO serves three purposes: Keep the Russians out, keep the Americans in, keep the Germans down."

15

It is politically incorrect to say any of those things now, but if you cut through the humor in the statement and examine what it actually means, you will find the meaning of the alliance.

"Keep the Russians out." It is a fundamental American interest to prevent any hostile hegemonic power from dominating Europe. This intent can be accomplished even better by turning the former enemies into status quo powers in a world based on Western economic and political values. That is the current objective of the North Atlantic Cooperation Council and the Partnership for Peace.

"Keep the Americans in." The key to achieving this aim lies in determining whether or not the United States has lasting national security interests in stability in Europe. I would argue that the answer to that question is emphatically yes; we cannot afford for Europe to go the way of the Balkans. Europe may not be in immediate danger, but stability is certainly something an American presence promotes. Most Europeans, both in the alliance and those seeking to join the alliance, recognize that it is at least in part the desire to keep the United States engaged in Europe that enabled most of the principal protagonists of the last two World Wars to hold together in the same alliance—no mean feat, giving Europe its longest period of peace in recorded history.

This point brings us to the final purpose of NATO: "Keep the Germans down." I would argue that NATO keeps not only the Germans down, but every member of the alliance down. Since NATO has something no other multinational or international organization has—an integrated military structure, a tangible standing force—no member of the alliance has ever had to fear that it will stand alone in its own defense. The corollary, which I think is the most important for the post-Cold War era, is that no member of the alliance ever need arm itself to the point where it may be perceived as more of a threat than an ally to its immediate neighbors. This is what interests the Eastern Europeans most. They come to us and say, "You have to help us in developing a military structure compatible with the West that doesn't renationalize our own defense." This aspect of NATO, maintaining stability within the alliance in Europe, is perhaps the most overlooked key function that the alliance has served.

16

Colonel S. Nelson Drew, USAF

The question that Americans must confront as we consider our own policy is whether this is enough to hold NATO together without a massive external threat. I guarantee that we could not create the alliance anew today in the current circumstances. I believe it still serves a vital function, but I'm not yet sure, nor are its members, whether the circumstances that still cry out for its existence are sufficient to hold it together so that it can continue to meet the legitimate needs of all its members and remain a bargain for them in security. This is NATO's line: it's a bargain. It does something we would do on our own if we had to, but collectively NATO does it cheaper than it would be if we were trying to do it on our own. If it remains a bargain, the alliance will stand. Its cost-effectiveness will maintain the financial backing and political support of its members.

If NATO is no longer seen to be doing something we would want to do on our own, then support will evaporate and the alliance will wither. The alliance will not go away. Too much bureaucracy is embedded in it for it to actually go away, but it would become increasingly irrelevant and certainly not credible. If it is not credible, then it will not promote stability. That is where the test case we face in Bosnia comes in.

QUESTION: I think you are right in saying that the purpose of an alliance is security, and if you can't figure out some threat to your security, an alliance is difficult to maintain. This is the dilemma. It seems that the great challenge of NATO is to define an international interest that will sustain it. Has any effort been made or can it be made to define an international interest that would involve NATO and would conform to the complexities of the contemporary world?

COLONEL DREW: The main issue that you raise of defining a sustainable international interest is complicated further by the fact that if NATO does expand to embrace Russia and Ukraine and a number of others, the consensus principle would become unworkable for any situation in which actual use of force might be required. As we have seen in Bosnia, every nation that is being called upon to provide forces is having to ask the question, "Can I

17

justify to my public and my legislative bodies the loss of American lives, French lives, British lives, for the purpose of keeping Bosnian Serbs from killing Bosnian Croats and killing Bosnian Muslims and vice versa?" The answer generally is, "No. We can't justify that on a national basis."

What about the commitment made at the end of World War II by the international community to never again tolerate genocide? The unfortunate answer—at least the one the Serbs are drawing from what they see in Bosnia—is what we really meant was never again under Adolph Hitler in Germany in the 1940s. If the issue is ethnic cleansing on a scale comparable to the holocaust, committed not just by one side against the others, but by all sides to varying degrees, then the issue is more complicated. It may be that the only reason the Serbs are more guilty than others is simply that they have been more efficient at being barbarous than the other parties. The history of the region suggests that given the right tools, the other parties could be just as barbarous and just as efficient.

QUESTION: Serbia is very volatile, and if it continues its aggression without being challenged effectively, it is going to be dangerous and unstable in Macedonia, Greece, Turkey, and the general southern area. Unless NATO recognizes its fundamentals and purposes—an attack against one is an attack against all—NATO will not survive. Do you have any contingency plans if Serbia meets it territorial objectives in Bosnia? What will happen to NATO when Turkey and Greece are directly threatened?

COLONEL DREW: Part of the problem in coming to grips with that situation is that Turkey and Greece still see each other as being as much a part of the threat as a part of the solution. If it had not been for their desire to maintain solid European credentials through membership in NATO and subsequently the EC, Turkey and Greece would have probably had an all out war over Cyprus long ago.

One of the problems we had in procuring peacekeeping forces for a Bosnian contingent was with the German constitutional question; American reluctance to provide at a maximum any more than 50 percent of the total forces; and British and French defense drawn down to the point where they feel they are already committed to the maximum they can sustain over a long period, given a military requirement basically to have a 3-to-1 ratio. (If you have forces deployed, you need twice that many forces back—one reconstituting, having just rotated back, and the other in preparation to deploy so you can sustain a long-time deployment.) Britain and France are already stretched thin.

The only possible NATO country with the ground forces necessary to meet the numbers required in Bosnia is Turkey. Until a couple of months ago, the United Nations absolutely refused to consider the use of Turks in peacekeeping operations because of the explosiveness of the relationship with Greece and a long-standing U.N. policy that no neighboring state to an area of crisis should provide peacekeeping forces. Turkey, Greece, and Italy were considered in that category of neighboring states. The requirements have grown so fast that the United Nations has backed away from this policy and said that Turkish forces could be deployed. The Greeks have acquiesced—not willingly, but they have acquiesced.

If the threat turns south toward Macedonia, a totally different set of problems arises. It is less likely that the Serbs would try to annex all of Macedonia or even strike into Greece or the Turkish areas. It is very probable, however, that if the Serbs turn their attention to Kosovo and Macedonia, they would create a refugee problem of unbelievable proportions for Greece. The Greeks have already made it clear that they will not take in those refugees. They want a buffer against those refugees to hold them in southern Macedonia. They originally said they could do that by deploying Greek forces into the southern part of Macedonia, a move that was not greeted with any joy by the government in Skopje, and creating a buffer zone where the refugees would be held. NATO has studied the possibility of creating a humanitarian buffer zone, using neither Greek nor Turkish forces, as one means of preventing Greece and Turkey from coming in on opposite sides of a war in Macedonia.

The answer to your question concerning contingency military plans is yes, there are contingency plans if Serbia does foolishly lash out at a NATO member and, in fact, if Serbia should lash out at nations supporting the NATO effort. Hungary in particular has been allowing NATO aircraft to fly over its air space to monitor the no-fly zone over Bosnia. We have also worked closely with the government of Hungary and with NATO allies to ensure that response plans are available should the Serbs decide that they would retaliate, either against the aircraft over Hungarian air space or against the Hungarians themselves.

QUESTION: Is it correct that the United States deployed two units to Macedonia?

COLONEL DREW: The United States has forces deployed in Macedonia as part of the peacekeeping operation. Macedonia is a great case because it marks for the first time a willingness in the international community to deploy peacekeeping forces where the name really means what it says—peacekeeping. There was a peace to be kept, not the end of a war where we are trying to create the conditions for future peace. In this instance, it went to a place before hostilities broke out in order to keep the peace. This case holds some potential for the future—certainly for NATO—but again, generating consensus is going to be a problem.

NATO is positioning itself to address the consensus problem through the Combined Joint Task Force concept. The idea is eventually to develop the capacity to deploy in a "NATO minus" configuration, in which you have a coalition of the willing drawn from the allies. The unwilling nations say, "If you want to use NATO resources to do this, fine, but we are not going with you for this one because we can't generate the support domestically that the rest of you have been able to generate. If you want to do this in coalition with other nations that have trained with the alliance, then go ahead and do it." This may be what is necessary to overcome the consensus hurdle within a larger and larger organization—an agreement to accept a negative consensus. As long as no one absolutely insists on standing up and vetoing an operation, a subset of the alliance could be used for given purposes while drawing on alliance resources.

We have already moved in that direction by agreeing that the Combined Joint Task Force concept could be used apart from NATO by the Western European Union if the United States chose not to get involved in an operation requiring military force. The

American motive in accepting this arrangement is that it does not want a diversion of economic resources away from those forces that are committed to the alliance to create a duplicate, sans Americans, alliance for a European Security and Defense Identity. Thus, we in the United States actually led the way in putting on the table a proposal that said, "Here's how the European Defense Identity called for in Maastricht could be structured using alliance resources without the wasteful duplication of effort that would come about if there were competing organizations."

QUESTION: What do you see as the relation between NATO and the United Nations down the road?

COLONEL DREW: It is evolving. When we first began our work, we could not obtain agreement from the United Nations to even talk with NATO directly. For a month and a half, they insisted on going through CSCE. Then they wanted NATO member nations on the Security Council to speak for NATO. Only after it became necessary for them to pass a resolution calling for enforcement of the No Fly Zone did they begin to realize they needed direct communications with NATO. There are now dedicated phone lines linking NATO with the United Nations.

QUESTION: What can NATO do to rein in the United Nations, which may eventually affect its viability and flexibility?

COLONEL DREW: Already NATO has found itself at odds with the United Nations. The Danes called for NATO close air support four times during the month of April 1994. The U.N. secretary general's personal representative denied that request.

What can NATO do as NATO? Probably nothing, other than to make sure that when it is called upon to apply force, it does so in a manner that is seen as responsible by the bureaucrats at the United Nations and by nations represented at the United Nations who are not members of NATO.

It is necessary for the member states of NATO to adopt policies within the United Nations that foster the U.N.'s use of NATO in an efficient manner. That process is going to take more time than the crisis in Bosnia is liable to give us. But already progress has been made. Kofi Annan talked with Manfred Wörner (the late secretary general of NATO) not on a regular basis, but certainly on a periodic basis.

QUESTION: Are subordinate commands of NATO, such as northern Europe, central Europe, southern Europe, and so on, still staffed and in existence, or have they been disbanded? Also, I read that Albania is brimming with allied naval elements. I wondered if that were true. I read that the president of Albania said unequivocally that he would be happy to have U.S. military units based there in case they were needed.

COLONEL DREW: Although there has been some reorganization, the major subordinate commands are still standing and staffed. In fact, the staffing for the Combined Joint Task Force Headquarters will come from those commands. Members of those commands will be pulled out of their peacetime jobs and deployed with the combat force in exactly the same way that we used the CENTCOM staff to run Desert Shield and Desert Storm—by pulling the bulk of them out of their standing headquarters while the standing headquarters continued to exist. They still exist, but there is a great deal of restructuring below the major subordinate command level in NATO. Many of those commands will probably go away.

NATO has been working with Albania in enforcing the maritime embargo against Serbia. The Albanians gave NATO ships the authority to enter Albanian territorial waters. NATO provided communications gear so that the Albanians could be in constant communication with NATO. The Albanians were also engaged in spotting. We notify them if we are going in, and they notify us if they see any potential violators and invite us in if their own forces cannot intercept. It has been a good, cooperative arrangement. To date, we have not based any forces in Albania, nor am I aware of any plans to do so. We have, in fact, avoided basing in Albania as much as possible because we do not want to provoke a problem across the border in Kosovo by going in. Whether this policy will stand if Kosovo goes up in flames later on, as seems at least plausible, remains to be seen. There would probably be some deployment of a multinational force—not just the United States, but a multinational, NATO-style force with a humanitarian charter—into Albania in that case.

QUESTION: What credence do you give the year-old rumors that Croatian president Tudjman and Serb leader Milosevic agreed on a plan to carve up Bosnia, and Papandreou and Milosevic had come to a similar agreement to carve up Macedonia?

COLONEL DREW: To answer the first part of the question, I would say fairly strong credence could be given, although Tudjman's policies can also be advanced apart from Serbian goals. Both Croatia and Serbia have independent interests in consolidating control over their ethnic kin in Bosnia. The issue of carving up Macedonia is not really one that the Greeks have been pressing. Their concern is more with the use of the name. It has for some time simply been "that republic that we cannot name" in council discussions in NATO, because the Greeks refused to acknowledge that Macedonia applies to anything other than Greece. Macedonia's flag gives them a problem; its constitution also gives them a problem. These issues are being fought out in the United Nations. I don't think there is much credence in reports of alleged Greek-Serb collusion to carve up Macedonia. Greek sympathies do lie with Serbia in its striving to create a greater Serbia, however, which would include parts of Bosnia.

Milosevic is probably one of the shrewdest politicians on the international scene. He has played Western policies like a drum.

Over a year ago, I was tangentially involved in a week-long review of options for the former Yugoslavia. I provided some of the NATO options. I was told afterward that they analyzed every possible U.S. policy option from "off the wall" to "do nothing" to "mainstream" and subjected them to a rigorous analysis, lining up the pluses and minuses of each policy. In the end, every option, including the "do nothing" option, had more negatives than positives. There were no good options left.

The least objectionable seemed to be the "Lift and Strike" option, which would lift the arms embargo on Bosnia and provide air strikes to support the Bosnians until they could be sufficiently re-armed to effectively confront the Serbs. Secretary of State Christopher was sent to Europe to try to build support for "Lift and Strike." While Christopher was airborne, Milosevic suddenly became the greatest convert to the cause of the Vance-Owen peace plan that you could find. He signed it, leaving the Bosnian Muslims and the Bosnian Serbs as the only nonsignatories to the plan, thereby cutting the rug right out from under Christopher's entire mission with the allies. As a result, there was never a formal American proposal submitted to the alliance to get NATO to endorse it. The *Washington Post* account of how NATO rejected the Clinton administration's proposal for "Lift and Strike" is inaccurate. They didn't reject it because they were never asked to support it. At the time such a request would have come, the circumstances that gave rise to the policy had ceased to exist.

NARRATOR: As always when Colonel Drew is with us, we have gained much insight on complicated issues. We thank him for his informative presentation. In a day when many Americans are skeptical about government and public service, they need only know Colonel Drew to restore their faith in the virtues of public servants. In character and commitment, he exemplifies the best in the American tradition. The Miller Center is proud that we have been associated with someone of his values and high standards. We look forward to the distinguished career that lies ahead for him.

CHAPTER TWO

Partnership for Peace and the Future of European Security*

JOSEPH J. KRUZEL

NARRATOR: It is a great personal privilege and an honor to have the deputy assistant secretary of defense for European and NATO policy, Joseph Kruzel, with us. Some of us know him even better in the academic profession, in which he has high standing.

Mr. Kruzel is a graduate of the Air Force Academy. After serving in Vietnam, he received an M.P.A. and a Ph.D. from Harvard University. He has taught at Harvard, Duke, and Ohio State University, where he directed the program on International Security and Military Affairs at the prestigious Mershon Center.

Mr. Kruzel was a member of the U.S. Delegation to the Strategic Arms Limitation Talks (SALT I), and for that service he was presented the Distinguished Service Medal. He has had several assignments in the legislative and executive branches, including special assistant to Secretary of Defense Harold Brown and legislative assistant for defense and foreign policy to Senator Edward Kennedy. He has served as a consultant to the Arms Control and Disarmament Agency (ACDA), the Department of Defense, and the National Security Council.

Presented in a Forum at the Miller Center of Public Affairs on 31 May 1994.

Mr. Kruzel's numerous publications on defense policy and arms control include the continuing publication of the *American Defense Annual*, a yearly review and assessment of the major issues in U.S. security policy. He is a member of the Council on Foreign Relations, the International Institute for Strategic Studies, and the International Studies Association. We are pleased to have him at the Miller Center.

SECRETARY KRUZEL: It is a special treat to come to the Miller Center. In my happy days as an academic, I had a whole shelf of Miller Center publications, especially the works on arms control and presidential advisers.

I am in Charlottesville between two trips to Europe, the purpose of which reflect the dramatic changes in Europe and NATO. Last week I was in Brussels for a meeting of NATO defense ministers. On Thursday, 2 June 1994, I will depart with the President and secretary of defense for the D-Day commemorations, beginning in Italy, then going to England and finally to Normandy.

Last week's meeting in Brussels had two special attractions. First, Russian Defense Minister Pavel Grachev came to NATO and lectured the defense ministers on Russian military doctrine. The Russians had rented a room at NATO headquarters to host the meeting. Whenever a country rents or borrows one of these rooms, they put the country's name on the door so attendees can determine where their delegation is seated. Our delegation included the United States, France, and the United Kingdom. We found the sign that said "Russia" and went inside. Grachev was there, and he said, "Welcome." He then added, "That sounds a little funny for a Russian defense minister to welcome an American defense minister to NATO, but these are new times."

At the end of this ministerial meeting in Brussels, we went to Mons, Belgium, where the Supreme Headquarters of the Allied Powers in Europe (SHAPE) is located, and opened the Partnership for Peace (PFP) Coordination Cell. The Coordination Cell, where the delegations of the peace partner countries will be housed, is in a modest building next door to SHAPE headquarters. After a small ceremony, the members of the Partnership for Peace were announced. As each announcement was made, the flag bearers for

26

each of the countries came forward, raised the flag, and dipped it. Seeing the flags of the 18 PFP members, some of whom we had planned to fight in World War III, flying alongside those of the NATO allies was one of the most moving moments of my professional life. This presentation of the PFP members' flags exemplified the new vision of NATO: the opening up to new states and the new geostrategic realities of Europe.

The second trip will be as extraordinary as the first. I have spent a great deal of time preparing for the World War II Commemoration during the ten months I have held this job. The amount of planning related to this event is extraordinary, and for me it will be a particularly special time. My dad, a retired Air Force officer, was a fighter ace in World War II and flew two missions over Normandy on D-Day. He will be there, and we will meet for that special occasion.

At the end of World War II, Europe was in ruins. Freedom-loving nations were looking forward to rebuilding their continent, which was the vision presented by George Catlett Marshall and Dean Acheson. Their plan was to include all of Europe, from the Atlantic to the Urals, including the Soviet Union and Eastern Europe. Their vision in the late 1940s was a continent of prosperous democracies cooperating in international relations for the mutual security of the whole continent. As we know, events intervened. Stalin declined that offer, the Iron Curtain descended, and only half of Marshall's vision was realized.

Now, half a century later, the Cold War is over and the United States has an opportunity to pick up where those great leaders left off and to rededicate our country to Marshall's vision of a Europe that is whole, secure, and free. That vision is one that five years ago most people thought would never occur. It is now within our grasp. To seize it, we have to face three challenges.

The first challenge is to reaffirm that the United States is in Europe to stay. As far into the future as anyone can see and as long as Europeans want the United States to be part of their security domain, the United States will be there not just in spirit but with a substantial military presence. President Clinton said at the January NATO summit, "We will be there, not until something happens, not unless you do this. Our security is inextricably linked

27

with yours, and we will be here with about 100,000 troops for as long as we can see into the future. That is the commitment of this administration, and, I hope, of administrations to follow."

The second challenge the United States must confront is to support the success of democratic and economic reforms in Central and Eastern Europe, and that support area includes Russia, Ukraine, and other republics of the former Soviet Union. The Defense Department can only do part of this job. It can work on the security architecture of Europe, but other parts of this puzzle may be more important for the long-term security of Eastern European countries than just traditional military conceptions of security. They need to complete their economic transitions. After the first excitement of democracy and market reforms, there has been a retreat. In the recent Hungarian elections, the Socialist party, whose members are former Communists, returned to power. The transition of Eastern European countries to pluralistic societies, democratic ways of government, and market mechanisms is by no means assured, and the United States needs to focus on those areas as much as the security domain.

The third challenge facing the United States is to develop a new security system based on the realities of a Europe that transcends the historical division of post-World War II Europe—the division that prevented Marshall's vision for half a century. The purpose of the Partnership for Peace is to avoid that division of Europe and to welcome the new Europe. The PFP program has already begun to help transform European security.

Last August, I entered government as an innocent academic and was immediately thrown into the process of deciding what to do about NATO in the post-Cold War era. During the January 1994 summit meeting of the heads of state, some countries were clamoring for membership in NATO. Some American pundits wrote op-ed pieces saying, "Admit Poland, Hungary, the Czech Republic! These countries deserve to be in Europe." Some U.S. traditionalists and even more in Europe said, "Don't fix NATO; it's not broke! It's a very successful military alliance that still serves a useful function in the post-Cold War world."

Lord Ismay, the first secretary general of NATO, said, "NATO has three purposes. It keeps the Russians out, it keeps the

Americans in, and it keeps the Germans down." He must have regretted making that statement for the rest of his life. The Russians no longer need to be kept out, or at least Russia is not so immediate a threat as it was during the Cold War. The other two functions are still important, however. For those reasons, many people have argued that we should keep NATO the way it is. They have argued that it is hard enough to do business with 16 members and have warned against admitting states that don't share our values and are not able to contribute to NATO's collective defense. Such points were argued back and forth, and finally the idea of the Partnership for Peace program emerged.

The decision to propose a compromise provoked criticism from both sides. Those who claimed that you shouldn't fix something that isn't broken criticized policymakers for opening the alliance to new members. Even more criticism was heard from those who claimed that the mandate was to expand NATO eastward, bringing in new states. As such, policymakers failed because Eastern European countries are neither in nor out but somewhere in the middle. In the eyes of these critics, the Partnership for Peace is a "gutless bureaucratic compromise."

I will try to answer this criticism. Bureaucracies constantly compromise; it is in their nature. One must sometimes hold one's nose and accept a compromise proposal as the best possible outcome between two groups that strongly hold two contrary opinions. No one likes such an outcome. The Partnership for Peace program is different from most compromise solutions, however, because it has produced better results than either of the alternatives it was intended to reconcile.

The PFP is a mechanism for detailed operational military cooperation that keeps NATO at its core but opens up the business of the alliance to new members. The nations that join in the Partnership for Peace will participate with NATO in a range of military activities, including joint planning and training, search and rescue missions, peacekeeping, and crisis management.

The idea of the Partnership for Peace program was launched at the NATO summit. Any European country or former Soviet republic is eligible to join, and there are no preconditions. All the prospective member country must do is sign the framework declaration. So far, 18 countries have done so. Minister Grachev said that the Russians will sign within a couple of weeks. Once the framework declaration is signed, each member submits a presentation document to NATO. Again, there is no negotiation. The presentation document is simply a list of the facilities, resources, and forces a country commits to the PFP.

Each country that joins the PFP must also state specifically what it will do to meet two objectives of the Partnership for Peace. First, each new member must outline its plan to make its defense budget process transparent. All PFP members must create their defense budgets in a way that is open for review and scrutiny. Second, each new member must explain how it will turn its defense ministry over to civilian control. Almost all of these states have had a ministry of defense dominated by general officers. Grachev, for example, wore his general's uniform to a meeting of defense ministers. Members of the PFP are required to increase transparency and civilian control of their defense ministries.

It is important to note the two things that the PFP will not provide. The PFP does not confer a security guarantee on member states. Such a guarantee is at the heart of NATO; each NATO member signs a treaty stating that its territory is the same as the territory of any other NATO state. Therefore, an attack on one NATO state is the same as an attack on any other NATO member and requires the same kind of response. The PFP countries do not receive such a commitment. They have a right to consult with NATO, but they do not have an automatic security guarantee. Furthermore, the Partnership for Peace does not confer on participating countries an automatic path to NATO membership. The PFP makes NATO membership possible for those states that want it, but it is not guaranteed.

In late January 1994 I was in Central Europe and had dinner with the chief of defense of one of the states demanding admission to NATO. These demands had received some support in the United States from the academic community, and before dinner I mentally rehearsed all of the arguments in favor of the PFP—that it is an apprenticeship program, a step-by-step process that will perhaps lead to full membership, and so forth. As I sat down to dinner with this general, he began our conversation by saying, "I would like to thank you for not admitting us into NATO." I certainly wasn't expecting to hear that. When I asked him why, he replied, "We are not ready for membership." He went on to say, "I know many of my political colleagues want to be in NATO, but I am a military man. I know that we're not ready today. Few soldiers in our army speak English. We do not have the capacity to communicate with your army. We don't know how you do business. We don't know how you formulate strategy or tactics. We are not ready to be your ally, and we do not want you compromising your standards to admit us when we are not ready."

I replied, "General, this reminds me of that old line from Groucho Marx when he said, 'I would never want to be a member of a club that would have me as a member.'" As I waited for the interpreter to translate this common American saying, I could see that it wasn't working. I asked the general if he knew who Groucho Marx was, but he had never heard of him. He thought that I was referring to another Marx whom he knew well and that somehow I was saying something nasty about his country. After I explained my meaning to him, he said, "That's it exactly! What we like about NATO is that it's a serious military alliance. We don't want you to stop being a serious military alliance so you can take in a country that today—I tell you because I'm its boss—does not have a serious army. Everything in its own time." That time is what the Partnership for Peace gives these countries.

One issue that I confess I did not really appreciate then but that I do greatly appreciate now, is what the likely consequences would have been had the new states been admitted to NATO membership in January 1994. These states continue to have terrible problems. The transition from communism to pluralism and market economies has put an enormous strain on their societies, and as a result, it is difficult for them to find funds for defense. If these states had been admitted as full NATO members in January 1994, many of them would have been tempted to do away with their army, air force, and other defense measures and to proclaim that their powerful friends only a few hundred kilometers away would defend them if necessary.

These new states have been told that if they are interested in NATO membership, they should join the Partnership for Peace.

Two things are asked of them before they will be considered for full membership. First, these countries must show that they are worth defending; they must prove that they have a democracy, are committed to a market economy, and have made an unalterable commitment to democratic values and processes. Evidence that these requirements have been met would be, for instance, free elections and the turnover of governments over time. The real nightmare for NATO would be to admit a new state to the alliance and then have it become fascist or revert to communism. NATO would not want to be obligated to defend such a country.

Second, prospective NATO members must prove that they can contribute to collective defense. It is clear that they have problems and worry about their security, but they will not be admitted to NATO by impressing the West with the extent of their problems. To become a member of NATO, these countries must show that they can contribute to collective defense and that they have the forces to join in the fight, if necessary, to defend the West's common values and common strategic space. They can demonstrate that kind of capability and commitment through participation in the Partnership for Peace.

An advantage of the Partnership for Peace is that it does not draw lines across Europe. That lack of division may be its greatest virtue. Those who wanted to admit Poland, Hungary, the Czech Republic, and maybe Slovakia into membership tended to overlook or minimize the fact that admitting those countries would mean excluding other states. It would mean, in effect, telling those countries outside that "this is the new line of Europe. The West won the Cold War, celebrated the tearing down of the Iron Curtain for a couple of years, and then drew a new line across Europe. Some people are fortunate enough to get in, but the remainder will stay outside." The Partnership for Peace does not redivide Europe. It creates the right incentives by requiring aspiring members to prove that they are capable of assuming the responsibilities as well as the benefits of membership. It also keeps NATO at the heart of European security, thereby keeping the United States involved in European affairs.

If the truth be known, the conventional wisdom may give NATO too much credit for ending the Cold War. Many factors, including the collapse of communism and the domestic situation in the former Soviet Union, contributed to the demise of the Soviet Union in addition to the prowess and firmness of the Atlantic alliance.

One thing for which NATO has not been given enough credit is making defense policy multinational—not just keeping the Russians out of Western Europe but keeping the peace among the states of Western Europe. This achievement seems so much second nature now that it is hard to get excited about, but remember that before NATO was created, these member states were not known for being at peace with each other. In the 70 years before the formation of NATO, France and Germany fought three terrible wars. Two of those wars became world wars. No NATO country has fought any other NATO country since the formation of the alliance, with the exception of the "Cod War" between Iceland and the United Kingdom, an exception so trivial that it proves the point.

Political scientists measure "dyad-years" of conflict as a measure of violence in the international system. One war between two countries for one year equals one dyad-year of war. Viewed in this way, one could say that the history of NATO represents over 10,000 dyad-years of peace. This long peace is NATO's second greatest accomplishment, one much less heralded than the stand against communism. Many scholars say this nonviolence is a consequence of democracy, but I have another interpretation. It is not simply democracy that steers states away from fighting; rather, it is multinational defense planning.

One of the most interesting things I have done in this job was the presentation of my American defense plan for 1994 in Brussels. Representatives of all of the countries that participate in the military side of NATO were gathered in the conference room at NATO. A total of 15 representatives sat around the table. I laid out American defense policy for the next year as it pertained to NATO: the number of fighter wings, the number of ship days in the Mediterranean, the number of divisions of troops in Europe, and so forth. After my presentation, I was questioned by the representatives, many of whom were troubled about the reduction in ship days in the Mediterranean.

My first reaction was to say, "Who are you to criticize the United States? You aren't doing too well yourselves. Everyone's defense budget is declining." I caught myself, however, and realized that making defense policy in a multilateral context means that each country starts in its national capital and decides on a defense policy. Then each country sends some poor bureaucrat to Brussels to stand in front of this group, present the policy, and get rocks thrown at him. However unpleasant that experience is, it means that anyone in NATO who wanted to plan a war against anyone else in NATO would have a hard time doing it because the defense budget and policy processes are transparent. Everyone knows what everyone else is doing.

Over time, the Partnership for Peace member countries will be brought into this process. If they want to become members of NATO, they will have to learn NATO's business. They will have to send military officers to the Partnership Coordination Cell to begin planning with NATO, training with NATO, and making their defense policy in a multinational context, just as the United States does. They will need to take their defense policies out of the half-light of ministries in defense of Eastern Europe and into the cold light of NATO conference rooms in Brussels. If history is any guide, the 10,000 dyad years of peace that NATO has contributed to the world for the past half-century will be replicated when these new states are brought into a system where they can see that they do not pose a threat to each other.

I mentioned at the beginning of my talk that my two trips symbolize the change and continuity in European security. So far I have talked about the change, represented by the discussion of the Partnership for Peace program. I would also like to say a few words about the continuity, or perhaps I should say the fear of continuity, that is in the back of many minds. My upcoming trip to Normandy reminds me that the threats of authoritarianism and imperialism are still in Europe. An extraordinary change has occurred in the strategic landscape of that continent, but there is still a risk that Russia might go bad and that the new NATO, like the old NATO, might have to work to contain an expansionist Russian empire. That possibility is the great question mark hanging over European security at the moment.

34

The Partnership for Peace is the right answer because it allows the Russians to participate. They can have the same peace partner status as Ukraine or Poland; they can see how NATO does its business; they can, at least in theory, aspire someday to be a member of the NATO alliance. The Partnership for Peace program is built around an optimistic scenario, and its goal is an optimistic outcome. It avoids drawing new security lines in Europe. As Strobe Talbott, deputy secretary of state, has put it, the objective is a Russia "integrated into the West rather than contained by the West."

There is also a hedge against pessimistic outcomes. If reform in Russia falters, NATO will be there to provide for the allies' collective defense and will already have been working through the PFP with the active participants to promote regional security. This year in Poland, NATO will conduct the first military exercises with some peace partner states. Russia will not participate in that first exercise. This process will begin developing habits of cooperation and interoperability in tactics, strategy, and doctrine with countries that are afraid Russia may again become an imperial threat to the rest of the continent. NATO is now beginning to work with those countries, and if Russia happens to become the enemy and a line has to be drawn across Europe again, that line will leave on the NATO side states with which it has worked and with which it has been engaged in learning how to cooperate.

Today, NATO and Poland would not be able to conduct a joint military mission. Next year, NATO will know something about Poland, and Poland will know more about NATO. The following year, NATO and Poland will have achieved more interoperability and a greater capacity to work together for some common purpose. We hope this common purpose is the collective security of the whole continent. It may be something else, but this program is a realistic way to get there without telling the Russians that they are forever consigned to be the threat.

In conclusion, I would like to answer James Chace's (professor at Bard College and former managing editor of *Foreign Affairs*) argument that NATO has served its purpose and should be put out of business. This argument is often heard in the United States. Whenever I travel, I encounter people who ask why, since the Cold

War is over, NATO does not just declare victory, have a party, and go home. I have told you why not and why I think this alliance may actually serve a greater purpose in the next 50 years than it has in its first 50. Furthermore, in all my travels in Central and Eastern Europe, in my conversations with hundreds of citizens and government officials from Estonia to Albania, no one has ever questioned the relevance of NATO. The question is always, How do we get in? They see the relevance of this middle-aged institution and understand its contribution to collective defense and collective security. They welcome association with this so-called relic of the Cold War.

The West stands to gain enormously from this move to expand. These new states will bring a new enthusiasm to NATO, a new vigor. Their participation will give NATO greater breadth and relevance. Their engagement will reassure all states in Europe that NATO is not a threat to anyone's security, but an instrument of collective security. If that result follows, 50 years from now I will say, "Jim Chace, you got it dead wrong. This alliance that we thought was useful for the first 45 years was actually much more useful in its second half-century."

QUESTION: If NATO is expanded a few years from now, what will be the tactical implications of admitting a country that does not border on other NATO members?

SECRETARY KRUZEL: The admission of noncontiguous countries does create a strategic problem, but to my mind not an insurmountable one. The perfect way to evolve or expand NATO would be to do it contiguously; that is, to move outward. Most people think that Poland will be the next state to join NATO, and they are probably right. It is contiguous with Germany, and the Germans are eager for Poland to be admitted because the leading edge of NATO would then no longer be the eastern border of Germany.

It is conceivable that a noncontiguous state could become ready for NATO membership earlier than states bordering on NATO countries. NATO must be prepared to accept that prospect. The U.S. position has been that any country satisfying the two conditions for membership can join, as long as it is part of a

36

European community of states. Membership of noncontiguous states would be conceptually messy, but not a problem in a practical sense. The West European Union, the European Union, the Council of Europe, CSCE, NATO, and Partnership for Peace all already exist simultaneously. In the future, many contending and competing organizations will still exist. Some states will belong to all of these organizations; a few states will belong to most. Each of these organizations will have a different set of obligations. The organizational diagrams will look confusing, but the system should continue to operate fairly well. In short, the admission of noncontiguous members to NATO, as long as they are democracies and are able to contribute to both their own and the collective defense, will produce no more of a strain than all of the other strains on Europe. After all, the United States is detached from the rest of Europe.

The question that is constantly asked is when do we expect to admit new members to NATO. Officially, this question has never been answered because no one wants to create expectations. My answer when the Poles or Czechs ask is that they will get in when 16 countries decide to allow it. At least in the case of the United States, two-thirds of the Senate has to agree to the admission of another country. President Clinton cannot say in 1994 that in 1999 they will be admitted. Thus, the official answer is that no promises can be made yet. The unofficial answer is that most people feel that new members will be allowed to join the alliance by the end of this century.

NARRATOR: Secretary Woodworth, since you are Secretary Kruzel's predecessor, would you care to comment or raise a question?

SECRETARY WOODWORTH: I was delighted to hear the kinds of things mentioned by Secretary Kruzel, and I think the direction we are taking is an excellent one, and I agree that the eventual expansion of NATO must be anticipated. My own feeling has been that in the fullness of time, expansion probably is the sensible way to go. As Secretary Kruzel pointed out, there is no easy answer to the question of how and when expansion will be achieved, but I think that in the coming years, the answer will be found.

Throughout its history, NATO has worked its way through many problems where the answers were not immediately obvious. Through much consultation and interaction, the right answer has tended to come forth. No one can be certain that the answers will always be clear, but the process of intensive interaction has served NATO well in the past, and I am hopeful it will continue to do so in the future.

Another subject Secretary Kruzel mentioned, one that is extremely important to the goals of the Partnership for Peace, is the habit of cooperation we have developed in NATO. People who see NATO exclusively in terms of countering the Soviet threat and who believe that there is no need for it now that the Cold War is over fail to understand the significance of the 40-odd years of cooperation among NATO members. The political and security cooperation that took place during that time, which transformed the nature of the organization and its purpose, was largely a result of this habit of cooperation and its effect on making defense planning procedures multilateral. NATO has produced an amazing array of personal interaction among those involved in the alliance, which has had a tremendous sustained impact over the years. To the extent that NATO members can develop such an avenue of activity with these new countries—these new friends, if you will—I think it will serve NATO well. I therefore strongly applaud the direction in which NATO is moving today.

QUESTION: You talked a great deal about the cooperation and sharing of knowledge between the NATO member states and those countries seeking to join NATO, but you have said little about economics. It is possible that this cooperation can only succeed if economic cooperation occurs as well, through the European Community, the OECD, and other agencies, for instance. Where does that economic aspect fit in this situation?

SECRETARY KRUZEL: In this decade, economics is more important for the security of these countries than military arrangements. These countries have been brought into a security association that is very reassuring to them. However, I cannot think of an equivalent way of bringing them into an economic association; the natural one, the European Union, wants to accomplish this goal in a much more gradual way. In some ways, these countries are potential competitors with the European Union in low-wage, basic manufacturing.

These countries worry about being invaded by Russia. That possibility won't happen in the next ten years. They also worry about their economies collapsing and the people turning to something else in frustration. That prospect is the real threat to these countries in the near term. Almost everyone accepts the fact that economic issues will pose the greatest challenge to these countries in the next few years. Creating a workable economic association is even more difficult than establishing a common security structure.

QUESTION: In the last two years with the problems in the former Yugoslavia, there seems to be a terrible amount of conflict and lack of cooperation between the United Nations and NATO. Can that conflict be resolved?

SECRETARY KRUZEL: The United Nations and NATO have had and continue to have problems on the question of Bosnia. This conflict is an inevitable consequence of the way the world is trying to resolve this terrible and complicated crisis. The U.N.'s engagement in this process is on the ground. UNPROFOR (United Nations Protection Forces) troops are present to deliver humanitarian assistance, so they are in charge of the ground war. NATO has said it will not become involved in the ground war except to implement a peace agreement. NATO does not want to be dragged into the war, but if there is a peace agreement acceptable to all parties, NATO will take over because it knows how to operate these types of situations. The United Nations doesn't know how to run a big operation like this one. Until there is peace, however, the United Nations will run the ground part of the war, and NATO will do what it can in the air. It will prevent Serb aircraft from carrying out aerial bombardments and will prevent attacks by heavy weapons and artillery on Sarajevo and other populated areas. It will also protect humanitarian convoys with close air support. With the ground war being run by the United Nations and the air war by NATO, there is a prescription for disaster.

It took a long time for the U.S. Army and Air Force to agree that ground wars and air wars should be coordinated. Having learned that lesson, the United States will not make those mistakes again, so NATO has promised to use air power only with the permission of the United Nations. This decision was made not out of deference to the United Nations but because the use of air power would never be allowed without the permission of a ground commander. The United States will not challenge that prudent dictum of military strategy just because it controls one part of this operation and other people with a different conception of the operation control the other part. NATO and the United Nations need to work together to bring the varying logics within these two organizations to some common understanding of how these two instruments will be used. Such coordination is an inherently complicated business simply because the reporting channels go in different directions.

QUESTION: Will Hungary be rejected by the Partnership for Peace because of its Communist-type government?

SECRETARY KRUZEL: It has a socialist government, and they have learned their lesson. Today's *Washington Post* has a complaint from hard-line Communists who say this new socialist government sounds a lot like the liberals. Obviously, we cannot interfere in Hungary's domestic political decisions. If these leaders are part of a socialist government that commits itself to pluralism and market reforms, the West can live with it. If after a couple of years the government is defeated in an election and leaves office peacefully, then the West can certainly live with that as well.

QUESTION: I do not agree with the administration's apparent reluctance to draw lines. NATO would never have been established in the first place if lines had not been drawn, so I do not consider the need to avoid drawing lines a persuasive argument against its expansion.

The critical questions are, what will the Partnership for Peace's relations to Ukraine be, and what will give the PFP strategic coherence? What is the threat, and against what is the strategy directed? What are the force projections to implement the strategy? The Partnership for Peace is an invertebrate mammal, hardly a backbone structure like NATO.

SECRETARY KRUZEL: Regarding the drawing of lines, of course NATO will eventually draw lines. It will draw lines when the next member is admitted to this alliance. The year 1994 is the worst possible year to draw lines, which is why the PFP is a good compromise. Five or six years from now, if Russia is an active member of the Partnership for Peace, it will see that NATO expansion is not a threat. It is not excluding Russia from some engagement in European security. It is thus better to draw lines then than now.

I agree that Ukraine is the vital question. The key part of that question at the present time is, will Ukraine survive? What strategic interests of the United States and Western Europe are engaged in that question?

The short answer to the question of strategic coherence is that NATO was a collective defense organization and a collective security organization. It holds the promise, if Russia's evolution continues along a positive path, of being a collective security organization for the whole of Europe. If Russia again becomes the enemy, NATO can become the collective defense organization of its members. No one yet knows which of these paths NATO will take.

That choice depends on what happens in Russia. NATO can affect the outcome only minimally because the answer depends mostly on what will happen internally within Russia. Above all else, the West should not strengthen the hand of the hard-liners by admitting some states but telling others that they will forever remain outside the European security community. Such an action would create a self-fulfilling prophecy and be a colossal mistake. If strategic coherence is lacking in 1994, it is because the world is not very coherent in 1994. Putting off the answer to an unanswerable question is a good reason for compromise.

NARRATOR: Secretary Kruzel has served several administrations, and he is following his usual pattern by serving the Clinton administration well. We thank him for his insight and knowledge on the subjects of NATO, the Partnership for Peace, and European security. At a time when scholars and policymakers often go their separate ways, he has helped to bring them together by his example and service to his country.

CHAPTER THREE

Structures for Security in Europe[*]

GENERAL JOHN R. GALVIN

NARRATOR: We are honored that General Galvin could join us at the Miller Center. General Galvin was supreme allied commander in Europe, the commander in chief of the U.S. European Command. He has a master's degree from Columbia and has also done graduate work at the University of Pennsylvania. In the Army, he advanced in grade from second lieutenant to general and won respect for his leadership in a series of commands: the 3rd Infantry division, the 24th Infantry division, and the 7th Army corps in Stuttgart, Germany. He was also commander in chief of the U.S. Southern Command. He has received numerous awards, including the Silver Star, Legion of Merit, DFC, Bronze Star, and Soldier's Medal.

General Galvin has also commented and written authoritatively on security and stability in the post-Cold War era. We have looked forward to his presentation.

GENERAL GALVIN: I would like to begin by recognizing that the presidential election is approaching. It has been unfortunate that the election campaigns have focused on domestic issues. There are

---

Presented in a Forum at the Miller Center of Public Affairs on 30 October 1992.

many things happening beyond the borders of the United States that have a deep effect on our country, and I wish we didn't feel the need to confine the election to domestic questions. I realize that the economy is in bad shape, but other things need attention, too.

I would like to describe the direction in which the world is heading, what we can do about it, and how we should view the future. We are all self-satisfied and happy, basking in the great victory we won at the end of the Cold War. It was the toughest of all of the confrontations and crises that the world has seen. Two superpowers faced each other. The Soviet Union had 30,000 nuclear weapons and 200 divisions; we had 20,000 weapons and about 100 divisions. The crisis couldn't have been worse. It was also long, about 41 years. I think we are too euphoric, however, and should take time to evaluate the current world situation. There are still areas that face enormous problems, including Nagorno-Karabakh, Ukraine, Georgia, Russia, China, and Cambodia, where there are currently around 15,000 blue-helmeted United Nations people. There are also U.N. troops serving in the former Yugoslavia, where they number approximately 16,000 with 5,000 to 6,000 additional troops expected to join them. Also, about 4,500 soldiers will soon be stationed in Somalia. Then there are all the other places where crises exist, from Afghanistan to Northern Ireland.

At the same time, there are some good things happening. The United Nations is much more powerful than it was during the Cold War, because the Security Council confrontation no longer exists. There have been more U.N. peacekeeping operations over the last four years than during the previous 43 years.

Interestingly, Secretary General Boutros Boutros-Ghali has said that the United Nations needs help in regional areas, and needs more regional structure. The need is based in part on the fact that last year U.N. peacekeeping efforts cost approximately $750 million. This year that amount is projected to increase to $3 billion.

We ought to look at the role of the United States in the future. Do we want to be the dominant nation, the cop on the block? I'm not sure we do, particularly if the block resembles Fort Apache and we would be a cop in a bad neighborhood. We will need other cops with us, so maybe we should think in terms of a whole police force, not simply our individual role. I'm not sure we should try to be the dominant power in creating a kind of Pax Americana or return to a balance-of-power global strategy.

Over the past half century, we proved that a balance of power works if there are two superpowers. It doesn't work within a multipolar world, however, especially with shifting powers. A balance of power doesn't stop proliferation of weapons of mass destruction; in fact, it encourages it. Instead of pursuing a balance-of-power strategy, I think the United States ought to play a powerful role under a security architecture that includes the United Nations and regional structures. There is already a Conference on Security and Cooperation in Europe (CSCE), comprised of 52 nations. We could build a similar organization in Asia, as many countries, particularly Australia, have suggested.

Currently, China is booming. The country reminds me of a big locomotive where the crew shovels coal to the economy and holds back hard on the political brakes. Also, China is looking at the South China Sea, the Spratly Islands, and questions of petroleum in that region. Questions involving the Asian Pacific rim need to be discussed among regional members, including the United States. We belong to the Pacific, too.

There is a role in the security structure for alliances such as NATO. NATO's main advantage is that it is a political-military alliance. It is not merely political and it is not merely military. Therefore, NATO can act, as was evident in the Gulf War that followed the end of the Cold War. Gulf War forces were comprised primarily of NATO member forces that had experience working together, with similar training, doctrine, organization, and the ability and political-military sense to carry out missions. For this reason, we were successful in the Gulf War. There was an eight-nation coalition—again NATO nations—that undertook the rescue of 450,000 Kurds in northern Iraq.

Given these successful operations, why hasn't the West been able to resolve the crisis in Yugoslavia? When analyzing that situation, we should not respond impulsively and say, "We have military forces and we have a problem. Let's combine the two and resolve it." Introducing the massive use of military force into

Yugoslavia at this time could reduce the level of fighting, but then it would grind along and smolder in the form of guerilla warfare. The will to continue fighting is still there, so military intervention would be long and costly in terms of money and U.S. casualties. Instead, we ought to evaluate the Yugoslav crisis in terms of the question, what is a crisis? We just finished managing the toughest crisis yet, the Cold War, a 41-year crisis that was relatively short compared to many others.

The brief hiatus during Marshal Tito's leadership makes the Yugoslav situation look like a newly emerging crisis or one that began during World War II. Yet the crisis involving the Serbs, Croats, and Muslims began centuries earlier. We need to study crises and their nature. Crises can be long and spiked by great activity, with interludes of quiescence. They must be resolved through collective action, if they can be resolved at all.

While we have not intervened militarily, we are still taking actions in Yugoslavia. The United Nations has stationed approximately 16,000 troops there, and NATO nations are now involved. The NATO headquarters, which had been responsible for defending the north German plain, is now in Belgrade and heading toward Sarajevo. The NATO staff includes ten U.S. officers; the British, Spanish and others are also involved. In part, NATO is responsible for air-monitoring operations. The Western European Union and the North Atlantic Alliance are also present in the Adriatic. There are further actions that could be taken. Sanctions could be more strongly enforced. The United Nations resolutions that created the sanctions are strong resolutions, but they are not being enforced.

I wouldn't want to convey the impression that simply because we didn't solve the Yugoslav crisis quickly, the whole idea of a global architecture for security and stability is flawed. It is a good idea and provides the only means for the United States to contribute to that stability without exceeding limits on what this country would be willing to do.

We entered World War II on 8 December 1941, when the Germans were at the gates of Moscow, and all of Europe—France, the Netherlands, Belgium, Denmark, Norway—had fallen. Great Britain was teetering, yet it still took the destruction of the Pacific fleet to bring the United States into the war. Even then, Franklin Roosevelt initially only declared war against Japan, not Germany, because he wasn't sure he had sufficient support in Congress. Likewise, we had entered World War I in 1917, two years after that war had begun. We are not a warlike people; we are not anxious to send our sons and daughters off to war. Therefore, our reluctance to act militarily in Yugoslavia shouldn't be surprising. Naturally, the United States and other like-minded nations would take all actions short of exercising strong military force in an unpredictable situation.

There are other reasons why a global security architecture would work now. There is a general recognition that the world is growing smaller, which we see in everything we do, whether it's the environment or international law. For example, three weeks ago, El Salvador and Honduras resolved a long-standing border problem through The Hague. Resolution in this form would have been impossible a few years ago.

There is also a recognition of the destructiveness of today's weapons and that we have just lived through the worst century in terms of people killed in warfare. In those giant wars, we lost millions of people, more than half of whom were noncombatants. Those recognitions guide us in choosing a path for the future. We can build a structure, an architecture of security, starting with the United Nations. We can utilize processes such as nuclear nonproliferation and arms control. We can depend on the far greater communication that we now possess. If we can understand crises and crisis management, we will have an opportunity to have a more stable world in the 21st century.

Since World War II, there have been 125 small wars, primarily in the Third World, that have resulted in 40 million deaths. In order to accomplish our goals, we still need standing forces that are small, well-trained, and capable of acting in conjunction with other nations.

QUESTION: How do we move in this new direction when we make so much money selling weapons to approximately 125 countries worldwide, about 60 of which are led by dictators or authoritarian governments, with all the concomitant political pressures? How do we extricate ourselves from that business and move away from an orientation geared toward blocs in which we bolstered our friends and watched other countries bolster their friends?

GENERAL GALVIN: The biggest obstacle is the old argument that if we don't sell something, someone else will. My comments thus far have dealt with collective action. We are in a world where we have to recognize coalition effort and collective action. In the United Nations, we should discuss ways that countries can stop the armament trade. Currently, 36 Third World nations have a frightening military capability. These nations each have more than 700 tanks, more than 100 fighter aircraft, and more than 100,000 armed troops. The arms trade fuels this situation. We must recognize that if we sell guns and are then shot by them, we have little grounds for complaint.

QUESTION: From a military perspective, looking at the civilian administration, what can be done in an open society to get people to think about the long-term, overall benefit for the country rather than short-term, personal, monetary gain?

GENERAL GALVIN: I liked John Kennedy's book *Profiles in Courage*. Kennedy wrote that if you are a leader, you are not elected just to reflect the views of your constituency. You are elected to think and act and make decisions. It is the responsibility of a political leader to act accordingly, but I don't think recent political leaders have done so. During the election, I think the American people would have welcomed a greater emphasis on what the political leaders intended to do or thought they wanted to do about our relationship with the rest of the world. It is the duty of our leaders to outline their plans for the people. Fora such as this one also provide an excellent atmosphere for discussion of geopolitical issues. There may be other things that could be done, and our leaders need to set an example in this area.

COMMENT: We benefit greatly from using our free-market system to export our economic capacity abroad, thereby increasing the receptivity of the rest of the world to our goals. We should promote the idea that it is in our best interest to work in this direction. Our efforts would be wasted if we tried to convince the American people that they aren't interested in their own personal welfare. If they see that the U.S. economy generally benefits from our actions abroad, they will support those actions. President Bush pursued this strategy in trying to gain support for our policy on China, given the general antipathy toward that country's political system and human rights record.

GENERAL GALVIN: We are right to condition our relationship with any other country in terms of our own principles and should continue to do so. Respect for human rights is an important value for all Americans; none of us liked what occurred in Tiananmen Square. Nevertheless, we have oversimplified human rights issues and have hidden behind them. If we support the development of democracy in China, human rights will follow. Human rights is a symptom of something else; it is not an end in itself.

When I visited China recently, I noticed that the querulous Americans there were uncomfortable and that they demanded great privileges in order to stay there. American businessmen contend that the laws are too difficult and that the environment is just not good for business. Some American companies, including Ford, McDonald's, and Kentucky Fried Chicken, have entered the market, but their presence is infinitesimal compared to that of the Japanese. For at least a dozen years, the Japanese have slowly and carefully built their business relationships in China. There is also a Korean presence in China, and China just recognized Seoul. Even the Taiwanese are in China. Hong Kong, Singapore, Australia, and New Zealand are in China. The place is booming, yet Americans find it too hard to work there, too hard to get started.

While there are some legitimate reasons for not investing in China—it is still nominally a Communist country and a dictatorship—we need more public education about the current situation and what the United States could possibly do about it. Simply cutting ourselves off from China on the basis that we won't deal with anyone there until someone apologizes for Tiananmen Square is not the best approach to take. It is simplistic, considering that this country contains approximately 25 percent of the world's population and considering its presence in world markets. There are political and business reasons behind our efforts to improve communications with China and to have an influence there.

There is a similar situation in Europe. We have grown accustomed to going to Europe and saying, "If you don't take this action, we will go home." That approach might have worked in the past when we were strong and Europe was destroyed, but it does not work well now. There must be better arguments and more articulate reasoning that the United States can make in the world arena than it is currently doing.

QUESTION: The type of command that you were in charge of in NATO and that has been so successful would have been an absolute miracle 75 years ago. From your experience, please analyze it in terms of the political and personal relationships that had to be built. What makes it work? A similar environment must exist if we are to establish the same kind of organizations regionally and in the United Nations.

GENERAL GALVIN: NATO has worked in ways we don't often recognize. All of the Western European countries have refrained from stationing troops on each other's borders or expressing any concern about each other, with the possible exception of the burgeoning new united Germany. Germany has gone to great lengths to demonstrate that it is not a threat. It has said that it would be a united Germany, but within a united Europe. Chancellor Helmut Kohl told me, "We don't want to have the presidency of a united Europe. We think that a country such as Luxembourg or Belgium should hold that position." That aspect has been important to the alliance over the past 40 years, and the United States can take a great deal of credit for having been, as Eisenhower said, the glue in NATO.

Another aspect of NATO's success is that a political coalition has controlled a strong military force for 40 years. It is historically important that it has been a subordinate, disciplined military force throughout that period.

More important than the togetherness, training, military forces, and stabilization of Europe, though, is the political-military

50

relationship. NATO is an organization unlike any other alliance. It has a military committee, an infrastructure committee, and a budget committee. It has the ability to act on a day-to-day basis. When we are in situations with a mission, the task for the multinational military will change. One day it might be peacekeeping; the next day, humanitarian assistance; the next day, deterrence; the next day, conflict; the next day, peacemaking. This situation occurred with the Kurds, and to a great extent, is taking place in the former Yugoslavia. Someone must be able to control that organization on a day-to-day basis. It would be wonderful if we could reach the point where the United Nations would provide the mandate, because the United Nations speaks for the whole world.

Even in Europe, the CSCE can provide the mandate. Then the day-to-day operation in a political-military sense can take place within an alliance such as NATO. Hopefully, we can build similar alliances.

The United States has seven alliances that could be strengthened. One thing encourages another in these alliances, but we need to recognize the absolute historical uniqueness of the North Atlantic Alliance.

QUESTION: A precondition to multilateral activity in Europe, at least in terms of a wider role for NATO, would be an active German military force. How realistic is the possibility for a greater German military role in such actions as U.N. peacekeeping forces or CSCE?

GENERAL GALVIN: I think it is coming. The Christian Democratic Union–Christian Social Union (CDU-CSU) coalition recently said, "We definitely think we ought to be able to go outside our borders for a number of different reasons—for stabilization in the world, under the mandate of the United Nations, or indeed, under mandates of other coalitions." I thought that statement would cause the Social Democratic party (SPD) to explode, but the SPD is evaluating the idea. As Germany develops a new constitution, the parties in Germany are moving closer to advocating a change in the basic law. I don't think a country as powerful as Germany currently is and will be in the immediate future, can retreat from a broader military role.

QUESTION: Could the absence of much discussion about foreign policy in the current election be interpreted as reflecting a substantial degree of consensus about what the U.S. international role should be? Bill Clinton, if he were to be elected, wouldn't follow an isolationist approach and actually is committed to the same institutions that Bush is, although they might disagree on the specific level of U.S. forces in Europe. The absence of comment on foreign policy may be a positive rather than a negative sign.

GENERAL GALVIN: I think you are quite optimistic. I feel that the candidates have instead agreed to neglect those issues, and they may be doing so simply because they lack an effective program. If any of the candidates had a strong program, he should have promoted it. It would have been a big advantage to have been discussing it over the past year. I don't think the American public would have felt that the candidate had forgotten the fact that many people don't have jobs. He could have shown that a strong foreign policy program greatly affects whether Americans have jobs.

QUESTION: I interpret what you mean by a European security structure in terms of institutions, often with an organizational capability. While most people would agree that structure is important, the question is, which structure? Please comment on U.S. policy toward the development of a Western European security identity. Do you think the United States has taken too negative an attitude toward such an identity, and even if it hasn't thus far, is there a point at which the development of such an institution begins to threaten U.S. interests and ought to be discouraged?

GENERAL GALVIN: The United States has supported the development of a general Western European identity or unity since the end of World War II. During the early postwar years, congressmen and senators repeatedly spoke of the Marshall Plan and a United States of Europe, linking these two ideas. In 1948 and 1949, those ideas were also linked to NATO.

General John R. Galvin

Every administration since Truman's has supported European unification, and the United States should continue to hold that position. We have not yet recognized all of the implications for us when Europe, instead of being many little states that we can deal with individually, is one big state that we have to deal with as an aggregate. We haven't considered the business aspects of a united Europe and potential problems with the GATT rounds.

We have been right to support the unification of Europe, which is a strong, stabilizing move in terms of our own security. As unification moves forward, Europe obviously will seek a security and defense identity. That identity will serve as a stabilizing force. We have probably taken too conservative an approach in this area. In terms of the structure's formation, organized growth is a good idea. What has taken place in Europe over the past 50 to 100 years that has resulted in the present-day institutions has been a matter of aggregation and assimilation. The European Community evolved from the European Economic Community, which originated in the European Coal and Steel Community. Previously, the Western European Union (WEU) was the Western Union. These entities have been aggregated to move forward into an even greater European entity.

We now have the WEU that serves as a defense identity for the European Community, in addition to the CSCE, the European Council, NATO, and the United Nations. We should not try to develop a ten-year plan delineating which institutions will be eliminated and which will be strengthened. This process has to occur naturally. The structure is too big and complex for us to simply assemble it like an erector set. There will be a natural competition between the WEU, NATO, and the French-German military arrangements. There will be questions about the role of CSCE as compared to the United Nations and the EC, as evidenced by events surrounding the Yugoslav crisis. Yugoslavia provides a test for these structures, but it is only one test. The European Community responded first, because the four major NATO nations couldn't reach a consensus on what to do. Then the United Nations became involved, and NATO and the WEU belatedly assumed a role. We have to see how this situation is resolved.

QUESTION: Clearly, the United States effectively dominated the United Nations, not without some diplomacy. As the United Nations becomes more of a real power, why does China see it as advantageous to let the United States continue its dominant role? Without the United States it would never succeed, yet China seems to be indifferent.

GENERAL GALVIN: I don't think China is indifferent. China is extremely interested in the United Nations and only reluctantly refrained from opposing the Gulf War in the Security Council. China's actions demonstrate how much that country wants a strong relationship with the United States. It does not want to cross the United States in the Security Council. Even though the United States is dithering over Most Favored Nation status and is harassing China in other ways, with some good reason, about topics such as human rights, the Chinese still feel a strong tie to the United States. The United States irritates them and they speak of forcing the Pacific Fleet out of the Pacific and so forth, but China hasn't been willing to take any high-profile action against the United States. We have some powerful influence over China, but we are not using it a great deal.

QUESTION: Experts have convinced me that direct military intervention in Yugoslavia would be ineffective and costly. The only alternative would be to isolate the country and enforce the embargo that already has been approved. Which organizations have resisted this move?

GENERAL GALVIN: There is a generalized avoidance of the sanctions, primarily because they aren't being enforced. As soon as enforcement began, any violation would be embarrassing to anyone who is providing assistance, arms, or anything else. There are a couple of steps that we need to take now. First, we need to enforce the sanctions in the Adriatic, along the Danube, and on the borders of Romania, Albania, Greece, and the other surrounding countries. Second, we need to take preventive action, especially with reference to Kosovo. The Serbs consider Kosovo their birthplace and will return. When they do, they will drive out the Albanians. As a result, Albania will become involved, and Albania has friends such as Greece and Italy that will also become involved. We need to station troops in Kosovo now. Third, monitoring the air space has apparently caused the Serb air force in Bosnia-Herzegovina to stop flying, and we need to ensure that they continue that way. If they do fly, we should destroy their planes on the ground; it would be a simple operation. Therefore, there are still measures that we can take.

Who is delaying such measures? There is a feeling among the nations of the world, including the United States, that they could become entangled in this situation and not be able to extricate themselves. People have seen what happened in Vietnam and Afghanistan. They don't want a long, smoldering 25-year war. There is a natural reluctance to commit to something that will last for a long time.

While everyone bemoans the whole problem and disaster that Bosnia-Herzegovina is today, they are careful about becoming overly committed. The British have always been forward about peacekeeping and stability operations, yet there is a great deal of discussion in London about whether British troops should move into Bosnia.

QUESTION: Why don't we enforce the sanctions?

GENERAL GALVIN: I'm not sure I understand it myself. It's certainly not the fault of the United Nations. The United Nations created the sanctions, but nations have just not been willing to begin a blockade. They just patrol and monitor.

QUESTION: What do you think will happen in Russia?

GENERAL GALVIN: We realize that the destruction and ruination of Russia is much more extensive than previously thought. It is costing the Germans $100 billion annually to rebuild eastern Germany, and those expenditures will continue for at least ten years, even though East Germany was probably the most prosperous of the Communist states. The others have been utterly destroyed. World War II didn't destroy Germany that badly. Despite the physical destruction, it still had entrepreneurs. Currently, Eduard Shevardnadze is in trouble in Georgia. Ukraine is a mess. There is no way of knowing whether the breakup of the Soviet Union into its republics will be followed by the breakup of the republics into smaller entities.

It is therefore another problem, the dimensions of which are currently unknown. If we were mindful of what could occur in the future, we might be willing to make more sacrifices now to bring Russia, Ukraine, Georgia, Kazakhstan, and other places through this transition to a market economy, democracy, free enterprise, respect for human rights, and so forth. No one appears to know what to do, however. Everyone seems to say, "We have so many troubles ourselves that there is not much we can do."

Those nations are moribund. Re-creating them will take decades of sacrifice, and I don't know if we are ready. Certainly, following World War II we supported all of Western Europe and were ready to support Eastern Europe with the Marshall Plan. Today, however, all of Central and Eastern Europe is in shambles.

NARRATOR: Nicholas Spykman used to say that whenever the pressure on one side of a boundary became so great that it intruded on the other side, the only way to avoid either war or appeasement was to equalize the balance on each side of the territory. For 400 years, the balance of power and international law were seen not as incompatibles but as reinforcing one another. Churchill preached that gospel for many years. Even in this post-Cold War era, in areas such as the Middle East, where we seek support from Saudi Arabia and where we even talked about Iran in relation to Iraq; in areas such as Europe, where there could potentially be some balance in the future; and in China, which is never discussed without a reference to Japan as a threat, don't we still have to live with the balance of power as well as the emerging institutions that to some extent still depend on it?

GENERAL GALVIN: My answer would be yes. The United States has a choice of being the cop on the block and trying to dominate the world or working within a balance-of-power framework, which hasn't ever really worked. While you could argue that it has

56

worked, it has only done so through wars that followed any imbalance.

In reality, we must combine these choices. We need to see an American dedication to collective approaches to security and stability. It would be wrong for us to consider surgical strikes while we sit in fortress America and lash out at people who do things that we dislike. We need to forget about fortress America.

Within the whole idea of an architecture for security and stability, elements of the balance-of-power framework would still exist. It is sort of like benevolent cynicism. You shift yourself around to ensure that things stay balanced. If Japan becomes too strong in Southeast Asia, we would try to balance their strength by supporting China. There would still be a balance-of-power aspect to the security architecture, but it would not be the same aspect. The solution is never that simple, however.

NARRATOR: Members of the Miller Center Council tell us we ought to deal with the most important problems in the world. We have looked forward to your visit because of who you are. In expressing our appreciation, I want to thank you for addressing one of the most important, if not the most important, problems in the world.

II.

IS NATO OBSOLETE?

CHAPTER FOUR

Is NATO Obsolete?*

JAMES CHACE

NARRATOR: Formerly the managing editor of *Foreign Affairs* in New York, James Chace is the Henry Luce Professor of International Relations at Bard College. He has written numerous articles and books, including *Endless War: How We Got Involved in Central America and What Can Be Done.* Professor Chace is the editor of the *World Policy Journal* and is currently working on a biography of Dean Acheson. We are delighted to have him at the Miller Center.

MR. CHACE: I will be as provocative as possible in order to generate discussion. Let me begin, therefore, by saying categorically that the Western Alliance is dead. It seems likely that history will record NATO's failure to respond effectively to the Bosnian war as evidence of its demise. One reason for this failure is that NATO remains largely designed to preserve Western Europe from external threats, and what are these threats? An expanding Islam that would threaten the gates of Vienna is a far-fetched idea, though perhaps not for Samuel Huntington. A nationalist Russia is more likely to be bogged down in conflict within the former Soviet Union than

---

Presented in a Forum at the Miller Center of Public Affairs on 9 September 1994.

poised to strike a powerful, reunited Germany. Therefore, if President Clinton is not willing to take the lead in transforming NATO, he should perhaps abandon it.

As it is, NATO is little more than an expensive fiction. Even had the administration decided to use military force in Bosnia, it would have involved not NATO per se, but a coalition of America, France, Britain, and Russia. By failing to push our European allies to take concerted action and by refusing to act unilaterally outside NATO, President Clinton may have paradoxically "saved" NATO while at the same time demonstrating its irrelevance.

With NATO moribund, European security concerns are likely to be met by coalitions that will vary from crisis to crisis. Nonetheless, if the United States remains concerned with European stability, as I believe it should, it will have to keep some troops and bases in Europe for an indefinite period. In addition, Washington will have to find allies willing to prevent borders from being changed by force rather than by negotiation. For example, the United States, France, and Russia might intervene in a Hungarian-Romanian conflict over former Hungarian lands in Transylvania, now part of Romania. Even if done under a U.N. umbrella, this would be a very traditional way of enforcing the peace.

There is an alternative to this 19th-century model. NATO could be transformed into a broader organization that might eventually include the members of the former Warsaw Pact, including Russia itself, Ukraine, and Belarus. The new NATO would deal with security problems arising from the disintegration of the two blocs that once divided Europe, maintain post–World War II borders, contain ethnic conflict, and aid in the transition to democratic institutions by monitoring elections and verifying arms control agreements. NATO would undergo a transformation from a military organization designed to deter an attack from the East to become a Pan-European security organization, including the United States and Russia. That transformation is being resisted, however, not only in Washington but also in London, Paris, and to a lesser extent, in Bonn. A transformed NATO would resemble in many respects a kind of supranational police force, and like any other police force, it would require police on the beat. NATO today is not doing that kind of policing. A few air sorties over Serbian-held

Bosnia is not evidence that NATO is prepared to fulfill the kind of mission just outlined. Only with the full participation of the Eastern as well as the Western countries could NATO begin to assume this new post-Cold War role. Moreover, such a transformed NATO would have to move its borders east to the Urals, and Russia would have to move its security zone west to the Bay of Biscay. Though it may seem far-fetched, this schema nonetheless has a logic of its own. Only as part of a Pan-European security structure could NATO uphold the standards that are being violated every day in the former Yugoslavia.

While the countries of Central and Eastern Europe ardently seek membership in NATO, and Russia wants to establish a new relationship as an equal rather than a defeated subordinate, Washington has come up with the Partnership for Peace (PFP). At least rhetorically, the PFP is supposed to be the initial vehicle for creating new relations between the West and the former Warsaw Pact adversaries. In part, PFP was supposed to dampen the Central European countries' enthusiasm for joining NATO while appeasing Russian sensibilities. In fact, it was invented to buy time. There was no overall strategic concept.

What the East Europeans wanted was a mechanism to reassure them against a resurgent Russian threat. The sense of exclusion that would accompany such a reassurance, however, was exactly what Moscow most feared. It was impossible to reconcile these two objectives. In short, will Russia be a key player in the partnership, or will the partnership serve as the foundation of a new anti-Russian coalition? In fact, a partnership that focuses on military cooperation does not truly ensure the democratization of the military forces of the former Warsaw Pact and the Soviet Union. Nor does it do much to ensure the stability of the East. By placing excessive emphasis on the relations between individual partners and NATO, the partnership may be missing an opportunity to act as a catalyst for intraregional cooperation.

There are two ways in which NATO could become part of a larger European security organization. First, an unrestricted expansion of NATO would eventually transform NATO from a military alliance to a nascent collective security organization. It is important to distinguish an alliance designed to counter a specific threat posed by an external enemy from a collective security organization primarily concerned with preventing conflict among its members. Such a large organization might compromise its military effectiveness and its decision-making capability.

An alternative vision also entails the creation of a Pan-European structure but does not rely on NATO to accomplish it. This alternative would entail a kind of nesting process: NATO would remain intact, but other regional groupings that evolve in Central and Eastern Europe and the former Soviet Union would serve as vehicles for erecting a Pan-European security organization. This would preserve NATO's integrity as a fully functioning military alliance. This version also presupposes the continued democratic evolution of the East. Otherwise, such a structure might amount to little more than sanctioning Russian domination of its periphery.

I prefer an expanded NATO as a foundation of a new European security system, accompanied by a five-power steering committee. This core security group would consist of the major military powers: Britain, France, Germany, the United States, and Russia. The group would be expected to ensure that the common interest in preserving the peace of Europe will prevail over short-term interests. In some respects, this arrangement resembles the Concert of Europe that prevailed from approximately 1815 to 1853. It is interesting at the end of the 20th century how often we are haunted by the 19th century.

The Concert system revolved around a small grouping of major powers that shared similar views of a desirable international order and was therefore able to forge cooperative mechanisms for preserving the peace. All five powers will not always agree, of course. Obviously, there were differences within the Concert—the Eastern powers (Russia, Austria, Prussia) were more conservative, while Britain and France were more liberal. Nonetheless, until 1853, the desire to avoid war in Europe was more important to the powers than their ideological differences. To preserve the balance of power in Europe today under new conditions and with a new policy of including Russia in collective security arrangements should now be the American goal. It would also help to ensure a continued, though reduced, American commitment to the stability of Europe, which has been the goal of the American government for the past half century and should remain the goal for the future.

President Clinton's general foreign policy posture and his seeming unwillingness to buck the military also encourages Americans to turn away from external commitments. The armed forces, in turn, seem to have an aversion to any military action that does not promise wholehearted public support and guaranteed success (including an exit strategy), The President has made no effort, or at least no repeated or clear effort, to define America's national interests, if indeed he has any idea what they are. I hope he does believe that the peace and prosperity of Europe rate high on the list of America's vital interests. There is no indication, however, that Clinton has drawn the necessary conclusions from the Bosnian debacle or that he intends to move in any direction other than the status quo. Reluctant to come to grips with NATO's obsolescence, unwilling to try to transform it into an effective instrument of American power and purpose, the United States may be making what former British prime minister Lord Salisbury once called "the commonest error in politics, which is sticking to the carcasses of dead policies."

QUESTION: How do you visualize this plan you propose for an expanded NATO being successfully developed and carried out?

MR. CHACE: I do envision success, although I was critical of the PFP as a stopgap. Nonetheless, facts are facts, and the Europeans were not eager to include Russia and some of the Eastern states in an extended NATO. We have to forge an American-European consensus. The PFP was probably the best that could be done in the short term, given the pressure from Hungary, Poland, and Czechoslovakia in particular to join NATO because of their fear of Russia. Pressure also came from Russia to keep them out because Moscow did not want an anti-Russian coalition to develop.

I attended a conference in Budapest recently with mostly younger security specialists from Eastern and Central Europe. I noticed a profound gap in perception between the Americans and the Eastern Europeans. At one point I was called an appeaser. East Europeans want to move the Iron Curtain 500 kilometers to the east. I understand why they feel this way, but a deep gap in perception remains. They want a NATO designed exclusively to deter Russia from doing anything aggressive, and they want to be part of that new NATO.

The Americans at the conference explained that the United States is a global power, while Russia, despite its weaknesses, is nonetheless a Eurasian power. Our interests can conflict but they also can coalesce at certain points, and therefore the United States wants to engage Russia militarily, politically, and economically whenever we can. As a result, the East Europeans considered us naive, and we considered them parochial and somewhat shortsighted. The difference is probably due to the nature of being a global power as opposed to a small power in Central Europe. They continue to press for NATO membership, and they certainly don't want Russia in at all.

The PFP could be an initial step toward a transformed NATO, first by including the East European countries in joint maneuvers and then in building relations with Russia. The ultimate goal should be to include Russia and the East European countries in an overall Pan-European security organization. Otherwise, the United States will retreat into some form of isolationism, which would be an utter disaster. If NATO has no real function to fulfill, it will fall apart. Historically, it would be a miracle if 20 years from now, or even 10 years from now, NATO were much of an alliance at all except on paper. If NATO's function isn't transformed, it is unlikely that it can continue to exist.

How, therefore, do you take an organization that does function reasonably well, transform it with a new mission, and preserve America's presence in Europe? The U. S. presence is going to be reduced to 100,000 troops anyway. It could be dropped to 50,000 if a decision were made to include the Russians instead of trying to keep them out. What I most fear now is the growth of American isolationism, fed in part by domestic politics. I am concerned when I hear Bob Dole, the titular head of the Republican party, inveigh against American intervention abroad again and again. President Clinton himself put out Presidential Directive 25, which contains so many conditions for American participation in peacekeeping and peacemaking arrangements with NATO as to make it almost impossible ever to send troops abroad. I think these actions and attitudes feed into one another, and I am trying to find ways in which we can strengthen American participation instead of withdrawing.

QUESTION: Until recently, the head of NATO had always been an American general. What influence does this indicate? Should a European general be head of NATO rather than an American general?

MR. CHACE: The Europeans have failed abysmally in the Yugoslav case, albeit they often remind us of the fact that French and British troops are on the ground in Bosnia. I don't blame them, by the way. We don't have any troops there, and in that sense, you can say they have done far more than we have. On the other hand, if you look further back in the development of the Yugoslav crisis, the United States, under Secretary of State James Baker, backed off from getting involved, in part because the Europeans, and German Foreign Minister Genscher in particular, said, "This is our show." The French agreed and said, "We will take care of this. We don't need you." As a result, by the time Clinton became president an ineffective policy had already been established.

I have been critical of President Clinton's waffling. It is not by accident that the new Doonsbury icon of Clinton is a flying waffle. A great power cannot make threats and then back off time after time. Secretary of State George C. Marshall (Dean Acheson's mentor) used to say around the table, "Gentlemen, don't fight the problem." This administration, in my view, constantly fights the problem.

Concerning the transformed NATO, the United States clearly has a major role to play. We have seen this even in the Bosnian case. Only when Russia and the United States became involved was it possible to propose a plan with some possibility of succeeding. Earlier, U.N. representative Cyrus Vance, followed by Thorvald Stoltenburg, and European Union representative David Owen had achieved little or nothing. Once the two major powers became involved, some progress was made. This outcome also reinforces my view that problems cannot be settled in Europe without the participation of Russia. It simply can't be done. Russia has been reasonably cooperative in Bosnia and Serbia. The fact that they have close relations with the Serbs has helped rather than hindered. The United States also has a major role to play.

With that in mind, should an American general be the head of NATO? My view is that in a Pan-European security force, in a transformed NATO with a reduced American presence, the leader should be a European general—not a French general or a German general but a Dutchman or a Dane. It is time to move away from an American head of NATO, while leaving 50,000 or so American troops under the transformed NATO. Furthermore, if Russia joins, it would be difficult for Russian forces to serve under an American commanding officer. Under an European, however, it might be more feasible.

QUESTION: Would you comment on the possible conflict or overlap between the jurisdiction of the United Nations and NATO?

MR. CHACE: As far as the jurisdictional overlap, in a given situation where the Great Powers have accorded the United Nations power, the United Nations would presumably decide whether or not to sanction a NATO action. We must remember that we are dealing with the traditional methods of governing. In addition, we are talking about a United Nations that was virtually impotent in terms of peacekeeping or peacemaking until the end of the Cold War. The United Nations began to function effectively in the Gulf War only under American leadership, but neither the Russians nor the Chinese opposed intervention. For the first time since 1945, the Security Council was beginning to act as a kind of Great Power condominium. This is exactly what Franklin Roosevelt intended, but the Cold War prevented it from happening. With the end of the Cold War, if the Great Powers can cooperate, they can accord the United Nations greater authority, but otherwise the United Nations is impotent. No one would admit this more readily than Boutros Boutros-Ghali.

The United Nations may be a useful mechanism for a number of things, but the Great Powers had been unwilling to accord the United Nations a peace enforcement unit. People such as Brian

Urquhart, former undersecretary general, urged a kind of military unit or rapid deployment force that would be under the control of the U.N. secretary general. The secretary general could not deploy the force, however, without the permission of the Security Council. Until recently, the United Nations has relied on ad hoc peacekeeping methods. Peacekeeping means that the two sides agree that they want the peace to be kept. The peacekeeping group also helps define a border. For example, there has been a peacekeeping force in Cyprus since the mid-1960s. Turkey and Greece do not really want to go to war over Cyprus, and the peacekeeping force simply ratifies the de facto border.

Peacemaking or peace enforcement is a different matter, and it remains unlikely that the Great Powers will accord the United Nations that kind of capability. Peace enforcement will probably still be carried out by regional organizations. A transformed NATO would become a Pan-European security organization concerned that borders not be changed by force—which is not to say that borders are immutable, but they should not be changed by force.

President Clinton is currently preparing for the invasion of Haiti, unless the Haitian generals leave at the last minute. In my view, the invasion must take place, because already the credibility of this administration has been gravely undermined by repeatedly threatening and then pulling back. President Clinton can no longer afford not to carry through with his threat, unless the Haitian generals retire.

We are basically talking about a useful U.N. sanction and the involvement of other Caribbean nations and, more directly, American behavior in an American sphere of influence. We are not talking about the Monroe Doctrine, which addressed threats from an external power like the Soviet Union. We are talking about something much closer to the (Theodore) Roosevelt Corollary, which stated that we will control what we wish to control in our own sphere of influence. Whether you think U.S. intervention in Grenada or other places was valid, at least we always invoked the notion that Soviet communism threatened us. When the United States intervened in Panama, no one invoked the Cold War; no one has invoked the Cold War in Haiti; nor will it be invoked in Cuba if something happens there. Instead, it is a question of American regional security concerns. In this case, the focus is on refugees.

COMMENT: In essence, the relationship of NATO to the United Nations would be determined on an ad hoc basis, dependent on the circumstances at the time—that is, dependent on the practical exercise of the United Nation's existing power on the alliance at the time.

MR. CHACE: Your statements approximate what I said about a five-power steering committee, which Professor Stanley Hoffmann has also suggested. If you enlarge NATO to form a Pan-European security organization of approximately 16 to 30 members, it becomes unwieldy. There must be some smaller mechanism within the organization for it to operate. You might group together the five major powers and two somewhat smaller powers representing different geographic regions—perhaps Spain or Greece from the Mediterranean and Poland from the east. In other words, there must be an effective form of representation and decision making.

I therefore oppose the use of the Conference on Security and Cooperation in Europe (CSCE) for security purposes. An organization of some 56 countries makes no sense as a military organization. Though we are talking about an organization with a political component, its main function is to be a military organization. Political organizations are fine, but NATO is a military organization, and the transformed NATO would be a military organization, and its mission has to be defined in military terms. A political component is behind it all, and the military serves as the arm of politics. Nonetheless, the focus is military.

QUESTION: If what you envision is an organization that will respond to a different kind of threat and in most cases a lower-level military threat, why do we need an elaborate organization? Why not just a political alliance?

MR. CHACE: That point is one I wrestle with. When no specific external threat exists, why not just have a political alliance rather than an elaborate organization? An alliance, particularly a military alliance, is usually directed against something. Alliances don't usually appear out of thin air. They usually are formed when a country has been threatened. I don't even think a Russian threat exists in the sense of threatening Europe, so what is the point of having an alliance at all? What would keep it from falling apart? My personal opinion is that it will fall apart.

Nonetheless, the long-term stability of Europe is in America's interest. I am not simply talking about a threat from Russia or smaller conflicts that may not spread far. I don't think many Europeans are worried that the Bosnian war will actually spread into a general European confrontation. After all, it is not 1914. NATO was designed primarily for the purpose of deterring the Soviet Union, but also as a means to anchor Germany. John T. McCloy once said that we never thought Russia could ever militarily threaten all of Europe. That might be an overstatement; there were moments when we were frightened of Soviet intentions and capabilities. Dean Acheson and George Kennan disagreed strongly in the mid-1950s about Germany's role. Acheson believed that West Germany had to be anchored in the Western alliance because a unified neutralized Germany might at some point become unstable.

People still discuss European security in terms of Germany. I don't believe that Germany necessarily threatens the peace of Europe, but there are those who do. Inevitably, 80 million productive Germans will come to dominate Europe. Will Germany always put its foreign policy at the service of an all-European policy? Not necessarily; it did not do so in Yugoslavia. A good case can be made that German policy helped spark the conflict in Yugoslavia. Bonn, against the express wishes of Paris and Washington, recognized Croatia and Slovenia. This was one of the few times in post-World War II history that Bonn had deliberately contravened the wishes of its two primary allies. Overall, German policy since 1950 has sought to keep Paris and Washington in balance. One cannot assume that Germany will not carry out what it believes to be German interests, which may or may not be seen as in our interest.

The stability of Europe entails a traditional view that the United States has had toward Europe since early in the century (with the exception of 1920 to 1940). American foreign policy seeks to ensure that no one power should dominate Europe to a degree that might threaten America's interest. That policy should not change. Therefore, a European security organization should not only aim to keep Russia within the polity but also keep Germany within it, which requires keeping the United States involved in Europe. Without a sense of the importance and relevance of U.S. involvement in Europe, the United States will withdraw and the alliance will eventually fall apart. Again, far from saying that NATO should come to an end, I'm trying to transform it. My initial remark was that the Western alliance is dead. It is. But that doesn't necessarily mean that a concern with European security is dead. Rather, events in Yugoslavia indicate that this concern remains as vital as ever.

QUESTION: You mentioned encountering, while at a conference in Eastern Europe, a pronounced feeling among Eastern Europeans that the Iron Curtain should be pushed back 500 kilometers. Do you place any significance on the first joint military maneuvers that took place last week between the United States and Russia, given that the other countries of Eastern Europe have been fearful of such U.S.-Russian cooperation?

MR. CHACE: I'm sure it made some of them nervous that the first maneuvers were between the United States and Russia. They are not united, however. We often construct a myth that the Central European countries cooperate and the Balkans cooperate. That is not true. The so-called Visegrad Group of Poland, Slovakia, Hungary, and the Czech Republic is a myth. The Poles are trying to cut their own separate deal with NATO and get in more quickly. The Czechs want to have as little as possible to do with the rest of the Central European partners and would like to tie themselves quickly into the West. My sense is that they are not a particularly united group of people. They were united with the Soviet Union against their will, but other than that, they are not much of a bloc in the way that one can say the European Community is.

If a country joins the West European security organization, it is also likely to remain a democracy. Democracy is the price of

admission, as it is for joining the European Union. The Greek
colonels could not have remained in power and become part of the
European Community. When Franco died in Spain and Portugal
had a revolution, it was not expected that those two countries would
necessarily become democratic. They had almost no experience in
democracy. Yet, today almost anyone would agree that both
countries are functioning democracies. They have had alternative
governments (the right and the left), and the military poses no
threat. In fact, when a leftist revolution took control in Portugal,
Kissinger thought it was too late for them. He was wisely overruled
by Helmut Schmidt of Germany and Giscard d'Estaing of France.

In short, the price of admission in Europe is establishing a
democracy. Control of military organizations is far more likely and
possible within a democratic polity. If Russia, Poland, and Hungary
are kept outside, they are much more likely to be a danger. A
policy of exclusion is far more dangerous than a policy of inclusion.

QUESTION: Did you say that an American presence within the
NATO structure is necessary for the indefinite future?

MR. CHACE: Yes. America should maintain a presence in this
transformed NATO, this Pan-European security organization. I
don't want America to withdraw from the European continent, but
we certainly don't need to keep as many troops there.

QUESTION: Was the decision by Germany's foreign minister
Genscher to recognize Croatia and Slovenia, which accelerated
Yugoslavia's disintegration, a decision he made on his own or was
it made at the cabinet level?

MR. CHACE: I don't know enough about the intricacies of German
politics to say for sure, but I doubt that Genscher could have made
a decision on his own to recognize Croatia or Slovenia without the
agreement of the cabinet or Chancellor Kohl. Croatia and Slovenia
are within the traditional German sphere of influence, and that was
one of the reasons they received diplomatic recognition. The
German economic zone includes Eastern (or Central) Europe and
extends into Slovenia and Austria. It seems ironic that after a long

hiatus Germany has simply picked up where it left off in 1913 after the horrifying experiences of war and almost total extermination of the Jews. Today's German economic zone is similar to the German economic bloc of 1913 that John Maynard Keynes described in his book *The Economic Consequences of the Peace.* Keynes explained that Europe revolved around the axis of German power; this is happening again. Thus, it would be historically impossible for Europe not to be dominated one way or another by Germany—but not necessarily by a German military bloc. A similar situation is Japan, which is not a threatening military power in the East, but nonetheless has a yen bloc extending almost to Thailand. These are the historical consequences the United States didn't necessarily foresee.

In current economic ranking (Russia and China aside), the United States is first; Japan, second; Germany, third; and France, fourth. Until Germany was unified, West Germany and France could still act somewhat in tandem. West Germany was more powerful economically than France, although not by much, so it took the lead economically, while France led politically, and that has lasted for the last 20 years. When Germany far surpasses France, as it doubtless will, then the relationships will change. No longer will there be a French-German alliance working in tandem to set the tone of Europe. Instead, the tone will be permanently German. The French by now are aware of the inevitable change and don't know what to do about it.

QUESTION: Do you agree that the reconstitution of Imperial Russia is inevitable?

MR. CHACE: Yes, and interestingly enough, it is being done with the approbation of the United States. When we use the term *Imperial Russia* in the contemporary world, I doubt it would include the Baltic states. The Baltic states became such an important issue in the West that Russia will not jeopardize relations with the West by menacing the Baltics. What the United States is sanctioning is a larger Russian sphere of influence—but not expansion into the Baltics, Poland, Romania, or Central-Eastern Europe—and I do not think the Russians intend such an expansion. By overreaching,

Russia would lose the International Monetary Fund (IMF), foreign investment, and military cooperation. No Russian leader, except perhaps Vladimir Zhirinovsky, can take that risk. Even Prime Minister Viktor Chernomyrdin toned down his hostility to reform after the elections, and he has accepted many of Yeltsin's policies.

In any case, Russia considers the "near abroad" their sphere of influence, which includes Uzbekistan, Kazakhstan, Georgia, Armenia, and other adjacent areas. Russian influence has already been exerted in Georgia, Armenia, and Azerbaijan. The United States has more or less consented to this Russian sphere of influence out of fear that major conflicts raging at the Russian borders could involve the Middle East and Islam. America would prefer that Russia handle that area. Besides, we could do little about it. It is one thing for NATO to extend its domain into Eastern Europe. It is another thing for the United States to become involved with more peripheral areas that were once part of Imperial Russia.

Similarly, Russia can do little when we intervene in Haiti. Yes, the United Nations is a tool, but does anyone honestly think the United States would choose not to act in Haiti if the United Nations did not give its approval? We didn't use the United Nations for Panama. In other words, within this particular sphere, it is unlikely we will be challenged, and I don't think we will challenge Russia in their respective sphere.

COMMENT: American troops in Germany have no idea of what they are doing there. They no longer patrol. They literally walk around Frankfurt or Nuremburg. A similar situation exists in South Korea, where American troops no longer patrol the demilitarized zone. I would argue from a global perspective that this is a good situation; fewer U.S. troops engaged in patrols means lower tension worldwide. From the viewpoint of keeping the United States engaged in world affairs, however, this condition seems disturbing. American soldiers do not understand why they are still in Germany or South Korea. Germans are not stationed everywhere in the world and neither are the South Koreans. American troops abroad may become a source of domestic conflict.

MR. CHACE: I agree with you. The most important question is why should we keep troops in Europe. What is the mission? During the peak of the Cold War in the 1950s, the U.S. mission was very clear, but it is less clear now. This is the reason the United States can no longer keep 100,000 American troops in NATO. The overhauled security organization I am proposing will mean fewer American troops, 50,000 or less. Basically, we should have a reduced American presence with a specific mission, such as border security or peacekeeping. I am speaking of a professional army, by the way. Naturally, I don't want to see anyone die, but when you have professional rangers, marines, and others, they are occasionally killed in combat, and you can't suddenly pull all American troops out of a danger zone. With small professional armies, it should be reasonable to deploy them with particular missions. For example, the French Foreign Legion was an intervention force.

The American people will not support large numbers of American troops under arms much longer. A small American presence under a Dutch general in a different kind of organization that could train for specific purposes such as verification and border wars could be acceptable. A reduced force that included an aircraft carrier in the Mediterranean could be used to intimidate—the old gunboat diplomacy. It is often said that if the Bush administration had sent a warship in the earlier stages of the Yugoslav war (the Croatian-Serbian battle over Dubrovnik), the destruction might have been quickly stopped. Sometimes intimidation early on in a conflict is useful. Americans would probably support such a limited presence, particularly if the president articulates the U.S. national interest.

It is amazing what Roosevelt did with the U.S. Lend-Lease Act. Britain ran out of money in the fall of 1940 and could no longer pay for the munitions they needed. The American people were unwilling to lend Britain any money outright after our experience with debts from the First World War. Thus, Roosevelt proposed the idea of lend-lease, using his famous Garden Hose speech to explain his proposal in which he said if your neighbor's house is on fire, you lend the neighbor the garden hose, and when the fire is out, he returns the hose or pays for it in kind. Such action is a question of presidential leadership and persuasion. Any continued American military presence abroad demands that our interests be clearly defined so the people can understand our position. The President of the United States is the person to do the job.

NARRATOR: Professor Chace has certainly stimulated our thinking and we hope he will visit again to provide us with further enlightenment on this subject.

CHAPTER FIVE

Is NATO Obsolete?*

RICHARD L. KUGLER

NARRATOR: Richard Kugler is a senior social scientist and former analyst of the RAND Corporation and is an internationally recognized expert on national security and defense policy, global military strategy, force policy, the defense budget, European security affairs, and NATO. He has worked as executive manager and adviser to the secretary of defense, deputy secretary of defense, and the chairman of the Joint Chiefs of Staff. His knowledge is therefore widely recognized not only in the public eye but also within the government—in the State and Defense Departments, Joint Chiefs of Staff, and the National Security Council (NSC).

Mr. Kugler holds a doctorate in defense policy and management from MIT and a bachelor's degree in international relations from the University of Minnesota. He currently teaches not only at RAND but also at the National Defense College and George Washington University. Within the vast format of the RAND Corporation publications, he has published the equivalent of six books.

Many other things could be said about Mr. Kugler's experience, but the sum and substance is that he is one of the

---

Presented in a Forum at the Miller Center of Public Affairs on 17 November 1993.

nation's preeminent authorities on security and defense matters, as well as the history of the Cold War, on which he has recently written an important book, *Commitment to Purpose: How Alliance Partnership Won the Cold War*. Today he will speak on the same subject he recently addressed in *Foreign Affairs*: Is NATO obsolete?

MR. KUGLER: For those of you who have read the *Foreign Affairs* article authored by Ron Asmus, Steve Larrabee, and myself titled "Building a New NATO," you already know my answer to the question, "Is NATO obsolete?" My answer is that NATO must go out of area or out of business. This thesis is the shorthand, sound-bite formulation of a complex answer that I would like to delve into today. I will draw on our *Foreign Affairs* article and talk also about some of the things that have happened since then, including the evolution of American foreign policy and NATO policy.

I do not think NATO is doomed to extinction simply because the Cold War is over and the Warsaw Pact threat is gone. Although formerly alliances often ended when the external threat vanished, that is not necessarily the case any longer. NATO has always been based on more than a reaction to an external threat. It has also been a community of Western values aimed at laying a security foundation that would allow democracy, a market economy, and cooperative diplomacy to take hold. The Cold War was won and communism receded in large part because of this legacy. Mainly because of this role, the governments of the alliance do want to keep NATO alive. They also value it, however, as an insurance policy against an uncertain and turbulent future. The defense cooperation NATO affords can be useful in dealing with other threats.

Nonetheless, if NATO is going to remain alive and vital, it must be relevant to the needs of the new era and to the dangers ahead. Simply stated, those dangers lie outside of NATO's borders, especially to the east along the so-called arc-of-crisis zone stretching from Poland through East Central Europe, down into the Balkans through Turkey, and on into the Caucuses. (When I use the phrase *arc of crisis*, I will be referring to that zone.) Dangers are coming from this crisis zone and the rest of Europe in general. My contention is that if NATO is going to remain not only in existence but alive and vital, it must be capable of handling those dangers. I stress that the goal is not to keep NATO alive in its own right as an end in itself but rather because the cause of peace and stability requires a healthy NATO. Restating the theme, if NATO does not go out of area, Europe will go out of business.

Indeed, we need a new NATO to deal with an endangered Europe. A year ago, the common judgment among many observers was that Europe was a permanently peaceful place owing to the ongoing triumph of market democracy and community, and furthermore that an optimistic future of peace and tranquility was a foregone conclusion. The last year, however, has dealt cruel blows to that vision, and many observers—not just myself and my co-authors, but other people such as Zbigniew Brzezinski, John Lukacs, and William Pfaff—are rapidly becoming pessimistic. Many believe that in one way or another, Europe is rapidly entering into a silent crisis—silent because the effects and manifestations are not readily observable, but a crisis nonetheless of deep proportions. This silent crisis is being brought about by five interacting dangers, which I will briefly list.

First is the decline of cohesion and vision in the West, not only in NATO but in the European Union (EU). We have seen the visions of Maastricht stagnate and fade in many ways, bringing about weakened Western resolve, weakened Western activism, and weakened Western leadership.

The second danger is that of mounting ethnic violence in the Balkans that threatens to spread outward and consume the surrounding area in an atavistic ethno-nationalism. Aggressive war may be again accepted as a romantic ideal and as a legitimate tool of statecraft, especially for resolving historical animosities in the Balkans and the surrounding area stretching up through Hungary.

The third danger is that of an emerging power vacuum in East Central Europe that threatens to spawn worrisome security dynamics, including nuclear proliferation (of which Ukraine is only the first example), competitive military rivalries, renationalized defense policies, and tremendous security tension in an area of significant historical animosity and unsettled borders. This threat could spur the emergence of new security alliances—between Poland and Ukraine, for example, or even potentially among Poland,

Ukraine, and Germany. The history of alliance formation is littered with many different permutations and combinations in Europe—hopscotch alliances and shifting alliances. History tells us, however, that multiple alliances in Europe, including tripolar structures, are not at all a remedy for stability.

The fourth danger is the turmoil in the Commonwealth of Independent States and the growing doubts about the ease or certainty of Russia's transition to a market democracy. In addition, there is increasing fear that diplomatic trouble of one kind or another with Russia probably does lie ahead. This fear is magnified by the perhaps harsh Western reactions to Russia's seemingly renewed design of coercion and imperial control over the commonwealth. I don't make this statement to tarnish Russia's image before the American people. I recognize that the Russian government must face many complex problems. I would refer you, however, to Foreign Minister Kozyrev's recent article in the *Washington Post* and to his speech to the United Nations in which I have based my interpretation of Russian foreign policy. We should take Kozyrev quite seriously.

Kozyrev offered the vision of a Russia that would not be an intimate partner of the West. This Russia would not be an adversary but would pursue its own national interest, meaning that in some cases Russia would be aligned with the West, and in some cases not. We should accept that condition. He also made the case for Russian predominance on the territory of the former Soviet Union. The activities of the Russian government lately indicate that this agenda is being carried out, even under Yeltsin's current regime.

The fifth danger is a forecasted product of the first four; if events truly deteriorate, it is one to be taken seriously even though it is in the distant future. This danger is the forbidding prospect that a clash between Russia and Germany may eventually emerge as Russia recovers its balance and moves westward, and as Germany, which is entering into a new period of restored power and influence in Europe, moves eastward. Separating these two countries now is this so-called arc of crisis, a zone of instability and danger in itself. Germany and Russia have a long and checkered history and are very proud nations. In some cases they have been able to cooperate with each other and in other cases have fallen into deep and bitter rivalry.

What do these five dangers and the emerging silent crisis they entail mean? I don't mean to imply that all hope for a positive future is doomed, but rather that a successful outcome is not foreordained. If a positive outcome is to be achieved, it will have to be gained through hard work, not passivity on the part of the West.

If the West does not become active, Europe could be lost for the fourth time this century—not to the reappearance of a totalitarian hegemon but to a chronically chaotic and anarchical system—a Europe of 19th-century politics, 20th-century passions, and 21st-century technology. In other words, we could have a Europe of multipolarity, rampant nationalism, and modern weaponry, meaning a highly unstable and volatile Europe, the nature of which could drag even responsible countries into conflict and potentially into war.

What is NATO's role in dealing with all of these conditions? NATO isn't a cure-all, nor is security policy a cure-all. Ultimately, peace in Europe will probably be a product of economic renewal, if it can take hold. Yet security does play an important role, and indeed in the absence of security, I'm not certain that economic prosperity would be possible.

NATO isn't the only security institution in Europe, but it does play a critical role. While I support the European Union and Conference on Security and Cooperation in Europe (CSCE), both institutions are nonetheless too weak in the absence of a strong NATO. Indeed, a strong NATO is critical to their vitality for a variety of reasons.

The question is, what is to be done? The proposal articulated in *Foreign Affairs* by my two fellow authors and myself is to create a new and revitalized NATO, anchored on a new transatlantic bargain. We propose to reorganize the West to deal with the East—to create a NATO that can export security outward and eastward instead of just within NATO's borders.

There is no expectation that this kind of NATO can solve all of the problems of Europe, but I believe a revitalized NATO could help in two ways. First, it could help lay a foundation of security reassurances in the arc of crisis that would foster a healthier political climate in which market democracy could take root.

If we look back to the Cold War, it seems highly unlikely that democracy would have taken hold in Germany had that country not been bought into NATO. Many Germans will attest to this fact. It was the foundation of Western security reassurances that created the favorable climate in which democracy was able to grow. The same applies to the future of areas east of those borders.

Second, a strong NATO would help deter aggression and provide the means for military intervention if such a step were necessary. In our *Foreign Affairs* article, we outlined a seven-point program for NATO reform to be carried out over the coming decade. The first point is to adopt a revised strategic concept reinterpreting NATO not as an alliance that solely defends its 16 members, but as an alliance that promotes common values and collective security across all of Europe. This concept presents a fundamental change in NATO's purpose.

The next two points bear upon the political dimensions of crafting a new transatlantic bargain. During the Cold War, NATO was basically dominated by the United States. The principal partners—Britain, Germany, and France—played subordinate roles in many ways. Indeed, France sat sullenly on the sidelines for many of those years. That basic relationship must change for many reasons, not the least of which is that the United States can no longer carry the burdens. Also, our allies are becoming stronger and more powerful themselves. What we therefore propose is much more co-equal relations among the United States, Britain, France, and Germany. Certainly continued relations with Britain will be important, but the key will be our relations with France and Germany. We especially need to improve U.S.-French relations. During the Cold War, there was cause for a fair amount of animosity, largely rooted in Gaullism. The geostrategic equation in Europe is rapidly changing, however, and America and France are now on much closer strategic wave lengths.

The next point—one that is critical and, admittedly, controversial—is to bring about the strategic emancipation of Germany. We need a Germany that actively and constructively leads the West in managing security affairs to the east, though not a Germany that lies outside of NATO or operates in a renationalized way. Nonetheless, an assertive, strong, and active Germany is needed.

The next step is equally controversial: to adopt a plan that would provide credible security reassurances to non-NATO nations and perhaps admit new members into NATO, particularly Poland, the Czech Republic, Hungary, and maybe Slovakia. Concurrent with this development would be a strategic outreach to Russia as well. Everything possible must be done to aid market democracy there and help foster constructive relations among our nations.

The sixth point is to treat Ukraine as a viable nation, for its emergence also fundamentally changes the geostrategic architecture of Europe. If it were ever to fall back into the Russian fold, which may regretfully be happening, it could bring the prospect of renewed hostilities with Russia. Yet, as long as it remains an independent nation the size of France in territory and population, it acts as an important strategic buffer. If Ukraine acts in constructive and responsible ways, it is a potential contributor to European stability. In order for it to behave that way, we need to treat it not as a nuclear problem to be solved but as a country to be reassured and brought into the community of nations.

The final point is to strengthen NATO's civilian institutions, military command structures, and force structures to improve NATO's capacity to project military forces beyond its borders. NATO's forces, contrary to popular interpretation, are not in free-fall decline. The reduction is fairly well planned. Its forces are oriented to border defense, however, rather than to operations beyond those borders.

While American forces have the capability to extend operations beyond NATO's borders, they are in a separate category. The allies, for the most part, are not equipped for such an operation. For example, the German army of the future is projected to have between 24 and 28 brigades. While this number is down from the 42 brigades of the Cold War, it is still a lot of combat power. Yet how many of those 24-to-28 brigades are capable today of projecting beyond Germany's borders? The answer is one. Most of the other Western European nations are in a similar boat, including France and Britain. Looking at their command and control, their transport assets, and their logistics, they lack the capability to project sizable force. NATO has a reaction force of nearly ten divisions; nevertheless, the alliance simply cannot deploy, equip, and sustain a force anywhere near that magnitude. The most it could handle would be two to three divisions, and even that would take weeks.

If we are to project security and democracy outward, respond to the contingencies, crises, wars, and demands of the future, we must have adequate military power for that purpose. We do not have it today. If this agenda or any other is to be carried out, NATO must improve. It can't be done overnight—budgets are tight and resources diminishing these days. Despite the many constraints, however, if the challenge is managed carefully, important improvements can be made over the next five to 15 years.

The publication of our *Foreign Affairs* article, which occurred in the Fall 1993 edition, generated much publicity and some controversy. We are thankful to have had some good allies, including Senator Richard Lugar and former National Security Adviser Zbigniew Brzezinski. We showed the article to some within the government before it was published and were told by a confidential source that only three people in the executive branch had any sympathy for our ideas: Tony Lake, Warren Christopher, and Bill Clinton. If those were our only allies, they certainly were interesting ones to have. I will not presume to speak for those men—their support was not stated directly—but nonetheless I believe their actions demonstrate their leanings.

The Council on Foreign Affairs gave us a great deal of help, and the *Wall Street Journal* and *New York Times* widely publicized our ideas. We had a lot of media attention, both in the United States and in Europe. NATO Secretary-General Manfred Wörner, German Defense Minister Volker Rühe, various French and Polish officials, and other governments as well were very supportive.

Some important objections were raised that need to be addressed. The first argument maintains that NATO lacks the political consensus and resources to carry out these ideas. I agree that there are real constraints, but our proposal is for a ten-year plan that begins slowly with the existing consensus and only increases the involvement over time as the consensus builds and resources become available.

NATO has always faced this same problem. Every time it has made a strategic innovation, it has faced a probable lack of consensus and lack of resources. Fortunately, the vision to move ahead has each time been strong enough to surmount these obstacles. If a lack of consensus or resources had paralyzed NATO in the past, it would still be defending the Rhine River, Germany would not be a part of NATO, and communism would still rule in East Central Europe.

The second argument holds that NATO will acquire commitments to nations outside our vital interests. True, the nations in East Central Europe are outside the traditional interpretation of our vital interests. Upon closer examination, however, these interests—economic, political, strategic, and moral—are steadily marching eastward. Moreover, our interests in East Central Europe go far beyond economics. These countries are struggling to become democracies. For the last 45 years, we have called upon them to embrace our values, and they are finally answering that call. We cannot abandon them at such a moment.

Regardless of our position, many of these countries, including Poland, are in one way or another going to gain membership in the European Union over the next ten years. At that point, they will automatically, by law, be offered membership in the West European Union, the security alliance for the West European powers that itself is a collective defense alliance yet lacks the military wherewithal to carry out collective defense commitments. The result of some of these nations not being brought into NATO would be a system of interlocking alliances. Commitments would be offered under one alliance that, if activated, would require NATO to come to the rescue. The United States would be vulnerable to a war in which it had had no opportunity to control the crisis and was still dragged in after the war had escalated. This situation is an unacceptable strategic state of affairs. It is one of the things that brought about World War I, and we cannot allow it to happen.

Furthermore, if NATO does not extend security guarantees eastward, Germany most certainly will. In speaking with German defense, security, and foreign affairs officials, it has become clear to me that they consider their security line to be not on the Oder River but on the Bug River, joining Russia, Poland, and the Commonwealth. As such, a security threat to Poland would be seen as a threat to Germany's own vital interests. Germany will therefore provide the security assurances to the East that the West as a whole fails to provide. If Germany and the West do not act in concert, Germany will then be pulled in the direction of a renationalized defense strategy, which we do not want.

Of added concern to some is the idea that taking NATO out of area means that intervention in Bosnia should ensue. That potential concern is not at all our argument. Bosnia is a separate issue. While I am sympathetic to the problems there, the strategic goal for the area is purely to stabilize the terrain north of the Balkans.

The final and most important argument lodged against NATO's expansion eastward is the concern that it will antagonize Russia. Staunch opposition to Poland's joining NATO was first voiced by Russian Foreign Minister Kozyrev. Yeltsin soon tempered this situation somewhat, at least on the surface, when he repudiated his own foreign minister and declared the issue none of Russia's business. Poland could join NATO if it so desired. According to press reports, however, Yeltsin shortly thereafter sent a letter to President Clinton requesting a different approach to NATO's expansion, in effect throwing cold water on hopes for Poland's inclusion in NATO with Russian cooperation.

Russia needs to be handled very carefully, perhaps with a positive outreach program. Prudent restraint is key, as we use the utmost care not to in any way threaten the legitimate interests of a democratic Russian state. The true source of Russian worry, and understandably so, is the appearance of German military power at the Bug River backed by American nuclear power. This concern is legitimate, and one that we cannot allow to become a reality. Many militarily viable ways exist, perhaps with an integrated military command in that area, to reassure Poland and the Visegrad nations without posing an offensive military threat to Russia.

An important point to remember is that by promoting democracy and stability in East Central Europe, we will increase the prospects for the same in Russia. It is instability in Russia's eastern flank that is most likely to bring about restored authoritarianism and imperial conduct in Russia. Should we, in fact, act as though Eastern Europe is Russia's permanent strategic playpen and therefore forsake NATO expansion? I don't think so.

In any event, Russia's future will be determined by events inside that country, not outside of it. If Russian democracy is so unstable and fragile that an eastward-looking security involvement by NATO destabilizes it, how much more damage will be caused by those powerful internal factors that already threaten? Russia is already beginning to pursue a neo-imperial foreign policy of sorts. If the West is passive, this neo-imperial foreign policy will flow westward, probably reabsorbing Ukraine and eventually again casting its shadow over Poland. The key strategic issue is not to keep from offending Russia, but rather to craft stability, a balance of power, equilibrium, and legitimacy. So as Russia begins to move westward, which is already happening, NATO contemplates moving eastward.

Briefly turning now to emerging Western policy, I am greatly encouraged by the current directions of both the Clinton administration and NATO. In light of the decisions taken by Defense Secretary Aspin at Travemunde, and Secretary Christopher in his parallel trip, the West seems to be moving in the strategic direction we have outlined. The core elements are present. I anticipate a NATO summit and declaration in January that will lay down a similar strategic vision, although certainly in guarded and prudent terms.

The Partnership for Peace (PFP) idea is a good move. While it does defer the question of full NATO membership for these partner nations into the indefinite future, the central idea behind it is still a good one. It will extend bilateral security commitments through bilateral agreements with nations such as Poland. NATO would offer not Article V collective defense guarantees but rather Article IV collective security guarantees. This distinction means that if any partner in the PFP framework were attacked, NATO would consult with them and, within the framework of sympathetic consideration, might intervene.

Along with the Partnership for Peace will come an agenda of growing military involvement in humanitarian operations, peacekeeping operations, common defense planning, and so forth. I hope that through such actions, other nations will be brought closer to NATO and ultimately may join NATO. Priority should and will be most certainly given to Poland and the other Visegrad countries.

NATO will also most likely unveil a proposal to increase reliance on combined joint task forces, allowing NATO not only to project power through the integrated command but also to form "coalitions of the willing" per Article IV—contingencies that are beyond NATO's borders. In operation, this endeavor might take the form of the WEU or the Euro corps, or it might be a formal coalition of the willing. The point is that NATO is now beginning to develop the military command relationships that would allow it to act flexibly beyond its borders.

We face a race against time. Will NATO move swiftly enough, or will the situation in Europe deteriorate too rapidly? If we are hesitant, the race will be lost. I am nonetheless optimistic, because I have confidence in our country and in NATO. The action of the United States will be critical in the debates ahead, both here and in France and Germany. We must show leadership that is visionary and also prudent. A stable Europe and a stable world can only further our goal of economic renewal. As such, our domestic priorities, though important, must not be allowed to hinder our overall goal. The summit in January will bring the establishment of a new strategic canvas in Europe. The picture to be painted upon it has yet to be decided, but we now have the opportunity to create a portrait of Europe that will be pleasing to all.

NARRATOR: John Duffield of the University of Virginia Government Department is here. His book was reviewed by Dr. Kugler, and he will be asking the first question.

MR. DUFFIELD: I enjoyed reading your piece in *Foreign Affairs*, but I wonder if the developments you outlined in it weren't more or less already underway. If your article had appeared in 1990 or 1991, it would have been visionary and served to set the agenda, but it seems now that NATO has already taken many of the steps for which you have called.

Richard L. Kugler

I'm not certain of the timing between plans for the Partnership for Peace and the appearance of your article, but my sense is that it was already in the works for some time. Certainly German Defense Minister Volker Rühe was calling for that type of outreach earlier this year. Also, there are some things that I'm not certain America can do much about; namely, the vision of the strategic emancipation of Germany. That problem will have to be worked out by the Germans. They know where we stand, and they know what we want them to do. Before they can move forward, however, they have to develop a domestic consensus.

MR. KUGLER: Those comments are both fair. It is not my role to determine what impact an article we happen to have written might have had. Policy in our government emerges by consensus. It is a pluralistic process, and that is the way it should be.

We began our enterprise last spring. At that time other people were beginning to develop the same ideas. How fast they would have developed had we not written our article, I couldn't say. Recently, Senator Sam Nunn visited RAND and told us that had our article not been published, the PFP would not exist today. We had no concept of what we were getting into when we began the article. It is likely that our article was propelled to higher visibility because of the growing concern surrounding this issue, giving it more attention than it might otherwise have received. Nonetheless, I believe it did help move the debate along in a constructive way.

As to your second comment, no, we certainly don't control everything. Unless our allies come to the fore, none of these proposals will be possible nor will NATO be able to come to grips with the future. Within the German government, Volker Rühe has been a tremendous help, and Foreign Minister Klaus Kinkel seems to be coming along. The Germans face a tough debate as they come to grips with their own history and take on a new role in the world. The British and French also face new roles and responsibilities.

Yet in the end, it is the United States who leads this alliance, and our words and actions will have a large impact. Note that in the past, every time NATO has been confronted with a strategic problem, it has taken the U.S. government to step in and table a coherent and credible vision, backing it with American power, influence, and prestige. When we have shown action and commitment, the other nations have joined us. This pattern will likewise be the case in the future.

MR. DUFFIELD: While a redefining of the transatlantic relationship is both desirable and necessary, I'm not sure that it can be written down in any kind of contractual form. It seems it is something that must be worked out step-by-step, in an ad hoc fashion.

Also, one of the key ingredients that makes NATO unique is the leadership role the United States plays in reassuring relations among the countries of Western Europe. While NATO is usually not discussed in the context of preventing the Germans and the French from fighting each other, this result is ultimately one of NATO's important, if unsung, contributions.

MR. KUGLER: I agree with that statement.

QUESTION: Do you see any future link between NATO and the United Nations?

MR. KUGLER: Of course, although much of it depends on how far the United Nations is going to grow in terms of its own security involvements. A great deal of optimism concerning this development was prevalent some months ago, but that interest has recently declined.

Clearly, cases may arise where NATO will function basically as a military arm for carrying out a U.N. mandate. This prospect has in some ways been contemplated in Bosnia's situation. Had NATO intervened in the Persian Gulf, an operation with a U.N. mandate, it would have been acting in that capacity. Certainly, it is a possibility for the future.

At the same time, we should not put ourselves in the position of acting only when the United Nations authorizes it. The United Nations itself is not a fully developed collective security alliance to be entrusted with that kind of capability. Yet, I expect that we will increasingly be able to use the United Nations for security operations, at least as far as in crafting the political strategy. In cases where NATO is militarily perfect for carrying these operations out, its use would be good.

QUESTION: I have some questions concerning the links in your argument between the arc of crisis and the larger role of NATO. It seems that the crises we now have are crises of a collapse of state power and of societal enclosure, with Bosnia being the most horrible example. Rather than threats from new Hitlers or Saddam Husseins, as powerful states emerge and threaten to overrun their boundaries, we have instead what appear to be fission types of crises. I question whether a link exists between this type of crisis and an external security threat. If enclosure creates a vacuum, an external threat may not necessarily be created. Realignments may be necessary, but this situation is not necessarily something against which we need to actively defend.

Second, I question if democratization is necessarily served by an imposition of foreign troops and a framework created without the participation of the newly democratizing nations. Do we distort the potential for democratization in a crisis area by massive external intervention, or do we really help it along?

MR. KUGLER: These are good issues and good questions—ones not to be reduced to sound-bite formulations. One risks that when formulating strategic arguments. These issues are valid terrain for the political science literature and should be studied carefully.

I am satisfied that the basic arguments we have outlined are correct. As to implosion or explosion, I think we are seeing implosion in the Balkans. Serbia's army, however, is showing an interesting capacity to engage in extraterritorial explosions.

To the north, we are looking at interstate frictions potentially developing. Ukraine is not imploding (at least not yet), but it is talking about keeping its nuclear weapons. It is very serious about this possibility, not because of ethnic fighting, but because of a perceived lack of security. All of the governments in that northern terrain have deep-seated fears about the future because of their lack of military security.

Last year I went to Ukraine and taught a week-long course on defense planning to its government. After a full week of lectures, I was asked, "Why shouldn't we keep our nuclear weapons? You taught us the planning methodology; we agree with it." If you spend some time there, you begin to develop a certain empathy for their situation. They face a tough problem: a lack of security assurances. Looking ten years down the road, their government sees a country in many ways surrounded by adversaries.

The core problem is an imbalance of military power in that area of the world. There is a big Russia and a medium-sized Ukraine. Poland is a little smaller than Ukraine, but bigger than everyone else. There is no balance—any of those nations, minus Russia, could easily view itself as encircled and potentially threatened. This type of situation breeds chronic insecurity.

The link between democracy and security is also complex. After World War II, we faced insecure and turbulent countries: France, Italy, and Germany. One of the solutions was to develop the Marshall Plan but then concurrently bring them into NATO in the hope that stability and security would enhance democracy. It did! Many Germans to whom I have spoken say there was a definite linkage.

Officials in the Polish government have stressed to me their perception of a direct relationship between their security and the furtherance of free-market democracy. Whether that is true or not can be debated. They say it is true, and I tend to agree.

COMMENT: I understand the need for Western Europe and NATO to move eastward. What I worry about is the likelihood that such a move will play upon Russia's historical susceptibility to xenophobia. I don't mean Russia's government, necessarily, because some reassuring acts can ameliorate their fears. I mean the underlying forces.

MR. KUGLER: You raise an important concern. One thing that will most definitely produce Russian xenophobia is an unstable power vacuum on its western front. Russia will be drawn to assert control over that region to prevent chaos there from infecting its territory. The result would be a confrontation with Germany and the European Union. At the same time, if we move in too aggressively to prevent this power vacuum, we could also antagonize the Russians.

Russia's military leadership is already grousing about NATO. One person, whose name I will not mention, came to see me last week. It seems that the Russian military's working scenario is that of a NATO attack on Russia. They need that scenario to justify their force posture for the future.

Let me say now that I don't look forward to NATO's expansion eastward with great personal enthusiasm. If we don't move in this direction, however, far worse things will happen. Definite risks do exist, and they must be carefully managed. Above all, there are ways to negotiate an understanding with the Russians about how the military relationship is to be conducted.

Although not discussed in the *Foreign Affairs* article, there are a couple of possibilities for NATO's relationship with Russia. Perhaps a security council for the CSCE or a security G7 involving Russia would be the answer. It would be like a resurrection of the Metternichian Concert of Europe, bringing the major powers together to negotiate with the Russians over the management of the so-called arc-of-crisis zone. After all, we are moving into it, and they are moving into it. This dual process of movement is destined to grow in the future, and the potential for a clash exists. This situation must be negotiated, beginning now. The situation is manageable, but it requires great care.

QUESTION: Would you comment on the present and planned force structure of the United States armed forces?

MR. KUGLER: I have written close to a 300-page document on that subject for the Joint Chiefs of Staff, and it will be published soon. We inherited our base force from the Bush administration; the bottom-up review of Secretary Aspin is reducing it by about 10-to-15 percent. Unquestionably this reduction diminishes our level of confidence and assurance. At the same time, the kinds of forces we still have, the size of the forces they are planning to maintain, the improvement programs that are planned, and the efforts to enhance the reserves should, according to technical operations research analysis, give us enough combat power. This level of combat power is at the margins, however, and suited to meet the future prospect of two regional contingencies. We are without question at the bare minimum level. If the budget spirals downward, out of sync with what is needed to support this posture, we could get a hollow force. This possibility worries me.

QUESTION: My first question is whether we don't require much more than a little luck in our relations with Russia, a nation that has had no tradition of anything resembling democracy or free enterprise for hundreds of years. Second, isn't it likely that the more nations that join NATO, the more ineffectual it becomes in keeping order? This situation is the case with the United Nations, which seems merely to fool around in places like Bosnia, while in other cases it cannot act at all because it has too many members with too many conflicting interests. The Gulf War was no exception in that it was not really the United Nations that acted. The Gulf War was President Bush's personal venture.

MR. KUGLER: I entirely agree with your point about Russia. Recently, I began to refresh my knowledge of Russian history. Few people realize just how long Russia and Poland have been fighting each other. While Peter the Great and Catherine the Great conquered Poland, war between these two nations actually extends back to the ninth century.

I have grave doubts about the appearance of market democracy or Jeffersonian democracy anytime soon in Russia. I expect to see a Russia of Gaullist nationalism—Slavic Gaullism, if you will—that would not be an enemy but yet would be a tough customer. It will probably be a matter of "Presidential democracy"—with a capital *P* and a small *d*.

I have deep fears about this coming era. In some ways, we may wind up looking back with a certain degree of fondness for the bipolar simplicities of the Cold War. We are entering into a multipolar era where nationalism will be the dominant ideology. That situation alone, with the disappearance of messianic conflicts between democracy and communism, will in a way complicate relations because it means a lack of organizing values. Nations and tribal groups will be acting on their own interests, with some nations imploding and others exploding. We face a highly unstable multipolar era, and I am afraid of it.

The answer to your second question is yes. If you expand NATO greatly, you will dilute it. It is already fairly diluted, with 16 members.

Also, the Gulf War was indeed George Bush's personal matter, and it was the perfect war. A hideous dictator was making a power grab at the world's oil supplies—a case of naked aggression. We had the military wherewithal to clobber him, and he behaved in the stupidest manner possible. Bosnia, however, exposes the West at its worst. When the 16 NATO members get together, the only thing they can agree on is not to do anything.

If NATO is going to project power beyond its borders, it is going to have to find a way to reach a consensus through new decision procedures. When part of the alliance wants to intervene but another part doesn't, the part that doesn't should not use its veto power. This veto mechanism would not allow the part that does want to act to employ its forces and common NATO assets in projecting power outward.

Not long ago I had an experience that has made me reconsider whether expanding NATO would necessarily make it militarily ineffective. In March 1993 I attended a conference in Poland. The Polish defense minister was also in attendance, and we were all gathered in the same hall where the Warsaw Pact Treaty was signed. The Polish attendees wanted to join NATO, and it caught me by surprise. I said, "You don't understand. The issue is not just about our defending you, but it is about your defending us. The issue is what you can bring to this alliance. If another war breaks out in the Persian Gulf, will Poland be willing to send three divisions to fight along side the U.S. Army?" The Polish defense minister looked at me, laughed, and said, "But of course. We'd be happy to. That is no issue."

Hearing that, I began to turn myself around. It occurred to me that they might be useful participants in this alliance. Actually, Secretary Aspin at Travemunde in effect said the same thing in a recent press conference. They said that one of the reasons PFP makes sense is that more participants will mean more forces contributed.

QUESTION: Is the SACEUR (Strategic Allied Commander-Europe) going to be an American in the future, and should he be?

MR. KUGLER: That is a tough issue. The French have complained at great length about the implications of an American SACEUR for their own sovereignty, and in many ways their arguments make sense. The rest of the Europeans, however, have always wanted an American SACEUR because it projects American power, American nuclear weapons, and American conventional responsiveness on to Europe.

I haven't seen a great deal of interest in a European SACEUR, at least not that has been expressed to me. I have written several times that it would be a good idea to rotate the SACEUR. After all, many positions are involved in NATO. The secretary-general position, which is equally important, is now occupied by a German. Why not have an American secretary-general and a West European SACEUR? If you examine NATO's command structure, many other general officer billets are seen. There are ways we could handle a European SACEUR, so I personally have favored it, and so has Henry Kissinger.

In the past, I read in the newspapers that General Shalikashvili would be the last American SACEUR. Well, we now have another one. I haven't see a great deal of pressure coming from the Germans and the British, in particular, for a non-American SACEUR. The French reaction, at least as I understand it, is that they don't want anything to do with the command structure. It is not a question of a French SACEUR; they don't want to be involved in it. They want an EU-WEU command structure of their own. I personally favor steps in that direction, and I think it would make great sense, provided NATO is not replaced.

NARRATOR: Thank you, Dr. Kugler, for a very thoughtful, lively, and informative session.

CHAPTER SIX

Why NATO Persists*

JOHN S. DUFFIELD

NARRATOR: It is appropriate to continue the Miller Center's series on NATO with a presentation by a member of the faculty at the University of Virginia. John Duffield is a member of the Department of Government and Foreign Affairs faculty. He received his doctorate from Princeton University in 1989 and has been at the University of Virginia since 1990. He teaches courses on Western Europe in world affairs, the transatlantic relationship between the United States and Western Europe, and military force in international relations. He has recently published a book called *Power Rules: The Evolution of NATO's Conventional Force Posture* (1995). He has also published several articles, including an article in the *Political Science Quarterly* concerning NATO in the post-Cold War era. He is continuing his research and writing to explore German security policy after reunification. The focus of his interest is thus squarely in the area of concerns with NATO.

Presented in a Forum at the Miller Center of Public Affairs on 2 May 1995. This presentation is an abbreviated version of "NATO's Functions after the Cold War," Political Science Quarterly, vol. 109, no. 5 (Winter 1994–95): 763–87.

MR. DUFFIELD: As made clear in the introduction, I have a keen professional interest in European security issues and in NATO in particular. I should also admit at the outset a strong personal interest in today's topic. The subject of my dissertation was the evolution of NATO's conventional force posture, which formed the basis for my recently published book. I finished my dissertation in 1989, however, which was not a good year to be completing dissertations on the subject of NATO. Within a few months after receiving my degree, the Berlin Wall was breached, the process of German unification began, the Communist regimes throughout Eastern Europe were overthrown, and the Warsaw Pact began to dissolve. Essentially, the Cold War had ended. As a result, many observers could legitimately ask whether there would be any reason to continue to maintain NATO.

For most people these were positive developments, but from the narrow perspective of a young NATO scholar, they made publishing a book on the subject difficult. Fortunately, NATO did not wither away, and within a few years publishers showed renewed interest in the subject. I am also pleased to report that despite or perhaps even because of the end of the Cold War, NATO has again become as interesting a topic of research as it was in past years, and I expect it will continue to be for some time to come.

Let me turn then to the puzzle of NATO's persistence in light of expectations that it would not survive the end of the Cold War and offer some observations about how well NATO is doing five years into the post-Cold War era. First, I will touch on international relations theory, which is the starting point of many early analyses that predicted NATO's demise. International relations theory teaches that states form military alliances in response to common external threats. Conversely, when those threats disappear, alliances tend to disintegrate.

When the Cold War ended, many observers thus expected that NATO might fall prey to just such a pattern. The alliance's primary purpose had been to address the threat posed by the Soviet Union to Western Europe during the postwar era. In the short span of less than three years, beginning with the overthrow of Communist regimes in Eastern Europe in 1989 and culminating with the dissolution of the Soviet Union in late 1991, this rationale all but evaporated. At the same time, the continuing costs of membership in the alliance, including the costs of stationing forces on foreign territory, hosting foreign forces, and other constraints on national freedom of action, threatened to undermine whatever public support was left for the alliance. In contrast to these pessimistic initial expectations, however, NATO has not only survived, it has even added to its already elaborate organizational bodies and has undertaken new activities. Indeed, NATO remains the leading security organization in Europe, with no obvious challenger in sight.

Let me offer one caveat at this point. Despite NATO's continuing importance, it is true that the military contributions to NATO—the national forces under NATO command—have declined substantially since 1989-90. Indeed, NATO is beginning to resemble the alliance of the early 1950s when it was still headquartered near Paris. This situation brings to mind one of the few jokes people tell about NATO. Soon after the Supreme Headquarters Allied Powers Europe (SHAPE), the military command structure of NATO, was established in 1951 outside of Paris, one wit compared NATO to the Venus de Milo in the nearby Louvre Museum, saying that NATO was all "shape" and no arms. Shortly thereafter, NATO did acquire substantial military arms. With the decline in the threat, however, NATO clearly does not need as many arms as it had during the Cold War.

Not only does NATO still exist, but the alliance continues to enjoy generally strong support from its member countries. For example, German political leaders, whose commitment to NATO was called into question by unification, have remained eager to maintain and strengthen the alliance. Even French officials, traditionally the most critical of NATO, have often acknowledged its enduring value. This favorable attitude, moreover, is not confined to the present governing parties and coalitions. Support for a strong NATO often ranges across the domestic political spectrum in member countries. In short, NATO remains the institution to which its members and many nonmembers primarily look to ensure their security.

If NATO is far from moribund, what was wrong with the previous forecasts of the alliance's demise? What are the sources of its persistence? The answer, in brief, is that although NATO

101

lacks a single compelling rationale as it had in the past, it still performs a number of valuable security functions for its members. As a result, all of the allies have found it in their interests to preserve NATO, notwithstanding the differing levels of importance they attach to each of these purposes.

These purposes or functions are of two basic types. First are the traditional external functions whereby NATO enhances the security of its members vis-à-vis external dangers. Less familiar but also important, especially after the Cold War, are NATO's internal functions.

The external functions are traditionally the types of functions to which people refer when talking about alliances. Despite the significant decline in threat, NATO continues to enhance the security of its members with respect to external dangers in three important ways. First, it preserves the strategic balance in Europe by neutralizing the residual military threat posed by Russian military power. Although the potential military threat posed by the Soviet bloc to Western Europe obviously declined dramatically between 1989 and 1991, it did not disappear altogether. Russia remains Europe's only nuclear superpower, and despite the Soviet departure from Central Europe, flank countries such as Norway and Turkey still face powerful Russian conventional military forces stationed near their borders. There is little certainty, moreover, that this military power will never again be used for hostile purposes. Under Presidents Gorbachev and Yeltsin, the Soviet Union and Russia have pursued cooperation with the West. In view of the twists and turns that have characterized Russian politics in recent years, however, it has not yet been possible to rule out the prospect of a return to a more confrontational and even expansionist posture. The tumultuous events of 1993 and 1994 only confirmed the view that the situation in Russia is likely to remain unsettled for a prolonged period, during which continued Western concerns about future Russian intentions are only natural.

Given these uncertainties, the countries of Western Europe have found it desirable to maintain a counterweight to the residual military power of the former Soviet Union, especially Russia's nuclear capabilities. Alone, though, they lack the means to do so. Only the United States is seen as fully able to neutralize the potential nuclear threat, however remote it may be, and more generally, as able to preserve the European strategic balance. And it is primarily through NATO that American military power is linked to the Continent.

A second important post-Cold War NATO function that has assumed greater prominence is the protection of alliance members against an array of newly emerging threats. Highest on the list of these new external threats are ethnic, territorial, and national conflicts within and among the countries of Central and Eastern Europe, as exemplified by the fighting in the former Yugoslavia. Such conflicts have the potential to generate large numbers of refugees and even to spread to the territory of neighboring countries, which include some NATO members. In a worst-case scenario, outside states might even feel compelled to intervene, risking an expansion of hostilities such as those that occurred at the beginning of World War I. Although unable to stop such conflicts thus far, NATO does help to address the concerns that they raise in several ways.

First, it protects its members against the possible spillover of military hostilities. Although no alliance country has yet been seriously threatened in this way, NATO's long experience with organizing the defense of its members leaves it well prepared to deal with such contingencies. NATO also helps to prevent other countries from being drawn into conflicts of this type and thus to prevent expansion of the conflict. Its presence helps to ensure that Western military involvement, where it does occur, is collective and consensual, and it inhibits other nonmember countries from meddling in such conflicts as well.

As the fighting in the former Yugoslavia continues, the alliance has been increasingly seen as having an active role to play in containing and even suppressing such conflicts. It has steadily enhanced its political authority and organizational ability to act, should its members choose to do so. Most noticeably, the alliance has gained valuable practical experience in the former Yugoslavia, where it has fired shots in anger for the first time in its history. NATO forces have enforced both the maritime blockade in the Adriatic Sea and the no-fly zone over Bosnia. They have provided protective air power for U.N. personnel on the ground, and they have used the threat of air strikes to try to establish exclusion zones for heavy weapons around Sarajevo and elsewhere. Although NATO's impact on the conflict has not yet been decisive, this lack of success can be only partly ascribed to the alliance itself. The alliance's ability to intervene effectively in future regional conflicts has clearly increased.

A third and closely related external function is that of stabilizing the countries of the former Soviet bloc to prevent the outbreak of conflicts in the first place. Following the collapse of communism, many of these states have undertaken ambitious political and economic reforms, and the West has a substantial stake in their success. That success is not assured, however. Reform among peoples with no recent experience with democracy or free markets is inherently difficult. These considerable domestic obstacles, moreover, are often compounded by an uncertain and seemingly threatening external security environment. In particular, many Central and East European states are concerned about possible adverse developments within the former Soviet bloc that could lead to a renewal of military coercion or armed conflict on their borders. If left unprotected, they may feel pressure to acquire additional military forces themselves or to take other precautionary measures that might nevertheless be viewed as provocative by their neighbors, thereby undermining rather than enhancing stability in the region.

NATO helps with this problem by promoting stability in the former Soviet bloc in two ways. First, it directly fosters the success of political reform in the region. Since 1990 NATO has established a wide array of programs and institutions of dialogue and cooperation on security issues, most notably the North Atlantic Cooperation Council (NACC) and the Partnership for Peace (PFP). Through these new arrangements, NATO assists the fledgling regimes in reshaping their defense policies, force structures, and planning processes. In particular, they help to reinforce democratic control of the armed forces and respect for civilian authority by exposing Central and Eastern European leaders to Western models of civil-military relations.

Second, NATO enhances the security of Central and Eastern European states by assuring them that they will not have to face

104

external threats entirely on their own. This assurance helps them to forego potentially destabilizing actions and to pursue their ambitious political reform agendas with greater confidence. The NACC allows former Soviet bloc states to voice their concerns and to discuss a wide range of security issues on a regular basis while sitting as equal partners with their NATO counterparts in Brussels. The recently adopted Partnership for Peace offers each participant formal consultations with the alliance, should the country perceive a direct threat to its security, as well as concrete military ties with NATO members through a variety of military activities and operations. Indeed, a number of joint exercises have been undertaken since September 1994.

Admittedly, such measures are not ideal from the perspective of the Central and Eastern European states. NATO has thus far steadfastly refused to offer these countries full membership and security guarantees for fear of antagonizing nationalist elements in Russia and importing potential territorial and ethnic conflicts into the alliance. Nevertheless, even the loose political and military links that have been offered promise greater security than any alternative arrangements. Moreover, participation in the Partnership for Peace is widely seen as an important step toward eventual NATO membership. Consequently, Central and Eastern European states quickly put aside any feelings of disappointment and embraced the PFP program.

NATO's internal functions are an important but infrequently discussed topic. Although analyses of NATO have typically emphasized its role in securing member states against external threats, it has not been as exclusively outward-oriented as alliances are generally viewed as being. From early in its history, NATO has played an important role in smoothing relations among its members. This subject has often been overlooked by outside observers because alliance officials have been reluctant to talk openly about NATO's internal functions. With German reunification and the disappearance of a single compelling external threat capable of forging alliance unity, however, these intra-alliance functions have assumed even greater importance.

The most important intra-alliance function is that of reassurance. The continued existence of NATO, including its integrated military structure and the U.S. military presence in Europe, assures alliance members that they have nothing to fear from one another. Of particular concern in this regard is newly unified Germany. As many analysts have noted, few if any concrete reasons exist for expecting a renewal of German aggression. Nevertheless, perceptions do matter, and the profound change that has occurred in Germany's position within the European state system will inevitably raise questions about its future foreign policy orientation. Western Germany's already substantial economic power and its long-term military potential have been augmented by reunification. In addition, Germany now faces fewer external constraints on its behavior while enjoying greater opportunities for self-assertion, particularly in Central and Eastern Europe. It would thus be natural for countries that have been victimized by Germany in the past to be concerned that Germany might someday use its new power in ways that are inimical to their interests. Just as it took some years for them to become comfortable with the idea of a re-armed West Germany, neighboring countries will need time to become accustomed to the presence of a unified Germany in their midst. In the meantime, the maintenance of stability requires forestalling the emergence of acute fears of Germany, or of any other West European country for that matter. NATO remains the leading institutional vehicle for performing this essential function of reassurance.

NATO reduces the possibility of tension and conflict among its West European members in several ways. First, it increases intra-alliance transparency. An important potential source of international conflict is misperception and misunderstanding among states. In the absence of detailed and reliable information, decisionmakers may exaggerate the offensive military capabilities of other countries or misinterpret foreign intentions, often perceiving other countries as more hostile than they actually are. As a result, international relations are often characterized by suspicion and mistrust.

NATO helps to prevent such destructive dynamics from arising among its members and instead promotes mutual confidence by facilitating a high degree of intra-alliance transparency. Frequent consultation at many levels and on many subjects allows members to inform one another of their activities and intentions, and if necessary, to register their concerns and misapprehensions. Participation in the alliance's force planning process requires members to exchange detailed information about their military forces, defense budgets, and future plans. As a result of such institutionalized openness, NATO members are able to keep few secrets from one another, and they have even fewer incentives to do so.

A second general way in which NATO fosters reassurance among its members is by integrating their security policies. To varying but usually substantial degrees NATO countries formulate and execute their security policies as part of the alliance rather than on a purely national basis. This denationalization of security policy tempers the natural rivalry and competition for military power that might otherwise occur among the major European powers. NATO promotes the denationalization of security policy in several specific ways.

At the most basic level, its consultative organs, force planning process, and integrative military structure help to forge a common identity among alliance members. Regular and in-depth consultation contributes to a high degree of mutual understanding. Joint force planning helps reshape each member's military posture to reflect alliance-wide rather than national interests, and assignments to the alliance's civilian bureaucracy and military organization socialize government officials and military officers into a common NATO culture.

In addition, participation in NATO's integrated military structure reduces military self-sufficiency on the part of member countries because it allows them to forego, or at least to de-emphasize, a number of the ingredients usually considered essential to an independent military capability. For example, many European states depend heavily on NATO's multinational airborne early warning force and its integrated air defense system. To husband defense resources, moreover, both small and large NATO members have sacrificed the ability to perform certain missions such as air reconnaissance and minesweeping, knowing that other allies would perform those types of missions for them.

At the same time, multinational integration establishes a degree of mutual control by increasing the level of collective involvement in organizational and operational planning. Indeed, Germany has never developed a full-fledged national planning and command capability above the level of the army corps, relying instead on multinational NATO staffs to conduct those vital tasks. The continued existence of the integrated military structure thus places constraints on the ability of member states to use their forces for exclusively national objectives and helps to ensure that the forces of one country do not raise alarms in another.

It is important to note, however, that the existence of the integrated military structure itself is no guarantee of continued participation by NATO members. Ultimately, their willingness to eschew a national approach to defense follows from the belief that working within the alliance offers them greater security with respect to possible external threats. It is in this area that the United States makes a unique contribution. Perhaps more than any other factor, it is U.S. involvement in the form of security guarantees and the presence of American forces in Europe that assuages the security concerns of other NATO countries. As a result, the renationalization of security policy appears unnecessary and even undesirable. In addition, the protection afforded by the United States allows NATO members to limit the size of their armed forces. In particular, it obviates any German need to acquire a nuclear capability, a move that many other countries in Europe would find particularly threatening.

Even in the absence of the integrated NATO military structure, direct U.S. involvement in European security affairs exerts a calming and stabilizing effect on West European politics. The U.S. security guarantee and an American military presence also help to ensure the maintenance of a balance of power within the region. Only the United States is perceived as powerful enough to play this internal, as opposed to an external, balancing role. As an extracontinental power, the United States does not stir fears of military domination, except perhaps on the part of the French, and even they do not make an issue of it these days.

Not surprisingly, U.S. engagement in Europe is seen as particularly useful for providing a counterweight to Germany's military power and potential. In the absence of the United States, Germany would dominate NATO, making the rest of Europe uneasy. This U.S. function is accepted and even encouraged by German leaders, who recognize that an American presence in Europe allows its neighbors to feel far more comfortable with the newer and larger Germany.

I would like to conclude with a few words about NATO's future prospects, about which I am cautiously optimistic. NATO's long-term survival is not assured. Its continued existence hinges not only on its ability to address the security concerns of its members, but also on their recognition of what NATO can do for them. It is conceivable that the alliance's contributions could become less and less appreciated.

Attitudes within two member states in particular will shape NATO's future prospects. The unique role of the United States has already been mentioned. Its ability to play this role depends in turn on Germany's participation in the alliance because Germany continues to host the bulk of the American troops stationed on the Continent. Germany's absence from NATO's political and military organs would greatly limit their usefulness for suppressing potential tension and conflict within Western Europe.

Concern has been expressed about Germany's willingness to preserve NATO and to host a significant number of foreign forces. Initial surveys of public opinion after reunification, for example, suggested a weakening of support for the alliance. Ominously, a majority seemed to favor a complete U.S. withdrawal. More recent polls have shown a fairly steady increase in public support for the alliance, however, and the percentage of Germans favoring a complete U.S. withdrawal has stabilized, if not declined.

More fundamentally, one should not necessarily expect German political leaders to take their cues from public opinion, especially on such complex and consequential policy issues. The values and beliefs widely shared within the German political elite clearly militate against a significant shift in policy toward NATO. First, German leaders exhibit a strong distaste for unilateralism, which they believe can only lead to isolation and conflict. Instead, they stress the need to pursue Germany's security interests in close cooperation with other countries, and thus they place a high value on multilateral security institutions such as NATO. This emphasis on multilateralism in turn causes German leaders to attach tremendous importance to *Berechenbarkeit*, or calculability, in foreign policy, a term they use quite frequently. They want their country to be perceived as a reliable, predictable, and dependable partner. As a result, there is a strong aversion to any German government reneging upon, let alone renouncing, the basic substance of established foreign policy commitments. Many Germans remain reluctant to see their country play a leadership role in international affairs. Consequently, membership in NATO—a NATO dominated by the United States—serves the useful purpose of enabling Germany to maintain a comfortably low profile. Finally, the visceral rejection on the part of many Germans of the development of a national nuclear capability helps to preserve a significant degree of security dependence upon the United States. In sum, there is little reason to expect a significant weakening of German support for the alliance.

Equally important, however, are attitudes in the United States, given that NATO's ability to perform its various functions remains critically dependent on American involvement. Continued American support beyond a mere token military presence in Europe cannot be taken for granted. The benefits of engagement to the United States are less direct and less tangible than they are for its European allies. As a result, some people fear that the U.S. military contribution to NATO could fall to the point where the alliance could no longer be sustained. The American presence in Europe has already declined by nearly two-thirds to some 100,000 military personnel, from over 300,000 in the late 1980s. Although a contribution of this reduced magnitude has generally been regarded as adequate, even deeper cuts cannot be ruled out. The United States is beset by a rapidly expanding federal debt, and NATO-assigned forces make an easy target for budget cutters. With the decline of the former Soviet threat, the need to maintain troops on the Continent—and NATO itself—is harder than ever to justify in the United States. Nevertheless, the danger that the U.S. military contribution to NATO will be eviscerated should not be exaggerated. Few influential voices have advocated a complete withdrawal from Europe, and as U.S. troop levels and their associated costs have decreased, the pressure for additional reductions has subsided.

One reason to expect continued U.S. support for NATO is that the United States has a significant stake in preserving a peaceful and prosperous Europe. In addition to the obvious strong transatlantic historical and cultural ties, American economic interests in Europe remain substantial. If history is any guide, the United States could also easily be drawn into any future major war in Europe, the consequences of which would likely be more devastating than those of the past, given the existence of nuclear weapons.

Continued strong American backing for NATO is further assured by the fact that NATO remains the principal institutional vehicle through which the United States can exert influence on West European policies. Alliance membership entitles the United States to play a direct role in shaping a variety of European security issues. Active American engagement, including the presence of U.S. forces on the Continent, endows the United States with considerable political leverage.

Finally, there is the intangible matter of American prestige. Perhaps no development would more vividly symbolize the decline of American power and international influence than the effective demise of NATO. Therefore, policies that could gut the alliance, whether intentionally or not, are certain to face strong resistance.

For all of these reasons, a serious domestic challenge to U.S. support for and participation in NATO is highly unlikely to materialize any time soon. To the contrary, the alliance's continuing value is generally recognized. This recognition is evidenced by the widespread interest among political and opinion leaders in expanding the alliance's membership and strengthening its ability to deal with conflicts outside its traditional geographical ambit.

In sum, at a minimum, it is still far too early to dismiss NATO. The alliance continues to perform several vital security functions, both internal and external, that were overlooked by initial analyses of its post-Cold War prospects. As a result, its members have found it in their interest to maintain the alliance, and their reasons for doing so are unlikely to become obsolete any time soon. Thus,

NATO's persistence as a highly integrated military alliance should come as no surprise, and solid grounds exist for expecting it to remain Europe's leading security organization well into the future.

QUESTION: Is it fair to say that NATO is primarily an evolving political institution rather than a military mechanism?

MR. DUFFIELD: The importance of NATO's political functions has increased both in prominence and with respect to NATO's military functions. NATO has always had important political functions, but its military functions will continue to be important, if somewhat less pronounced, in terms of deterring residual military threats and perhaps in an increasing level of out-of-area involvement. NATO countries will continue to approach the latter with great caution, but they are nevertheless moving in the direction of being able to exert military power to deal with conflicts outside of their borders. That is a significant departure from NATO's past military history.

QUESTION: Do NATO's current functions endanger the future of the United Nations? Unlike the United Nations, NATO already operates with an effective military capability when needed.

MR. DUFFIELD: The question touches upon an important issue: What kind of relationship should exist between these various security institutions? Although there is a potential synergy between them—and between NATO and the United Nations in particular—much more work needs to be done before it will be fully realized. In general, NATO will not infringe on U.N. prerogatives or responsibilities outside the European theater. The question is, what about conflicts within the European theater? In particular, there is the case of the former Yugoslavia. The United Nations entered the conflict partly as a result of NATO's, and particularly the United States', initial reluctance to become involved in Yugoslavia and the constraints that reluctance placed on any NATO action, especially after the failed efforts of the Western Europeans through the European Community. In 1991 and 1992, some argued that NATO was irrelevant and the future belonged to the United Nations. It was the only organization that seemed to be able to do anything—and even then, not much—about the fighting in Croatia. When it became clear that the ability of the United Nations to act as a military organization was extremely limited, however, it also became clear that NATO had a bigger role to play. Since then, it has incrementally become more involved in the conflict.

Ultimately, how effective NATO will be in the former Yugoslavia, and perhaps elsewhere in East Central, Eastern, and Southeastern Europe is constrained by the United Nations. For NATO to operate effectively in both a military and a political sense on the basis of some kind of international consensus, it will probably have to limit its involvement to situations in which a mandate exists from either the United Nations or the Organization for Security and Cooperation in Europe (OSCE, formerly the Conference on Security and Cooperation in Europe, or CSCE). There is thus a symbiosis with NATO serving as an agent of organizations such as the United Nations and the OSCE that provide the necessary political legitimacy. Without one or the other, action is not possible. On the other hand, an effective military organization is needed, which at this point only NATO can provide, to go in and get the job done. The more these institutions are able to cooperate, the stronger both institutions will be, and there is not necessarily a conflict of interest between them.

QUESTION: Haven't the United Nations and NATO effectively trapped each other in the former Yugoslav situation? The threat that the U.N. peacekeepers may become hostages if NATO uses air power in that area seems omnipresent.

MR. DUFFIELD: That threat is the result of the way the situation has evolved. In fact, it has arisen precisely because the United Nations and NATO did not communicate with each other at the beginning of the conflict. When NATO refused to become involved—again, mainly because of U.S. unwillingness—the United Nations by default was encouraged to take action. In Bosnia, its involvement consisted primarily of the deployment of military forces to ensure the delivery of humanitarian assistance. As the situation changed, people argued that military power should be used more assertively to punish combatant factions for violating the no-fly zone, and in particular, to punish the Serbs for attacking civilian population centers. The problem was that NATO and the United Nations were attempting to carry out incompatible functions. They could not on the one hand station nonpartisan peacekeepers there to provide humanitarian assistance in the expectation that they would be respected by the various combatants while on the other hand using force authorized by the United Nations to attack one side or the other. The present situation is thus a function of the way the international mission in the region evolved over time. Once the United Nations became involved in a humanitarian role, that placed constraints on what NATO forces operating under U.N. mandates could later do.

To put it starkly, there is a need to choose between the two missions. The peacekeeping forces can either remain there to perform their humanitarian functions or withdraw and regroup prior to becoming involved in a more active way, including the use of force against one side or the other to enforce international sanctions. These two functions cannot co-exist, however. One can only hope that there will not be another conflict like the one in former Yugoslavia. If something like that were to occur elsewhere in Europe, however, the experience that the United Nations, NATO, and other institutions have acquired in working together should enable them to orchestrate from the outset a more effective form of intervention that is not ambivalent as to what its functions are.

QUESTION: You began your presentation with a traditional definition of alliance, that of nations coming together to face some external threat. NATO is probably more interesting, however, for the internal dynamics than it is for the residual external threat that Russia poses. Should some new name be invented for the entity? Is it no longer simply an alliance? Are there historical precedents of old alliances with the same kind of dynamic?

MR. DUFFIELD: If an alliance is traditionally defined as a coming together of states for the purpose of defending themselves against external threats, then NATO is no longer simply an alliance. It certainly still has alliance-like functions, and there are reasons for maintaining them. But even some of the external functions that NATO performs are rather removed from the traditional function of defending against or deterring an external threat. In some ways, it performs a collective security function, though no one refers to it as a collective security organization—that is, one in which states come together to protect themselves against one another. I have not as yet, however, found a good alternative term to replace *alliance.*

In response to your second question, I should say that other people have recognized that alliances have often performed other types of functions. There is a particularly good article written by Paul Schroeder entitled "Alliances, 1815-1945: Weapons of Power and Tools of Management" that was published in *Historical Dimensions of National Security Problems*, edited by Klaus Knorr in 1976. He was one of the first people to develop that idea.

I am not sure, however, that the functions NATO performs fit so neatly into Schroeder's categories. He talks, for example, of the function alliances play in managing alliance partners; that is, one member might use the alliance not only to aggregate military power to defend against an external threat, but also to manage some other alliance partner that it wants to control. That function implies a certain amount of coercion. In the case of NATO, to the degree that there has been mutual self-management, it has been done on a voluntary basis, something for which the Germans deserve a great deal of credit. They obviously wanted to join NATO in the 1950s to enhance their security, but they also knew that by integrating themselves into NATO along with other Western institutions—the European Coal and Steel Community and subsequently the European Economic Community—they could benefit a great deal by volunteering themselves to be managed by their partners. It helped enormously in overcoming what residual fears and concerns there were of Germany and in allowing the powerful positive dynamic of cooperation within Western Europe to develop. Even in that regard, the so-called alliance literature is still inadequate, and there certainly is a need to broaden the conceptions, if not the definitions, of alliances.

QUESTION: Perhaps the primary issue currently facing NATO is the possible enlargement of the organization. Some on the Western side argue that NATO's future depends on resolving successfully the enlargement issue. Others in Russia argue that NATO enlargement would be a dire threat equivalent to the Cuban missile crisis for them. What do you believe the outcome will be on this issue?

MR. DUFFIELD: Although divisive, enlargement will not be a make-or-break issue for the alliance. There will always be a few people who will argue against expansion or involvement outside of Western Europe, and others who will argue that if NATO does not expand, there is little point in maintaining the institution. Even if it does not expand as quickly as some would like, however, cooler heads will prevail, and people will not end the alliance simply for that reason.

On this issue, the alliance is in a difficult position. There certainly is a great deal of pressure from the Central and Eastern European countries to join the alliance, and some people in the West (in the United States in particular) are sympathetic to those views. On the other hand, there is the very real question of how Russia would respond. An important distinction needs to be made here in that one can be sensitive to the effects of enlargement on politics within Russia without being guilty of giving Russia a veto power over NATO enlargement; that is, people within the present Russian government might personally not have strong objections to enlargement. However, to the degree that they feel any NATO enlargement would endanger their prospects in the next election and allow people who are more inimical to Western points of view to assume power, then it really is in the West's interest to proceed slowly. Therefore, moving cautiously is not simply a matter of giving the Russians veto power.

In this context, the incremental approach that has been taken is impressive. First, the North Atlantic Cooperation Council (NACC) was created. Then, when it was seen as inadequate, the idea of the Partnership for Peace developed. One of the virtues of PFP is that it allows individual countries to strengthen their ties with NATO at different rates. Every Eastern European country that joins PFP negotiates a separate contract with NATO regarding the types of military activities in which it will participate. The more these countries interact during NATO military exercises, training for peacekeeping operations, and so on, the more they will have and will feel that they have a de facto military or security guarantee. In other words, the more that NATO is involved with them and the more they restructure their forces and decision-making processes to be compatible with NATO, the harder it will be for NATO to refuse to act if their security is endangered.

At the same time, a parallel attempt has been made to establish a strategic partnership with Russia. Before the Soviet Union dissolved, it took a major risk in allowing German unification to proceed with Germany remaining in NATO. As a result, the Soviet Union, and later Russia, insisted that it continue to be regarded as an important state and be taken seriously. It thus behooves the West to try to engage Russia as much as possible in security as well as other areas. The Russians have not made it especially easy for the West by taking repressive actions in areas such as Chechnya, but the West should not necessarily give up. One development currently taking place to help pave the way for some kind of eventual NATO enlargement is the establishment of a direct link with Russia. This will signal that Russia is an important strategic partner and that the West wants to maintain a special dialogue with it. Thus, even if some people argue that Russia could never be a member of NATO, creating this separate link will be an important means of overcoming residual Russian concerns that NATO is somehow opposed to Russia's interest. Once people begin to view NATO differently in Russia as a result of that type of interaction, it will be easier for the Russians to countenance gradual NATO enlargement.

QUESTION: You are optimistic about the future of NATO. How will the rise of neo-isolationism in the United States affect NATO?

MR. DUFFIELD: Neo-isolationism is of concern to people who believe that NATO does serve American interests and ought to be preserved. The Clinton administration has taken a strong stand in support of NATO. Although it has agreed to continue U.S. troop reductions to roughly 100,000 troops in Europe, it will support a continued military presence at that level, which is significant, given the lack of a major direct threat to Europe. Isolationism itself is not a new phenomenon. It has appeared many times in the past. It is easy for someone who has never thought about international affairs and is elected to Congress to come to Washington and talk about how the United States is wasting a great deal of money overseas and how it should bring the troops home and eliminate foreign aid. Once these people are exposed to the counter-arguments, however, and are forced to make serious decisions that have important consequences for their country, they will not in general be swayed by their own or other people's demagogic rhetoric. Cooler heads tend to prevail. A number of Republican leaders feel strongly about the importance of U.S. engagement and maintaining NATO. Despite the many challenges to NATO that have occurred over the years, it has usually been able to weather the storm.

NARRATOR: Thank you for such a clear and well-focused presentation of the subject.

III.

THE ENLARGEMENT
OF NATO:
CHANGING FACES

CHAPTER SEVEN

The Changing Face of NATO: Partnership for Peace and the Combined Joint Task Force*

DOUGLAS K. BEREUTER

NARRATOR: NATO has been one of the pillars on which American foreign policy has been based since World War II and is more discussed and debated than during the Cold War. We are delighted to have Congressman Doug Bereuter with us, someone concerned with NATO in both theory and practice. He has represented Nebraska's first congressional district since 1979.

Congressman Bereuter is described as a conservative Republican member of Congress. He gets very low ratings from left-leaning groups such as the Americans for Democratic Action (ADA) and the American Civil Liberties Union (ACLU). Yet it is intriguing that he has also been a member of the Society of Statesmen—a group of about two dozen Republican members of Congress who see their primary role as legislators rather than as confrontational figures. They see their major purpose as being one of moving forward with legislation that is essential at this moment in our history.

Presented in a Forum at the Miller Center of Public Affairs on 16 May 1994.

It is also interesting that he is a practical politician with two master's degrees from Harvard, one in city planning and the other in public administration. Few conservative Republicans have an interest in planning. He is the exception. He is also a Phi Beta Kappa graduate of the University of Nebraska-Lincoln, having taught at the University of Nebraska, Kansas State, and Harvard. He has also served as a member of the Executive Committee of the Alumni Association of the John F. Kennedy School of Government at Harvard.

Congressman Bereuter brings to Congress experience as a state legislator, a businessman, a college educator, an urban planner, and a state agency administrator. He is a veteran, having served in the U.S. Army from 1963 to 1965. His congressional assignments include serving on the Committee on Banking, Finance, and Urban Affairs as well as on the Committee on Foreign Affairs. He has been a member of numerous U.S. congressional delegations and will soon be leaving for a meeting of the North Atlantic Assembly. Congressman Bereuter has been a member of the House observer group to the arms control talks since 1989. He is a major supporter of international trade and an active participant in internationally oriented congressional activities.

MR. BEREUTER: It is probably clear to everyone that the future of U.S.-European security relations are changing. A year ago my comments would have been very different because these relations change so rapidly. My reflections six months from now could be totally different as well.

NATO is clearly America's most important defense alliance and the anchor of U.S. security policy in Western Europe and the North Atlantic region. It is evolving to address changes around the world. I will address four major issues in my remarks. First, I will try to describe the evolution of the goals and purposes of NATO since the collapse of the Soviet Union. Second, I will discuss the pressures within the Atlantic alliance, specifically, how members of the alliance are developing different views on the responsibilities and privileges of NATO membership. Third, I will look at the pressures being applied from the outside, particularly by nations that seek immediate admission to NATO. Former members of the

Warsaw Pact and formally neutral countries are pushing hard for full and immediate membership in NATO. Fourth, I'll comment on how NATO is responding to these changes and challenges, including what happened at the January 1994 NATO summit in Brussels attended by President Clinton and other heads of state, where more important changes were made in NATO than at any time in recent memory.

First, NATO's goals and missions have evolved. When the Warsaw Pact began to collapse in 1989 and the Soviet Union dissolved in 1991, the leaders of NATO were faced with a dilemma. With the demise of its great adversary, specifically the Soviet Union and the Warsaw Pact generally, what was the future of NATO? Was there a need any longer for a European security organization involving Canada, the United States, and the 14 countries of Western Europe?

NATO has proven to be the most successful defensive alliance in the history of the world. Suddenly, however, politicians and pundits have begun to insist that there is no longer any justification for NATO. It is argued that at a minimum, its roles, missions, and organizational structure should be changed substantially.

When the NATO commanders and national leaders began to contemplate these changes in a serious fashion, they quickly recognized that the end of the Cold War had increased the likelihood of smaller, hot wars in various parts of the world. In any bureaucracy—and NATO is a bureaucracy, of course—people will try to find a new role to justify their bureaucracy's continued existence. This bureaucratic self-preservation must be kept in mind, but it is quite clear that those who thought smaller conflicts might erupt in Europe and elsewhere were quite right. It has become evident that while old hatreds and animosities had been capped or supplanted, they had not disappeared. They have reemerged in ethnic, racial, and religious conflicts such as those in the former Yugoslavia.

Western leaders concluded that in this new environment NATO still had a unique capability to respond to the new types of threats. NATO is the only multilateral security organization able to respond to serious security threats. NATO has an integrated military command structure, and it provides the essential forum for consultation and planning.

It was also recognized that NATO's 16 nations share a common belief in democracy and human rights with open political and economic institutions. NATO provides a model for behavior for the new democracies of Eastern and Central Europe. Indeed, when NATO leaders began to look at the issue seriously, they concluded that if NATO did not already exist, they would have to create it to deal with the new post-Cold War common security problems in Western Europe. Thus, the decision was made at the London summit in July 1991 and confirmed at the heads of state NATO summit in Brussels in January 1994 that NATO must continue its traditional missions. There are primarily two traditional missions: to serve as a forum for transatlantic consultation, and planning on defense matters and to provide for the mutual defense of the member states. The heads of state also agreed, settling a long period of discussion and controversy, to adopt the new mission of crisis prevention and management in out-of-area regions that alliance members conclude are areas of particular interest to NATO members. NATO finally concluded that it does have out-of-area responsibilities. That acknowledgement marked the beginning of the controversy.

In the 1993 meeting of the North Atlantic Assembly, a gathering of the 16 countries' parliamentarians, NATO members' governments were urged to expand NATO's missions to include crisis prevention management and out-of-area activities under certain specific guidelines. A second role that NATO was urged to take on is risk reduction in the former Warsaw Pact area. NATO has in effect already made this move, but it has not been formally adopted at the ministerial or head of state level.

Calls have also been made in all NATO countries for significant force reductions. Clearly, a need no longer exists for the alliance to preposition a large multinational army prepared to fight a static battle against advancing Warsaw Pact forces. That plan is obviously not necessary now or in the foreseeable future. The Warsaw Pact will never be put together again.

The United States has had approximately 330,000 American military and naval personnel assigned to the European theater. This kind of force and expense is no longer necessary. It was originally decided by the Bush administration that the United States

124

would keep approximately 150,000 military personnel in Europe. The Clinton administration reduced this total to 100,000. The United States is presently rapidly demobilizing to that 100,000 troop level. Some of the returning U.S. units will be disbanded, but most will be based in the United States, ready for redeployment in case of an emergency. Similarly, British, Canadian, Belgian, and other units were also withdrawn from forward positions in what was West Germany.

The members of NATO were supposed to begin reconfiguring their militaries to emphasize "rapid reaction" forces. These highly mobile forces are relatively lightly armed and designed to cope with crisis situations. The problem has been that many of our allies are simply dropping their force levels to a point where they are no longer able to respond to a crisis. For example, driven by domestic concerns, the already very modest Belgian forces have been cut by more than 50 percent in just a matter of two years. The Dutch had originally planned to cut their forces by about 30 percent and restructure according to NATO's new requirements, but what emerged from Parliament was a 60 percent reduction—double what had been planned. A cascading series of cuts are taking place among many NATO allies. This situation is also present to some extent in Canada. Without any overall plan about how defense spending is to be reduced, governments are trying to implement cuts now for reasons of domestic budgetary concerns. These reductions are leading to a situation where nations simply will not have the ability to respond to a crisis. NATO has yet to deal with that problem.

NATO is facing pressures from the outside as well. These pressures come mostly from would-be members, primarily the former Warsaw Pact countries that now want to be a part of NATO. NATO leaders have concluded that the alliance must address the security dilemmas posed by Eastern and Central Europe. The object is to help them in their economic transitions and in the creation of democratic institutions—particularly to help ensure that the armed forces and intelligence organizations actually do serve the democratically elected leaders.

The House Intelligence Committee, for example, has been visited by a variety of Eastern European parliamentarians, asking us how we conduct oversight of the intelligence community and keep them responsive and responsible to the elected civilian leadership. Candidly, we had to tell them that we occasionally have had our failures. As we all know, our failures are fairly notorious. We certainly have much to offer them, however, and we have tried to be as forthcoming as we can in those discussions with visiting parliamentarians.

To help NATO address these outside pressures, especially pressures for membership, the North Atlantic Cooperation Council (NACC) was created in 1991. NACC is a means for former Warsaw Pact countries or neutral countries who want to have some affiliation with NATO—perhaps even full membership—to begin to cooperate and associate with NATO countries. NACC provides training seminars, permits Eastern European political leaders and military officers access to the interworkings of NATO activities in Brussels, and provides for the exchange of technical information. Not everything is shared, but a high degree of interaction now occurs on a formal basis. Many military and civilian leaders from NATO countries are also working with military and civilian leaders in the former Warsaw Pact countries.

I was in Hungary in July 1994 visiting several refugee camps and military installations all over the southern half of the country, and I was amazed at the extent to which their military has collapsed. I was also pleasantly surprised to see how many American, British, and other NATO countries' military personnel had been there working with the Hungarian military and how many Hungarian military personnel had already been in the United States at some of our military schools. One could see the rapport being built up between American and Hungarian military officers.

Not surprisingly, however, most of the Eastern and Central European countries have not been satisfied with this arrangement. They feel they are being left in a vulnerable position. Most Eastern European countries want NATO membership now. They are worried about political instability in their own countries and in Eastern Europe in general. They are also worried about what might be happening in the former Soviet Union, especially in Russia. They fear that a very different kind of leadership could emerge from this chaos. Eastern Europeans want to sever the Yalta knot.

126

They want to ensure that the division of Europe that took place at the end of World War II is gone. They certainly do not want to be on the "wrong" side of any line that is drawn in the future. These feelings can be found all over, but such feelings are strongest in places like Poland, Hungary, the Czech Republic, and Slovakia.

Early NATO membership for these countries has been controversial in the United States as well. It divides members of Congress, and it is not a partisan issue. Republicans and Democrats can be found on both sides of this issue. Proponents of immediate or early NATO membership for these countries make five main arguments. First, expanding NATO would project stability eastward, which, they argue, is the most important function of NATO. Second, NATO has a moral and historic responsibility to open its doors to Central and Eastern European nations that subscribe to Western democratic values and traditions. Third, Russia must not be given a veto over Western security arrangements. Fourth, NATO membership is the quickest way to promote democratic values, market-oriented economies, and respect for human rights. Fifth, a resolution of ethnic problems in Eastern Europe would be best achieved within NATO.

Opponents of early NATO membership for former Warsaw Pact countries make six principal arguments, some of which are just the converse of proponents' arguments. First, rapid enlargement of NATO would be viewed as unnecessarily provocative by Russia and could perpetuate a nationalist backlash that would undermine the reform movements throughout the region. Russia must not be allowed to dictate NATO decisions, but one cannot totally discount Russia's position when making such momentous decisions.

Second, there is little enthusiasm among NATO members for extending NATO's collective defense commitment. This commitment, of course, is a core tenet of the NATO charter. If any of the 16 member nations are attacked, the other 15 must come collectively to their defense. This is a very big decision. The undeniable fact is that few NATO countries would want to send their young men and women to defend, for example, Lithuania, particularly when the people of Lithuania have recently reelected the old communists who ruled before the breakup of the Soviet Union and the Warsaw Pact. Many of these countries had high expectations about what would happen under a democracy. When things did not move as rapidly or in the direction that they anticipated, people were a bit disillusioned, and some of the old Communists were reelected under different names.

Third, admitting some nations (the Czech Republic, Hungary, Poland) while perhaps not admitting others (Ukraine, the Baltic states) would inevitably and unnecessarily draw lines across Europe, partitioning Eastern Europe and perhaps precipitating even greater instability. By what criteria does one choose among those who want to join NATO?

Fourth, many of the nations who seek NATO membership have not done enough to address their own security needs. They are looking to NATO to do for them what they have been unwilling to do for themselves.

Fifth, none of the former Warsaw Pact nations is ready to be effectively integrated into the NATO establishment. This view is held by senior NATO commanders such as Admiral Jeremy Boorda, the commander of NATO's Naples-based Southern Command, one of NATO's three major commands. (He is now the chief of naval operations.)

Sixth, some of these would-be NATO members have unresolved internal political difficulties that make them unsuitable candidates. Slovakia, for example, may want membership so that it can deal freely with the ethnic Hungarians without a fear of military reprisal from Hungary. Such ethnic and social problems must be resolved prior to NATO membership, otherwise they would simply be transferring these unresolved problems to NATO.

Neither the controversy over expanded NATO membership nor the dilemma over how to handle out-of-area contingencies have been resolved yet, although the January 1994 heads of state summit in Brussels did make progress on both issues. Two proposals emerged from the summit: the Partnership for Peace (PFP) program and the concept for establishing Combined Joint Task Forces. The Partnership for Peace program makes it clear that it is not a case of *if* new members would be permitted to join NATO, but *when*. It is an evolutionary process; a country will be judged on how well it is preparing itself for a full membership in NATO. The PFP makes it clear that NATO is not extending the umbrella of security over that country. The PFP is merely a framework that will allow members to move toward full NATO membership. NATO will work with the military forces of these aspiring countries through participation in joint exercises and the enhancement of existing exchange programs. The PFP remains intentionally vague on actual criteria and timetables for membership. This intentional vagueness is being resisted by many within NATO who want more specificity in the timetable and in the criteria. There are, on the other hand, some advantages in keeping things a bit vague and open.

PFP membership imposes some obligations. Nations participating in the Partnership for Peace must agree to transparency in their defense budgets and military planning in order that their publics and the other states might better understand their military capabilities. Second, they have to demonstrate civilian control of their armed forces. Third, PFP members must develop a capability in their militaries to cooperate in operations under the authority of the United Nations—for example, in out-of-area peacekeeping activities. They must also agree to build cooperative military relations with NATO, permitting interoperability of doctrine, weaponry, munitions, tactics, and so on.

We deliberately did not draw any lines. We did not say that PFP extends only to the countries outside of the former Soviet Union. We opened it to any countries that participate in the CSCE, which includes all of the former Soviet republics. It does not shut the door on Russia. It holds out the opportunity for it to become a member as well, although it is admittedly hard to imagine the conditions that would permit Russian membership.

The Partnership for Peace sets a process. Clearly, the Czechs and the Poles are most likely to qualify the quickest, with the Hungarians probably not far behind. Surprisingly, Albania—a country that was so isolated for so long—may soon qualify for NATO membership as well (probably the most pro-American country in Europe today is Albania).

The Combined Joint Task Forces is a plan to provide for greater flexibility in responding to potential crises. This approach recognizes that out-of-area operations, by their very nature, will be controversial, and therefore it will be difficult to convince all 16 NATO countries to support and participate in out-of-area operations. These operations may be hot wars, peacekeeping, peacemaking, or perhaps even nation-building. The Combined Joint Task Forces permit a group of NATO countries to act when they believe it serves a collective vital interest and to use NATO-assigned troops and planning assets in an ad hoc manner, if needed.

The Combined Joint Task Forces concept may also form the nucleus of a future European defense identity. It is the vehicle through which the United States has given a token kind of agreement to the creation of what might be called a European pillar within NATO. The United States has been lukewarm and less than sincere at times, but as a part of the January 1994 NATO summit, for the first time an American administration—the Clinton administration—formally approved of the establishment of a Europe-centered element within NATO. It is now possible that some of the countries of NATO might agree to act together under a Combined Joint Task Force, but without the agreement or participation of all 16 members. There could also be a combination of neutrals for peacekeeping duties—for example, if things go badly in the newly independent country of Macedonia. The Combined Joint Task Forces would require NATO agreement to gain access to NATO assets such as AWACS or intelligence, but they would not require the participation of all NATO countries. In fact, they would not even require that all of the participating countries be members of NATO.

This opportunity gives the Europeans the ability to act without the United States when European leaders feel it is in their interest. The Europeans may have an important stake in a situation, but the United States may be reluctant to deploy troops. This arrangement would, perhaps, permit the French, Italians, Spanish, and Portuguese to respond to threats from North Africa without involving the United States or the northern European countries. This program is designed to ensure that when NATO members believe there is a need to act, NATO will be able to respond more rapidly.

After the dissolution of the Soviet Union, it seems that we were caught short institutionally. Institutions were not in place to cope with this new post-Cold War environment. The West did not have the capability—even if it might have had the will—to intervene at the proper junctures when Yugoslavia began to disintegrate. NATO is now beginning to put in place some of the things that are necessary. The Combined Joint Task Forces concept is one of those institutional changes that will help us address the changes in the post-Cold War era.

The Combined Joint Task Forces are controversial, as is the Partnership for Peace proposal. These policy innovations will make foreign policy more difficult for the president, and they will multiply the chances for disagreements between the Congress and the president because more opportunities for out-of-area military action exist that could involve, but need not necessarily involve, the United States. Decisions will have to be made about whether to participate in the Combined Joint Task Force. Disagreements will also occur about expanding NATO membership. There will be less certainty about how the president should respond. The controversies are likely to be more intense and more numerous between the Congress and the president on these issues, as well as between the U.S. government and the NATO allies. All of these changes create many additional challenges for the president.

With so many challenges ahead, the future of the NATO alliance will depend on the ability of the United States, Canada, and the European allies to deal with these challenges in the same spirit of cooperation that has been the hallmark of our relations during the Cold War. Whether we are successful in that endeavor remains to be seen.

All this having been said, the snapshot picture I have sketched of NATO could be very different tomorrow. A great deal depends upon what happens in Russia itself.

QUESTION: I have two questions. First, NATO essentially is a military organization, designed for common defense and security. Many of these same countries are seeking association membership in the European Union. Is there any coordination in these membership efforts in terms of timing? My second question concerns the interaction between the United Nations and NATO regarding peacemaking and peacekeeping. How can the United Nations employ NATO in some of these crisis locations like the former Yugoslavia?

MR. BEREUTER: A relationship certainly exists between NATO and European Union membership. A European pillar for European defense and security will continue to evolve from the Western European Union (WEU). It was a moribund organization for many years. The only reason it was originally created was to accommodate French unwillingness to participate in the command structure of NATO, but it has become more active. The WEU now enforces sanctions against Serbia, with stations located in the Adriatic, the Danube, and elsewhere. The United States has now formally approved the creation of the European pillar. The WEU will clearly be that pillar and will evolve further as it takes in new members. The newest round of members to be taken into the European Union are Sweden, Austria, and Finland.

Increasingly, since there is such a significant overlap in the European membership of the WEU, NATO, and the European Union, those European members of all three organizations are going to push hard to ensure that those countries that want to be a part of NATO or the European Union also belong to the other two organizations. While an unofficial link among membership in these organizations will exist, it is going to become a very real link.

NATO assets have been used for quite some time now, especially U.S. assets within NATO, to assist U.N. peacekeeping operations in Yugoslavia. The biggest controversy within the NATO alliance today concerns whether or not NATO requires a U.N. resolution or the approval of the Conference on Security and Cooperation in Europe (CSCE) to undertake out-of-area operations. The American delegation to the North Atlantic Assembly (the parliamentary arm of NATO) unanimously agree, that America's national interests demand that the United States insists on NATO having autonomy of action. NATO cannot be subservient to the United Nations because when it is dependent upon a U.N. resolution prior to acting out-of-area, NATO is left vulnerable to a Chinese veto in the Security Council. This subservience could keep the United States from acting quickly in something like a new Yugoslavian situation. While it is certainly desirable to have a United Nations resolution or CSCE or OSCE approval of action, it cannot, from an American point of view, be a requirement. America and NATO must preserve the ability to act out-of-area when it is in the member countries' national interest to do so.

Events during the Gulf War and postwar efforts to help the Kurds in northern Iraq show that in a multilateral military effort, a NATO kind of involvement, training, and doctrinal commonality are absolutely crucial. Although NATO was not officially involved in Desert Storm, without the NATO underpinnings that stood behind the British, French, and American cooperation, coalition objectives would have been much more difficult to achieve. It would also have been much more difficult for any country to aid the Kurds in northern Iraq.

COMMENT: As NATO membership is broadened, the nature of NATO's mission inevitably broadens. Furthermore, as more units join an organization, there is a tendency to diffuse and dilute authority from an organizational standpoint. To some extent, the position you just mentioned vis-à-vis the United Nations cannot be avoided. A larger number of members will find it increasingly difficult to agree on actions. Issues are more likely to become controversial. There is a danger that NATO could degenerate into a debating society.

MR. BEREUTER: Your point is perceptive. That is exactly the kind of problem that could emerge. A traditional NATO action is likely to occur only in the event of a threat to Western Europe or North America. The Combined Joint Task Forces will become the more action-oriented element of the alliance.

One of the key issues to be decided is whether NATO will insist on unanimous approval of any Combined Joint Task Force in the future. A requirement for unanimity could immobilize the alliance.

QUESTION: Considering the decision-making procedures for Combined Joint Task Forces, could you elaborate on the dilemmas faced with or without a requirement for unanimity? NATO presently pretends to require unanimity, but if Denmark or Greece gets too obstreperous, there are ways of making decisions without unanimity. Reality has never been reflected in official doctrine. Will it be necessary to have flexibility on this issue in the future?

MR. BEREUTER: I think flexibility will have to exist.

QUESTION: Increases in membership need not make decision making impossible. Every time the European Union increased its membership, it found a way to lessen the number of circumstances that require unanimity. Will NATO pursue similar reforms? Should the requirements for unanimity be softened in the future?

MR. BEREUTER: I don't expect a rapid increase in NATO membership. New membership in the near future is unlikely, unless a radical change occurs in Russia. In such a situation, NATO membership could expand rapidly overnight. Three or four new members could join, and I think such a move would be smart. If the choice is between losing these Eastern European countries and reinstalling the Yalta lines or now granting them full NATO membership, I hope the West will have the will to quickly take them as new members. I'm sure contingency plans are in place to ensure that outcome.

An unofficial way of proceeding without unanimity in the European Union has evolved over quite a period of time. NATO would have to go through that same sort of evolution regarding the use of Combined Joint Task Forces. The more members there are, the more difficulty there will be. The potential exists for the resurfacing of current and long-standing disputes between nations that are both members of NATO, such as that between the Turks and the Greeks, now to be repeated between the Hungarians and the Slovaks, the Hungarians and the Romanians, or the Albanians and the Greeks. Thus, many more problems will occur within NATO as it is enlarged.

I imagine that NATO could not operate effectively unless near unanimity, if not complete unanimity, were required for the creation and use of Combined Joint Task Forces, even if the task force does not involve the participation of all or even half of the members. If NATO is going to permit central assets like command and control capabilities, AWACS, and intelligence resources to be used, approval for how these assets are being used must be unanimous.

QUESTION: Suppose one had reliable intelligence of one NATO nation planning a war against another NATO nation. Could you delineate the steps that it would take for such intelligence information to be acted upon by other NATO members?

MR. BEREUTER: I cannot imagine that this situation could arise among the 16 current NATO members. I do not think troops will ever again be crossing borders for belligerent purposes among current NATO countries. That is the major success of the postwar Europe. We may not, however, stick with just the current 16 members. If NATO expands, the scenario mentioned could become a reality.

Sufficient early warning systems are in place to alert NATO to any imminent hostilities between, for example, the Hungarians and the Slovaks. If Hungary and Slovakia were NATO members, the alliance would have to come down hard on those countries with all of the political and diplomatic force of the United States and the WEU to prevent the outbreak of armed conflict. If that effort failed, a need would exist for peace-enforcing activities within NATO.

For this reason, it is important that the evolution of democratic and human rights institutions proceed within those countries before they are granted NATO membership. They must be given help to overcome these ethnic and racial problems. In some ways, the United States is not well-equipped to handle these problems, but in other cases, it is extremely well-equipped. I am struck by the fact that every foreign policy issue taken up by Congress seems to have an American domestic constituency.

Recently, Croatian-Americans and Serbian-Americans testified on the same panel with great intensity and hostility toward each other. It is consequently more difficult sometimes for the United States to act in such areas. In other cases, America has the capacity to show that people should be able to live peaceably together. We also have people in Congress itself who fan the fires.

QUESTION: When it comes to NATO, the United States seems to be pushing for expansion, but when we talk about multilateralism at the U.N. level, it is just the opposite. The United States seems to want to have little to do with the United Nations. Isn't that a great dichotomy?

MR. BEREUTER: There is a dichotomy. The United States was badly burned by the tragedy of events in Somalia. Americans are now less willing to engage U.S. personnel in such activities. The United States had an insufficient appreciation of what is involved in peacemaking, peacekeeping, and nation-building. The President laid out some excellent intervention criteria in a speech before the United Nations, but these criteria haven't been implemented.

QUESTION: Undergirding the military part of NATO was always the assumption of political support. This political support was relatively easy to sustain as long as the common threat was generally agreed upon. What is the utility of pursuing parliamentary cooperation? What is the interest-based political underpinning of this endeavor? It seems very uncertain.

MR. BEREUTER: The North Atlantic Assembly serves as a modest legislative function for NATO, but in reality it is a powerless body. What it seeks to build is a consensus for the support of NATO and its objectives among member national parliamentarians. The assembly's membership was enlarged through associate memberships being offered to the parliamentarians of all of the former Warsaw Pact countries, including the Russians. This process is part of democracy-building for those countries.

Senator Howell Heflin of Alabama and I have prepared a resolution to give the six major committees of the North Atlantic Assembly specific sets of responsibilities to help strengthen democratic institutions and respect for human rights in those countries so that they are well prepared for NATO membership. One of the aims of this interparliamentary cooperation is to avoid a military dispute within NATO itself. I think such cooperation has a major role.

Douglas K. Bereuter

We are also providing direct aid to the Eastern European parliaments. This aid has taken the form of providing computer and library capabilities to the Polish, Hungarian, Czech, Slovak, and Albanian parliaments. Exchange programs also exist on the House side as well as the Senate side, but the United States is not alone in providing such aid. The Germans have provided more aid than the United States already. The British are also active. This effort is being made to reach out and develop a consensus not only behind Western ideals, but also behind the North Atlantic alliance.

NARRATOR: We appreciate Congressmen Bereuter taking time from his busy schedule to visit the Miller Center and address the changing face of NATO. We thank him for his contribution to our ongoing study.

CHAPTER EIGHT

Russia in NATO: The Fourth Generation of the Atlantic Alliance*

IRA L. STRAUS

NARRATOR: Ira Straus earned his doctorate in the Department of Government and Foreign Affairs of the University of Virginia. He has a long-standing interest in NATO and has written widely on the subject. He has continued the work of Clarence Streit and *Union Now.*

MR. STRAUS: When I wrote in 1985 about the hypothetical possibility of Eastern Europe and Russia joining NATO, people thought I had lost my mind. Even today, when one talks about Russia joining NATO, it sounds in the West like the wolf joining a flock of sheep. Currently, in Russia, the phrase is put the other way around—it is like a sheep (Russia) joining a pack of wolves (the West) that are gobbling up Russia. In fact, to some it sounds as it would have sounded 50 years ago to say that Germany should join the Western Alliance. In those days, the Western Alliance was engaged in a world war against German power, but only 10 years

---

Presented in a Forum at the Miller Center of Public Affairs on 19 December 1994.

later, West Germany did indeed join the Western Alliance. Thus, we have to allow for the theoretical possibility that the enemy against which NATO was actively directed for 40 years could become a part of the Western Alliance. For those trained in dialectics and the unity of opposites, this exercise may not be difficult. For the rest of us, it still takes some explaining.

The standard argument against having Russia in NATO is that NATO is an anti-Russian alliance. Therefore, NATO plus Russia equals zero. An alliance requires an enemy, and Russia is the enemy against which NATO is defined. If NATO were to include Russia, it would require some other enemy, like China, Japan, or the rest of the world; otherwise the alliance would likely fall apart. Russia's membership would cause it to become meaningless and ineffective. Henry Kissinger is the prime exponent of this view.

A mirror image of this view is held in Russia. Some Russians say it was a terrible mistake of Gorbachev, Shevardnadze, Yeltsin, and Kozyrev to stop defining the West as the enemy. It caused the Russian Empire to fall apart, and Russia itself is falling apart. These people of the "New Right" think the only way to hold Russia together is to again regard the West as an enemy. I say "mirror image" with full consciousness that in the Cold War it was often said that the Soviet-Western antagonism was just a matter of mutual misperceptions, mirror imaging, and so forth. In fact, there *was* a real dispute at that time. What we have on both sides today, however, is the beginning of the deliberate creation of an enemy image to hold something together—in Russia to hold the whole society together and reconstruct part of the old empire; in the West, to hold NATO together. No one expects that the United States, France, or Germany is going to fall apart, but the fear that the Western Alliance could disintegrate is very real, and there is a widespread notion that we need to have an enemy to keep it together.

This argument derives from Carl Schmitt, a brilliant and dangerous German political scientist who became a Nazi. He held that enemy relations are primary in politics; the category *friend* exists only in a dialectic with *enemy*, *self* with *other*. The state is the agency that defines the enemy by willful sovereign decision.

What is NATO? Is NATO essentially an anti-Russian alliance? I would argue that it is not. Certainly its main business in the first 40 years of its existence was to defend against Soviet power. NATO, however, is not just the institution formed in 1949 and defined by its functional activity up to 1989. NATO is the third generation of the Atlantic Alliance.

The first generation came in World War I. The second generation appeared in World War II. The third generation existed during the Cold War. The fourth generation is already under construction after the Cold War. It is not so much a question of whether there will be a fourth generation, but rather how it will be organized and which countries will be included.

Notice that the time lapse between the generations of the alliance has grown shorter. The first generation dissolved at the end of World War I, and 20 years later it was reassembled. The second generation virtually dissolved at the end of World War II, but within four years it was reassembled, and Dwight Eisenhower returned to Europe and reestablished the Supreme Allied Command that he had left off in 1945. The fourth generation is apparently going to come right on the heels of the third generation without any institutional break. This timing brings the tremendous advantage of retaining the existing institutions and building on them rather than having to start from scratch.

A need exists for this kind of institutional inheritance. If it is true that having a common enemy is important for building unity among countries, then we should cherish what unity we have built during the terrible period of enemy relations. In the Atlantic Alliance we have had three generations of enemy relations, which have allowed a great deal of unity to be built. If we were to throw that out and start from scratch, it is unlikely that we could build as much again, even if we faced a new enemy. So having this inheritance is good, but at the same time it would be ill-advised to create enemies for the sake of creating the new generation of the alliance.

If NATO is seen as the third generation of the Atlantic Alliance, and if we consider that the third generation included Germany, the enemy against which the first two generations were directed, then it is quite conceivable that Russia, the enemy of the third generation, could be included in the fourth generation, which is now under construction. If we consider the ideas that underlay the founding of NATO, this scenario becomes more than just conceivable; it becomes logical.

It becomes the appropriate and natural thing to do, because it was not just an external threat that led to the three generations of the Atlantic Alliance. There was also an internal idea of unification among the Atlantic countries that led to the Alliance. That idea was called Atlanticism.

Atlanticism proceeds from the predicate that the Atlantic countries are the leading countries of Europe and have been since the 18th century, and that Europe is the leading area of the world and has been since the Renaissance. As such, it holds that the unity or disunity of the Atlantic countries plays a decisive role in maintaining or dissipating world order.

The Atlanticist idea developed over several generations just as the Atlantic Alliance did. The generations of Atlanticism preceded the formal alliances. Benjamin Franklin was one of the founders, but the first major generation of Atlanticism came in the late 19th century after the American Civil War. At this point, after American federalism had seemed discredited in 1860 and then vindicated in 1865, the British began to look back and wonder, "Why did we lose America in the first place? What a mistake that was!" They reexamined Benjamin Franklin's ideas for reforming the British Empire into a sort of split-level union—a federation of the colonies within a trans-Atlantic parliament for the Empire—and thought that they made a great deal of sense. So they formed a movement for an imperial federation to save and consolidate what remained of their empire and a movement for an English-speaking union. Many Americans had great interest in these ideas, which paved the moral ground for the diplomatic rapprochement of the late 19th century between Britain and America. This rapprochement turned out to be an essential prerequisite for the formation of an Atlantic Alliance during World War I.

The second generation of Atlanticism developed in the 1930s and looked for a union of Britain, France, America, and all of the small countries in between. It received its clearest expression at the end of the interwar period in a book called *Union Now* by Clarence Streit. He was the *New York Times* reporter at the League of

Nations. The idea was that by uniting the Western industrial democracies that control the vast bulk of the world economy, the Germans would see that it was pointless to start another world war. They started World War I in the expectation of American neutrality, but if America were engaged politically from the start, they would not start World War II.

Moreover, this federation would be an open nucleus of an international union that other countries could join as they became democracies. Specifically, he thought of Germany, Italy, and Japan joining soon, and then Eastern Europe and Russia.

This perspective exemplified the Atlanticism that began as an organized public movement in 1939. In America the movement was organized as the Inter-Democracy Federal Unionists. In Britain a parallel organization, Federal Union, was formed to promote a European federation including Britain. Its members mostly also supported Atlantic federation, but they didn't think many Americans would be interested.

This movement and its ideas provided the basis not so much for the Alliance of World War II, which followed traditional lines, but rather for the postwar construction of the European and Atlantic communities through the Marshall Plan, NATO, and the European Coal and Steel Community, which subsequently grew into the European Community (EC) and today's European Union (EU). The European Union was always explicit that its ideas derived from this movement and that the European Union had the goal of becoming a federation of Europe. NATO was less explicit about this goal, which is why this part of its history is little known. NATO was more of a compromise. Not all of the founders shared the federalist idea, but most of them did. Lester Pearson of Canada did, and his ideas were embodied in a watered-down form in Article II of the North Atlantic Treaty. In the U.S. State Department, the two people most involved in creating NATO—Jack Hickerson (then-director of the Office of European Affairs) and Theodore Achilles (then-director of West European Affairs)—both not only shared this idea but were inspired by the book *Union Now*. Achilles attended lectures by Clarence Streit, and he told me in 1983, "If it hadn't been for *Union Now*, I don't think there would have been a NATO treaty." The public spirit of Atlanticism was the background music for the creation of NATO.

If the idea of Atlanticism was an open nucleus alliance of the Atlantic democracies to which other European or other industrial countries could join after they became democracies, then it is natural that it included Italy from the start and Germany a few years later, and it would have been natural to look forward to including Russia after 1991. The inclusion of Germany, however, was still almost incomprehensible to the French when it happened in 1954. Many of the same arguments they used against including Germany are being used today against including Russia.

One other facet of the Atlantic idea was that the unity of the Western democracies would serve to attract others. The other, "Eastern" countries would see that it was useful to be a part of the alliance and would throw off their dictators in the hope of joining. Before our eyes, this has happened. The strategy worked.

If one looks at Russian history, and even German and Eastern European history, one sees a curious ambivalence about relations with the West. On one hand, there is a recognition that Western Europe is the leading, more advanced sector that one wants to join.

On the other hand, what did it mean to join Europe in the time of Peter the Great around the year 1700? It meant joining an area where many wars were being fought and where the main system of international affairs was one of confrontation and the balance-of-power system. If Russia joined this system, it meant joining the effort of counterposing power against power. One of the perverse consequences was that Russia became involved in war—Western wars. During these wars, it was natural to "deepen" the war effort by developing ideologies to justify fighting against those "bad" people to the west. Thus anti-Western sentiments grew. This is the paradoxical dialectic, so to speak, of westernization: In the process of joining the West, relations developed that built up Russia's internal resistance to what it was joining. And when *world* wars would start and spill over into Russia—which happened with Napoleon, World War I, and World War II—the West would be discredited in a disastrous way. Russia might be following a policy of westernization, but then it would see that joining the West was not such a good idea. Joining the West meant joining world wars because the West couldn't manage its own affairs.

To be sure, it didn't always happen that way. For example, in the Crimean War, the West actually united against Russia, and Russia suffered a humiliating defeat. As a result, the anti-Western policy of Czar Nicholas I was discredited, which led to the second great westernization movement in Russia.

It was when general wars began in the West and spilled over to the East that an anti-Western reaction ensued. The ideological reaction developed not only in Russia but also in Germany, blaming the world wars on the individualism of Western society. Individualism was deemed to lead to conflict and lack of social coherence, resulting in aggression, warfare, and egotism (such as that of Napoleon). The cure for these problems was a romantic organic society. Not fully Westernized countries such as Germany and Russia were still able to preserve and develop their national characteristics and organic unity. They could show the world the moral way to conduct a society, and world wars would disappear. These ideas were developed by the German romantic nationalists. They were picked up by the Russian Slavophiles and later adapted by the Marxists. Lenin's basic idea of imperialism is just a translation into economic language of the romantic arguments against Napoleon—that Western individualism or bourgeois capitalism leads to conflict and wars, and the solution is to create a socialist, or in other words an organic nationalist, economy. These ideas are also expressed around the world in religious forms by ayatollahs and religious fundamentalists of many stripes. If we develop an organic religious society without so much individualism, we will have a moral society that will lead to world peace.

The unfortunate consequence of this nationalism is that it makes international conflict much more serious. It also put Russia in a 70-year struggle against the real existing world order in the name of a hypothetical future, socialist world order.

That cycle of attraction and reaction was the paradox of westernization in the past. Today the West is no longer divided, but rather is engaged in a process of integration. Joining the West no longer need mean involvement in conflict. Indeed, in the period of Gorbachev, Western institutions of integration were reappraised in a positive way. Instead of being seen as primarily anti-Russian, they were reinterpreted as positive steps toward international unity in which Russia should try to join.

The attractive nature of the Western nucleus played exactly the role that the original theorists in 1939 hypothesized. In this sense, the attraction to Eastern Europe and Russia in joining the West was not an accident; it was all according to the game plan. The West was supposed to form a nucleus of unity. The people under dictatorship were supposed to be attracted to this nucleus, and they were supposed to throw off their dictators and join the West. If we present the situation this way, Eastern Europe's attempt to join NATO is no longer paradoxical, but rather becomes so natural and inevitable that we should expect it to occur without delay. The final synthesis should be clear. The industrialized world should be marching onward straight toward unity without any problems.

One has to ask why the consummation is not working out in that manner. Why is integration of the East taking so long, and why is a negative attitude toward it prevalent in many circles? There are perhaps some good reasons for these delays, but the main explanations lie in the bad reasons; that is, in inertia.

Western unity didn't just begin in the 1940s and move straight to its fruition in the 1990s. In between, in the late 1950s and 1960s, came Charles de Gaulle (president of France), who basically ground Western multilateral institutions to a halt. The "era of stagnation" in the West parallels almost perfectly the era of stagnation in the Soviet Union. Before there was Brezhnev, there was de Gaulle. While Brezhnev was general secretary of the Soviet Union, Mr. Joseph M. A. H. Luns remained secretary general of NATO for so long that everyone recognized the amount of stagnation in NATO.

The same thing was true of the European Community from the Luxembourg Compromise of 1966 to the Single European Act of 1987. In this era of stagnation, the ideals of integration became buried under a mound of habits. In scholarly and political conferences about the European Community held in the early 1980s, the tendency was to talk as if the original federalist ideas were just a mistaken dream, and anyone who still talked like the federalists just didn't understand what the European Community (now the European Union) was about. Those types of comments

146

are no longer heard at meetings about the European Union, but that was the prevailing mind-set in the early 1980s.

In NATO, the early years were described as "the era of institution building in the Atlantic Community," as if the institutions built in the late 1940s were the last ones that would ever be built. The atmosphere of the 1980s was that the Atlantic Community, only 30 years old, had reached its final fruition for a thousand years to come. The ideals of unity embedded within those original institutions—of a political community something like the European Union—were excluded from discussion. It is not surprising that this era of stagnation made it difficult to overcome the inertia and return to the original ideas under which NATO was formed.

At least the European Union began to come out of its era of stagnation in 1984 on its own initiative. Its efforts led to the Single European Act, negotiated in 1985, ratified in 1986, and implemented in 1987, and then the new era of progress in the European Union that has led to the current situation. The Soviet Union began to come out of its era of stagnation a year later. NATO is decidedly the slowest of the three to come out of its period of stagnation. That extreme slowness is the primary source of the failure to live up to the original ideas of the alliance.

One could speak of this situation as a tragedy in three acts. If the original idea was a dialectic moving through thesis, antithesis, and synthesis, the failure to come to the synthesis has at least three acts—the first of which is that era of stagnation.

Additionally, the original ideas of NATO were never clearly spelled out in the treaty. The preamble contains beautiful rhetoric but is rather vague, whereas the preamble of the European Union's original treaty (Treaty of Rome) is very clear: "Determined to lay the foundations of an ever closer union among the peoples of Europe." The preamble further "call[s] upon the other peoples of Europe who share their idea to join in their efforts." Thus, the idea of expansion to include other countries was explicit in the European Union's treaty, as well as always being clear in European Union rhetoric. Further, means are provided in both the treaties of NATO and the European Union for including more countries. The point was that while the European Union was explicitly intended as a nucleus for expansion, NATO expansion was only implicit in the ideas of most of the people who created it. It was never written in as a deliberate goal of the alliance.

Yet despite all of these subjective disadvantages of NATO, a tremendous objective advantage exists. Objectively, NATO, unlike the European Union today, could expand rapidly. It is much easier to integrate a new military ally than it is to integrate an entire economy, as must be done in the European Union for new members. Furthermore, NATO's greater size would enable it to expand without losing balance. Whereas the European Union now includes approximately 300 million people, NATO includes about 600 million people and is thus better suited for including a couple hundred million more. In fact, NATO could include Russia without dramatically upsetting the balance, unlike the European Union. In the European Union they make a joke about this scenario: "Well, we might include Russia one day if we include the United States as well." That is the whole point. Since it is not in the game plan to include America, it is also not in the game plan to include Russia in the European Union. It is only NATO and the other Atlantic organizations like the Group of Seven and the Organization for Economic Cooperation and Development (OECD) that could include Russia and do so quickly.

Why hasn't NATO pursued this path? First, there was the lack of clear thinking about it during the era of stagnation and even since then. Second, there is the bad habit of power: He who is in power doesn't like to adjust; he likes to make others adjust to him. This was one of the key concerns of Karl Deutsch, who in most other respects served as an ideologist for the bad habits of NATO. One of the big challenges to people in power is to have the wisdom to adjust themselves to new circumstances. They are in danger of becoming dinosaurs if they just sit around expecting others to adjust to them until they come to the point that the others cannot or will not adjust any more.

NATO has been happily projecting the burdens of adjustment onto the countries that want to join it. This is partly what the Partnership for Peace is about. It aims to teach the former Warsaw Pact countries all of the adjustments they have to make. NATO itself is making *some* adjustments—in fact, it is proud of saying that it has adjusted more than any other international institution to the post-Cold War conditions—but how could it help but do so? Its main business had been the Cold War. Of course it is going to make some adjustments!

The sad point is that these adjustments have been far from adequate. Basically, the same organizational structure that existed five years ago is still present. The offices for dealing politically with Eastern Europe and Russia remain infinitesimal in comparison with the size of the military offices, which are essentially the same old ones. There is one assistant to the secretary general for dealing with Eastern European and Russian affairs named Chris Donnelly. He wants things to go much faster and much more in a political direction, but he is faced with the old structure with its old habits. NATO has made a minor adaptation, not a deep transformation as is needed for the new era.

Furthermore, a problem exists in all international organizations of how to make decisions about new problems. In NATO this problem was not very serious during the Cold War because there was only one basic decision to be made. This decision was made in 1950: that if the Red Army crossed the Iron Curtain into Western Europe, NATO would fight. In the meantime, it would prepare for this eventuality and organize collectively to fight against it. All of the decisions made in NATO from 1950 to 1989 were basically follow-ups to that one essential decision. Even the follow-up decisions were sometimes difficult to make, but since war did not break out, NATO never faced the consequences of doing too little too late.

Life is different nowadays. Real wars are being fought in Europe. The decisions about these wars have to be made while the wars occur, not through a process of 30 years of preparation. Political decisions have to be adapted to the response that was made to the first response—sometimes a military one. NATO's unanimous method of making decisions so far has been totally inadequate for this situation, as we have seen in the former Yugoslavia. Furthermore, if more countries are included in a system that makes its decisions unanimously, more possibilities for a veto exist. The decisions therefore become slower and harder to reach. This problem is one of the elementary points of wisdom in international organizations—how can these organizations function if more countries are around the table?

The European Union (EU) has been debating this problem ever since it was formed. It intended to include more members someday but knew that it would have more trouble making decisions when more countries became members. The EU eventually reached a brilliant conclusion: It would have to "deepen" or streamline the decision-making process when more members were included. The first time, when it allowed Britain, Denmark, and Ireland to become members in 1973 (Greece came later in 1981), the only deepening it tried was by making some new commitments to closer economic unity, more political consultation on foreign policy, monetary coordination, and so forth. It made one bad mistake: It didn't really streamline its method of making decisions, and the consequence was that the this supposed deepening didn't work. Instead, the result of the enlargement was more and more stagnation and what came to be called in the early 1980s "Eurosclerosis."

In the second occasion of expansion in 1984-85, the then-European Community debated letting in Spain and Portugal (which it did in 1986). The EC concluded that the earlier mistakes that had contributed to the state of sclerosis needed to be corrected. It decided that the way to correct these earlier mistakes was to streamline decision making by going ahead with two-thirds weighted majority voting on a number of economic decisions. This change was the essence of the Single European Act of 1987, and it worked. The inclusion of more countries did not lead to a problem this time.

In 1989, the European Union realized it faced the same problem again. The procedures were still not streamlined enough to include countries of Eastern Europe that were facing different circumstances. So they negotiated the Maastricht Treaty, the essential purpose of which was not just to complete economic union, but to further streamline decision making so more countries could become members.

I am far from satisfied with how that treaty turned out. In many respects, it concentrated on the wrong subjects when it came to economic union. In terms of streamlining decision making, however, it did make some progress, and now Sweden, Finland, and

Austria have been allowed to join the European Union. (They officially became members on 1 January 1995.) Negotiations for membership of additional countries will soon occur, and a further streamlining of decision making will be attempted during negotiations in 1996.

The great problem in NATO is that unlike the European Union, it has not had 20 years of experience and debate about how to handle problems associated with new memberships. Instead, it is suddenly faced with new external conflicts that its old decision-making system is not good enough to handle and with potential new members that are not used to just going along with the Western gang. NATO has no tradition of thought on this subject. Instead it has a bad ideology, one that was expounded by Karl Deutsch. His ideology of international integration was diametrically opposed to that of the European Union, which was always federalism, albeit sometimes disguised as functionalism. Federalism meant forming common governing organs in which decisions are made by democratic voting. Karl Deutsch's ideology was the exact reverse. It was to multiply communications channels and develop virtually unanimous consensus as the best way of developing unity among member nations. NATO used that sort of ideological justification for its habits of operating by consensus over the years, and once something becomes not only a habit but an ideology, it becomes difficult to dislodge.

When the question of new members came up after 1989, the prospect of much more complicated decisions left NATO in a bafflement that has continued to this day. One bright sign is the idea of administrative flexibility, known technically as Combined Joint Task Forces (CJTF) or "coalitions of the willing." Countries can form a coalition within NATO to carry out some specific action. Not all countries have to be engaged in every action. The only problem is that this reform is still only on the administrative level, not the political level. No one knows how decisions are to be made to authorize a coalition of NATO countries to go ahead and act in the name of NATO, using some common NATO resources but without involving all of the countries. The official position is still to say that this decision will be taken unanimously, and only then can some of the NATO members go ahead and do something.

What is the point of having a subcoalition if everyone in the original larger group has to unanimously agree? This condition contradicts the whole point of the CJTF idea and nullifies most of its advantages for flexibility. Not everyone agrees, by the way, that it should be maintained in this rigid mode. Congressman Doug Bereuter of Nebraska thinks there should be more flexibility in decision making for these coalitions. This idea is not yet official NATO doctrine, however, which is now in a state of paradox because of the unanimity requirement.

If this condition were changed and NATO took the next step and developed a flexible method of authorizing coalitions of member countries to undertake actions on behalf of the alliance, a weighted majority of NATO countries in terms of power and population would become able to make effective decisions about defense, security, and military affairs for the new era. Unfortunately, this is not yet the case. The essential question facing NATO thus remains: Will it transform itself for the new era, and thereby also include the new countries?

In the absence of a conception of self-transformation, NATO will continue to project upon the supplicant countries all of the burdens of adjustment. It will keep telling them they must adjust to this, that, or the other NATO habit or standard; to strive toward interoperability of weapons; to spend a larger sum of money; to reorganize the army; and to become stable democracies. Some even insist that they must become "irreversible" democracies. What country in the world *is* an irreversible democracy? There isn't a single one. All of the NATO members today would have to be expelled if the standard of irreversible democracy for NATO membership were to be used. The idea is farcical. Yet it has become a part of the NATO lexicon that these countries must continue to adapt themselves until others trust them so completely that they can become members without anyone worrying about these prospective members creating trouble for the other countries.

That is not the real world. The point of international institutions is to deal with real existing countries, and it is the nature of a country to create trouble. We want some basic standards for a country to become an ally: that they feel like an ally and our friend; that they believe their basic national interests are compatible

152

with ours and are shared with ours; that some common dangers confront us around the world—not necessarily a single permanent enemy, but a basket of common dangers and potential dangers. An orientation toward democratic government is certainly a pre-requisite for being a member of a democratic alliance—support for democracy as an ideal and an attempt to institutionalize democratic practices. These basic standards are met by virtually all of the post-Communist countries of the former Soviet bloc. A couple, such as Turkmenistan, may be questionable, but basically all of them are oriented toward democratic government, oriented toward the West as a friendly area of the world, and are seeking alliances with the West. They have met the standards for becoming allies. It is the West that is refusing to go through with or even conceptualize the fundamental adjustments that are needed for the Eastern European countries to become allies.

Various reasons are given for this. We in the United States have become tired of having allies; we are not sure if it is worth the effort. Isolationist ideas are again circulating. Many people in the United States say that the United States is not a European country, just as many people in Russia say that Russia is not a European country. This categorization is partly true, of course. We are not *merely* a European country, just as Russia is not *merely* a European country. But we are essentially European. Our institutions are essentially European, and our way of life is essentially European.

The real reasons why NATO expansion has been so slow and inadequate for the challenges in the new era are not good ones: inertia, habit, and loss of NATO's original ideas and spirit. These ideas are much better understood in Eastern Europe and Russia today than they are within the West and in NATO itself.

Solutions are slowly emerging. NATO is adapting to the idea of new membership. Its processes are becoming more flexible than they used to be. Eastern European countries are gradually prying the door open. Russia is playing an ambiguous role. Russia does want to join NATO, but it doesn't want to be the last country in. It certainly doesn't want to be told the other countries can join, and perhaps later NATO will let Russia join. For a very good reason, Russia fears being isolated as the only excluded country. It fears that the Henry Kissinger scenario will come true, which is that all of the other countries will be members of NATO for the purpose of joint opposition to Russia. Russia would be conceived as the enemy that holds NATO together, and the door would be slammed shut to Russia. So Russia's objections are real, sincere, and serious. The solution from Russia's standpoint is to develop close relations with NATO as a precondition to NATO letting in more members, with the door genuinely open to Russia to become a full member not too far in the future.

Although some part of these solutions are underway, it is an open question as to whether they will be realized before the problems explode and render the process of solving it moot and hopeless. Post-Communist parties are now in power in most of the former Soviet bloc, which is partly a consequence of disillusionment with the lack of Western leadership. A Communist party may well gain power in Russia in 1996 if the elections are held, which is uncertain. Even that Communist party would not be nearly as bad as the extreme nationalists coming to power. So I am far from optimistic that the problem will be solved before it explodes, but at least the method of the solution is known and some progress is underway.

MR. WALTER SABLINSKY: What is the purpose of NATO, and how can the Russian strategic position be integrated? NATO is essentially facing the possibility of external aggression and civil war in Russia. Does NATO want to become involved in Russia's internal problems? I can understand why those on NATO's side would be reluctant to become involved. Certainly other countries should be invited to join, but should we invite Serbia or the Bosnian Serbs to joins NATO as well?

MR. STRAUS: Certainly the northwestern parts of former Yugoslavia want to join NATO. What *do* we do, however, in the case of a civil war within a NATO country? Nothing has been done about it in the past, and we don't necessarily want to do anything in the future.

NATO's strongest line item is Article V, which says it will defend collectively against any country that attacks it. That type of defense is not all NATO is about, however. Article IV calls for cooperation in developing a peaceful international environment and preventing conflict, and Article II calls for economic and political cooperation. If NATO included Russia, it would be in the most secure and comfortable position ever in terms of Article V; no external country could conceivably attack any NATO member to its own advantage. China is a remote possibility, but it requires some stretching of the imagination to think the Chinese would be so unwise as to attack Russia, especially if Russia were a NATO member. Even without NATO, Russia has plenty of nuclear weapons to scare off any potential aggressor.

The only condition under which Article V would remain relevant is if Russia is kept outside as the enemy or the implied enemy. Then NATO countries would indeed need to be defended against the potential future threat of Russian military forces. If Russia is included in NATO, Article V would remain as an implicit guarantee to remind other countries that it would be incredibly stupid to attack a NATO country, given the enormous military power of the alliance.

Articles II and IV involve military coordination, preparation for various potential problems and threats, cooperation in peacekeeping and peacemaking, economic cooperation, and the collaboration of military forces so that they view each other as allies rather than enemies. It includes the defense of France against any conceivable threat by Germany, which does not involve any military preparation, but is assured simply by Germany and France knowing that they are both in NATO. Since France knows the military plans of Germany, it knows that Germany is not a threat to France. In the trans-formed NATO there would not only be the existing treaty but also the protocols of accession of the new countries, which would have to define some similar mutual responsibilities. What would be NATO's involvement in case of war between new member countries? This scenario was never defined in the past. When war almost erupted between Greece and Turkey in 1974, NATO was in some trouble. NATO would need a clear policy in the future because of the unstable mutual relations among some of the new countries. If they did in fact come into conflict, NATO would probably insist that they subject their conflicts to NATO arbitration or lose their NATO protection.

It seems to me that one would have a transformed arrangement if one were to include these countries, and I see no reason why it cannot be done. All of those commitments are already included in the Conference on Security and Cooperation in Europe (CSCE). It would be a matter of reaffirming them as a part of the NATO commitment.

MR. ALLEN LYNCH: The Partnership for Peace program was originally a bureaucratic idea to postpone and hopefully stifle the question of NATO expansion by covering it in the forums of consultation and assimilation and so forth. So the question would have to come to the political level because I don't see the interest in the Western European capitals. I suspect that the fate of NATO expansion will be similar to the fate of health care in this country, which is to say that the people who are proposing it did not have the constituent base necessary to implement it. It is the Eastern Europeans who are forcing this issue, not the Western Europeans. In the same way, health care was a technocratic initiative, not a popular initiative, and therefore it failed.

My second observation is that all of the Eastern Europeans see the main purpose of being in NATO as protection against Russia. Even if they do not see a specific threat scenario in the next three to seven years, they all see it, and every Russian knows it. Furthermore, most Western European diplomats see the basic function of NATO in the same way.

My third point is that an unstated premise underlying your whole analysis is that the United States remains committed to influencing the pattern of political order in Europe. I submit that this commitment is probably no longer true. Even though the United States maintains 100,000 troops in Europe, and even though it will remain economically committed to trade, investment, the G-7, and so forth, I am not convinced that the United States remains committed to using that presence to influence the distribution of political power in Europe. In this sense, we in this country are much closer to the period between the fall of France and Pearl Harbor (June 1940 to December 1941) than we are to the late 1940s and the era of forming new institutions; that is, the country remains divided over the question of whether we have deep and

156

abiding security interests in Europe. In the absence of an overarching external threat, I think we will basically come back to that debate that was never resolved but only interrupted by Pearl Harbor and then the advent of the Cold War.

What I am saying is that many of the political premises behind your argument do not exist because people do not see it.

MR. STRAUS: I think at least 90 percent of what you said is not only compatible with my arguments, but it is essentially the same as what I said. I believe we agree on the explanation of why NATO does not expand and the old habits of thinking. Political will is essential. It is the Eastern Europeans who are driving this issue because they have the political will. For them it is not a technocratic question. For some people in the West it is not a technocratic question, either. When I wrote about it in 1985, certainly it was no technocratic question for me, but I recognize that I was very much in the minority in the West at that time.

Gyula Horn was the first political leader to raise this issue in February 1990. He was then the foreign minister of Hungary and now is the prime minister. He is a reformed Communist. He advocated having all of the Warsaw Pact countries join NATO, including Russia. Joining NATO was not raised as an anti-Russian matter, and in the minds of the Eastern Europeans to whom I talked, it is still not essentially an anti-Russian matter. Certainly reassurance against Russia is a major part of their interest, just as reassurance against Germany has been a major part of France's interest in being in NATO from the beginning. But the issue was raised by the Eastern Europeans as a matter of building what Gorbachev would call a "common European home"—a united Europe in which they would get their full seat at the table, affirming and consolidating their European identity.

Even apart from the Russian question, they were not convinced that they would be stable, happy, peaceful democracies if left all to themselves. In fact, they distrusted each other so much that they didn't want to unite among themselves; they wanted to unite with the West. That was not just because we had more firepower than Russia; it was because of economic, moral, and above all, political reasons. The identity of their democratic movements impelled them to rejoin Europe, and Europe meant the CSCE, EU, and NATO.

NATO people would hear nothing of this federalist idealism from the Eastern Europeans but would listen somewhat to their anti-Russian talk. The rise of the Russian nationalist right wing certainly makes everyone afraid. But the essential reason the Eastern Europeans want to join NATO remains what it was in 1990, even if their rhetoric is no longer so strong. They know if they continue with that old rhetoric, they will get nowhere with NATO.

The reasoning of the Russians is more complicated. The Russians are not united on the question of joining NATO, as virtually every Eastern European country is. Russia has a different psychological, cultural, and geopolitical option. It can choose to try to be a non-European country—at a terrible price to itself, but it does have that option. Russia is divided on what it wants to be. If the option of joining Europe—which was the essential idea of the Soviet/Russian government from the beginning of Gorbachev's tenure until the Yeltsin era—is clearly closed to it, then the other option will be taken by default. That is the way the debate is tending to go in Russia.

Can the door be pried open? Can the United States remain committed to Europe? I don't have any final answers to this question, just as I trust you don't. I am not so optimistic that enough progress will be made before it is preempted by an explosion, but I do think that we are moving basically in the right direction.

The North Atlantic Cooperation Council (NACC), formed in 1991, was another method of postponing the issue, and yet it pried the door open ever so slightly. Nowadays the Republicans claim that it was a brilliant first step toward expansion of NATO, and that this is what it was always intended to be. To the contrary, it was intended as a way of putting off the Eastern Europeans, but it pried the door open and got the issue into NATO anyway. The Partnership for Peace program was also partly a method of putting off the issue, but the declarations issued when it was established set forth the goal of membership for all of these countries. That goal was not remarked upon at the time because there was so much criticism from the Eastern European side that the goal wasn't expressed strongly enough. Therefore, the people managed to overlook the more basic point that it established the goal on behalf of all of the countries, including Russia. The latest NATO declaration does little more than to reaffirm that and make it somewhat more definite in the sense that NATO is going to now conduct a study on how to expand and what the processes and problems are.

My greatest fear is not that NATO is not going to expand some day, but that this study will not focus on the right questions and will not define expansion in the most useful manner. I think the greatest danger is that NATO will in too many areas just continue with the old habits.

NARRATOR: You have certainly stimulated us to think more deeply about a controversial issue. We are glad you have provided us with new dimensions of thinking about opportunities.

CHAPTER NINE

NATO, East Asia, and Japan*

ALAN TONELSON

NARRATOR: The issue of NATO, what it is doing, and what it is failing to do has become more and more a public issue. Senator Dole has spoken out very strongly on the question of NATO, and it remains to be seen exactly what the view will be in Congress on NATO. Alan Tonelson, a superb writer on public affairs, is here to speak about the relations between the United States and its NATO and Japanese allies.

Currently a fellow at the Economic Strategy Institute based in Washington, D.C., Mr. Tonelson has written not only on Europe but has worked with Clyde Prestowitz, Jr., and others who have also written about Japan. The Economic Strategy Institute is devoted primarily to trade and international economic relations. Mr. Tonelson is also the former project director of Twentieth Century Fund, and before that he was associate editor of *Foreign Policy*. He has also served as associate editor of the *Wilson Quarterly* and of *The Inter Independent*, which is a publication of the United Nations Association in New York. In addition to many articles and reviews, Mr. Tonelson has contributed to *The New North American Order: A Win-Win Strategy for U.S.-Mexico Trade* and co-edited *Powernomics:*

---

*Presented in a Forum at the Miller Center of Public Affairs on 1 December 1994.

Economics and Strategy After the Cold War. He is also author of *A Foreign Policy for the Rest of Us*, in which he addresses the need for economic and strategic retrenchment in U.S. foreign policy. We are pleased he could join us.

MR. TONELSON: I recently returned from England, where I attended a conference on NATO's future. The conference took place immediately after President Clinton announced the lifting of America's enforcement of the arms embargo on Bosnia and in the wake of the recent midterm elections. As a result, most people at the conference, including a number of senior national security officials from the major Western European countries and Eastern Europe, concluded that NATO's future is grim. I happen to share that conclusion, but unlike these dedicated, even archetypical, Atlanticists, I believe that this development—which is also true of our security relationship with Japan—is anything but grim for this country.

Two reasons stand out in my mind. As I review these reasons, I will probably not spend much time on the front-page crises that the two relationships are undergoing—the present Bosnia crisis and our economic imbalances with the Japanese. These questions will come up, but I would like to focus more intensely on what I consider to be the more fundamental, structural reasons that these relationships are in serious trouble.

The first reason is that although the Cold War is over, we are still trying to pursue a Cold War-oriented strategy and Cold War-spawned objectives with regard to these two relationships. I am reluctant to use the term *alliance* to describe the U.S.-Japan and the U.S.-NATO security relationships because the sharing of costs and risks in both has been so unequal for so long that the kind of all-for-one and one-for-all implications of the word *alliance* seem to me to be rather inappropriate. What we call allies have really been client states, only they are ruled for the most part by white people, not black or brown people. We tend to shy away from the term *client state* when we talk about states ruled by white people, but in fact, that is exactly what they are.

Specifically, the United States is still using "alliance" policy to prevent Japan and the countries of Western Europe from pursuing their own independent foreign policies. However desirable this objective might be, I consider it to be unattainable in the post-Cold War era.

The second major problem with U.S. alliance policy is the larger failure to think through the new geopolitics of world trade—the questions of whether the world's three major trading and economic regions will deal with each other in fundamentally conflictual or fundamentally cooperative ways; whether today's intraregional trade arrangements will take on an exclusivist cast; and which countries or groups of countries will be the most influential in writing the rules of the new international economic system. U.S. alliance policy has handled all trade disputes with Japan and West European countries on a case-by-case basis, without any strategic framework or thought given to building economic alliances and coalitions or breaking them apart.

The first problem plaguing American alliance policies is the attempt to prevent the allies from developing independent foreign policies. The roots of this policy date back to World War II, when American officials began thinking systematically about the postwar world and about preventing a replay of the catastrophe in which they found themselves. Many different approaches were proposed by the national security bureaucracy, and many different approaches were, in fact, tried in the early post-Cold war years—some concurrently, even if they were not always perfectly consistent. Common to each approach was the determination to ensure that the classical pattern of European and Asian politics did not reemerge. These systems, after all, had collapsed into world war twice within 25 years. Moreover, in an age of nuclear weapons, American officials feared that a third world war might also be the world's last.

The basic solution that emerged was typically American in its optimism and its ahistoricity. The United States sought to prevent the classical pattern from reemerging by eliminating the need for the European countries as well as Japan to conduct any independent foreign policies in the first place. The United States would satisfy the basic national needs that require countries to conduct foreign policies. After all, foreign policies are not conducted for their own sake; they are conducted to achieve certain ends. The United States would provide military protection and grant extremely favorable terms of trade and commerce. In previous writing, I have called this strategy a strategy of smothering. The United States literally sought to smother the independent foreign policy impulses of its allies. It was an offer the Europeans and the Japanese could not refuse.

As long as the United States remained overwhelmingly superior militarily and predominant economically, this policy could be maintained at acceptable cost and risk to the United States. As these conditions faded, however, these alliances came under serious military and economic pressure during the Cold War in the form of disputes over détente, nuclear weapons strategy, and overall strategy toward the Soviet Union. Various dollar crises broke out as well, in addition to periodic debates over burden sharing. In my view, had the Soviet Union not collapsed, these problems eventually would have overcome American alliance relationships, or at least transformed them in fundamental ways. This point is more than merely academic, precisely because the prospect of a reconstituted Soviet Union or a genuinely nasty, uncooperative Russia has become such an important rationale for keeping NATO pretty much as it is. The Soviet Union, however, did collapse, but for perfectly logical and defensible reasons, the smothering strategy persisted.

The expression that NATO's particular purpose is "to keep the Russians out, the Americans in, and the Germans down" is widely known. It is often argued that the United States must also remain East Asia's major stabilizing force, lest age-old conflicts and rivalries among Russia, China, and Japan resurface, and that a primary aim of U.S. policy in both Europe and East Asia is to prevent a renationalization of security policies. The Bush and (to a lesser extent) Clinton administrations have been cool to the idea of a so-called Eurocorps that would carry out security missions in Europe when the United States elected not to become involved.

I would be the last person to argue that the Europeans and the Japanese have indeed grown up and have become competent to handle their own security affairs without getting us all into a global war. If I thought that the independent foreign policy impulses of these countries could be contained much longer at an acceptable risk and cost to this country, I might well favor the continuation of such a smothering strategy, but this option is no longer possible. The end of the Cold War revealed the fundamentally different strategic interests held by the United States and Europe on the one hand, and the United States and Japan on the other.

During the Cold War the United States could contain European and Japanese nationalism at acceptable cost and risk because the same forces and resources that were necessary for these particular missions and force structures were also used to contain the Soviet Union. They could help the United States achieve its traditional goal of ensuring that no hegemonic power would be able to marshal the resources of the old world to threaten the security, independence, and prosperity of the new world. With the hegemon gone and no plausible candidates visible to succeed it, the only remaining rationale for significant U.S. forward-deployed forces in these regions and their accompanying risk and cost is the distinctly secondary objective of maintaining or ensuring stability in these regions.

Unfortunately, military power does not readily address most of the threats to stability in Europe and East Asia—for example, the serious structural economic decline in Europe, the continuing economic stagnation in the newly independent countries of Eastern Europe and the Russian near abroad, and to a slightly lesser extent, the growing refugee flows coming into Western Europe from Eastern Europe and North Africa. Moreover, most of the threats that could be addressed through military forces are too local in their power and implications to be portrayed convincingly as threats to U.S. national security. Hence, the American public will not support risking American lives and expending significant American resources to actually deal with them. The most obvious example would be Bosnia, but consider another possibility.

Suppose that China—growing economically at about 13 percent each year, clearly feeling its oats politically, and clearly in no mood to be pushed around by this country on human rights or on anything else—has its eye on various minor territories on its rim; for example, the Spratly Islands in the South China Sea, which also happen to be located in the midst of what are probably fairly significant oil fields. Let us say that China invades the Spratly Islands. Is it really likely that President Clinton or President Bush would have sent the U.S.

Seventh Fleet to stop China? An argument for U.S. military action would be difficult to make because such an invasion of the Spratlys would be a simple grab for territory, not the opening shot in a campaign of world conquest.

North Korea illustrates a possible counterexample. It is difficult to establish what the Clinton administration, with the help of former President Carter, has accomplished for the present or medium term—much less the long term—with regard to its deal with North Korea. But I am not persuaded that the rest of East Asia sees Korea as a significant counterexample. Notwithstanding the U.S. defense commitment to South Korea, were I an East Asian leader, I might well conclude from this crisis that Washington will not militarily confront a country possessing or likely to possess nuclear weapons. Washington will negotiate and hope that we can accomplish our objective nonmilitarily. Nevertheless, when military force is needed, the United States probably will not act. Simple prudence will dictate that other leaders assume that the United States will not act. Asian leaders will conclude that they can no longer count on a U.S. military guarantee—and this will be an entirely reasonable conclusion to draw.

In the post-Cold War, post-Soviet period, most local problems, even in areas allegedly vital to American interests, are starting to look very local from the U.S. standpoint. An American standoffishness from these problems tells the rest of the world something critically important about the military backbone of our current alliance policies. It tells them that the presence of American forces in a region is no guarantee that they will actually be used. These countries will come to the conclusion—I believe reluctantly—that given the security problems they are likely to face, they will have no choice but to rely on their own devices, either individually or in various coalitions, to achieve their core foreign policy objectives of security and prosperity.

Moreover, the United States should not be struggling to stop a process that has been set in motion by the limits on its own power and by its entirely reasonable judgments that its security interests and those of its allies are no longer identical. The United States should encourage its allies to look to and work with it when genuinely common interests are at stake, but it should also encourage them to develop the capabilities necessary for independent action in cases where their interests, but not American interests, are at stake. In this vein, at a time when the U.S. military budget is shrinking rapidly and the American people are clearly in no mood to take on new security responsibilities, I do not believe that the expansion of NATO and the expectation that the United States will fulfill new commitments in peripheral areas like Eastern Europe and even the Russian near abroad will succeed in creating a new and more durable transatlantic relationship.

Moreover, I find very curious and revealing Secretary of State Warren Christopher's remark that Bosnia is not a NATO concern. If Bosnia is not a NATO concern, why are Poland, Hungary, Moldova, or any of the other countries people are considering as potential new NATO members, NATO concerns? In particular, why would they be American concerns?

The Clinton administration is not the only force in Washington that is guilty of incoherence on this score. For example, I do not understand why the mainstream of the Republican party in Congress is on the one hand very enthusiastic about extending NATO membership eastward, but on the other hand, very unenthusiastic about using American military power anywhere. In my view, these two opinions are not consistent. I do not expect that people like Senator Jesse Helms or Pat Buchanan or even Senator Bob Dole are going to be very enthusiastic about using American military power in places like Slovenia or the Transcaucasus; yet, the logic of NATO expansion would commit the United States to exactly that.

The second major problem with U.S. alliance policy is the failure to think strategically about its foreign economic policy. The Clinton administration entered office avowedly determined to give U.S. foreign economic policy a more nationalistic cast and in particular, to introduce a smarter trade policy. Some people would use the word tougher, but I prefer the word smarter, because in my view, what U.S. trade policy lacked in recent decades was not toughness, but minimal intelligence. Many of Clinton's efforts to introduce a smarter, results-oriented approach to trade policy are most welcome, although the execution of this policy has been quite poor. In particular, the administration's willingness to tilt at foreign trade barriers and to combat predatory foreign trade activities has had a worrisome side effect. By treating each such trade challenge on its own economic merits, the administration has ended up being just as confrontational with West Europe as it has with East Asia, if not more so.

I raise this issue because the Clinton administration has made it quite clear that it considers East Asia and the Pacific Rim to be where the economic action is taking place. Moreover, the United States has not been at all shy about conveying that impression to the West European countries—which are only now slowly emerging from deep recession. It has let the Europeans know that they are considered to be yesterday's news. Growing at 6 to 8 to 10 percent a year, East Asia is where the action is considered to be.

This stance is worrisome because our economic problems with West Europe and East Asia are very different. If the United States would focus on the forest rather than the trees with regard to foreign economic policy, it would see that treating these two regions in nearly identical ways in terms of trade and economic disputes—and especially tilting toward East Asia—jeopardizes America's central international economic interest for the foreseeable future. This interest consists of building alliances to ensure that the emerging international economic system is relatively congenial to American interests and to American values.

The Uruguay Round of world trade negotiations marks not the end of the process of writing the rules of global commerce, but a very modest beginning. The United States will find itself at many international economic bargaining tables in the years ahead. Once upon a time the United States was strong enough to ensure the establishment of what it considered to be the right rules. Such unilateral power is now gone. To get the rules the United States wants and needs, it will need help. It will need allies, and if it looks around the world and asks itself which countries are closest to it in terms of economic and social priorities and structures, the answer is crystal clear. It is the West European countries. They are the ones that are most like the United States, and their system of capitalism is the most like America's system. It is not exactly the same, but it is certainly closer to America's system than the capitalist systems of East Asia.

Moreover, lost amid this growing official infatuation with the Pacific Rim is the reality that trans-Pacific economic flows generally do not work to America's economic advantage. In most trade and technology transfer and investment activity, the United States has been the clear loser. In particular, enormous trade imbalances persist despite dramatic and continuing dollar devaluation and a stunning competitive comeback by major American industries. Economic flows between the United States and Europe, by contrast, are quite balanced and in fact mutually beneficial. They are also amenable to macroeconomic management. When the exchange rates with Western Europe are lowered, trade deficits go away. That has been our experience since 1985, when the first major dollar devaluation since the late 1970s took place. Our trade deficit with Western Europe, which had reached $25 billion a year, went away by the early 1990s, even though Europe had experienced slower growth than had the United States.

In areas like telecommunications and aerospace, the European Union's policies are clearly protectionist, but in these areas—in which American firms are world leaders—the United States has run consistent surpluses since 1980, even in the most troublesome areas.

Yet the administration continues to pick trade fights with the Europeans in these sectors where American companies already do quite well. It continues to bang loudly on doors that are already three-quarters open and as a result has created a significant economic rift. Prospects for the deepened cooperation that both West Europe and the United States need are seriously clouded.

A colleague and I argue in the *Atlantic Monthly* that this danger has developed in large part because security concerns, not economic concerns, remain the central focus of transatlantic relations and institutions. We argue that this security focus is based on a mistaken view of America's European interests and priorities. We believe that most common transatlantic security interests have in fact dissolved in the wake of the Cold War's end, but that common economic interests—including shared international and domestic economic problems—have greatly expanded and intensified. Yet without the right forums and institutions to identify these common interests, nurture common approaches, and manage the inevitable disputes, these disputes are likely to produce ever greater transatlantic economic estrangement at a time when the need to develop and maintain a common front is greater than at any time during the postwar period. Transforming the focus of NATO from security to economic issues offers a solution to the problem. Though this is a fairly drastic step to propose, the drastic changes on the world's stage demand such action.

QUESTION: Will the GATT situation ameliorate or exacerbate the situation between the countries when it is related to something like NATO?

MR. TONELSON: The GATT will probably make things worse because the GATT deals with economic questions in an indiscriminate way. The GATT is an indiscriminate form of multilateralism. It assumes consensus across regions of the world on questions where consensus simply does not exist. It has promulgated a series of new trade rules that are, for the most part, unenforceable, and its legacy is the new World Trade Organization (WTO), whose politics can only be anti-American, for two basic reasons. First, the rest of the world has an overriding interest in ensuring that the U.S. market remains wider open than their markets because it is the American market that has been the chief engine of international economic growth since 1945. Not surprisingly, they want to keep things as they are. In fact, the only reason the rest of the world agreed to the American idea for a new trade round in the mid-1980s was to dampen what they perceived to be growing American trade protectionism and unilateralism. The American political system was reacting to the faltering competitiveness of American industry and the high value of the American dollar, which priced even competitive American exports out of world markets. With this new World Trade Organization, other countries have in fact succeeded in stemming the tide of American protectionism. This is why I personally do not favor WTO ratification.

As for U.S.-European economic relations, one concern is that this indiscriminate global multilateralism will come to overshadow the need to cultivate transatlantic economic relations. It is going to be more and more difficult to perceive common economic interests that are purely U.S.-European in scope. In fact, West Europeans have already found it extremely tempting to side with the rest of the world against U.S. unilateralism and to support the kinds of international positions that deny the United States the right to use its own laws to protect American companies and workers from predatory trade activity. When Special Trade Representative Mickey Kantor says that U.S. economic sovereignty is completely unaffected by this position, he is simply not telling the truth.

QUESTION: How can we be sure that Russia will not once again be a superpower against the United States or Europe? Or, if not Russia, it might be China. How does this NATO concept diminish such possibilities?

MR. TONELSON: You are right in saying that we can't be sure about the future of the former Soviet Union. Neither can we be certain about future developments in China. Nevertheless, the reemergence of Russia or a Soviet Union II exercising power vigorously in its own immediate neighborhood has never been, nor will it be, a threat to significant American security interests. We never challenged Moscow's writ in Eastern Europe at any time after the end of World War II because we simply decided that, as lamentable and tragic as Eastern Europe's fate was, it was not, nor had it ever been, a vital U.S. interest. Eastern Europe was not so important that we would go to war for it. The same applies today. I cannot imagine the United States, whether under President Dole, Helms, or anyone else, ever confronting Russian military power in Turkmenistan, Moldova, or Lithuania.

I can't imagine any American president ever sending American combat troops into regions so close to the heart of Russian military strength. It did not happen in the closing days of World War II; it did not happen after the end of World II—a conflict in which Russia suffered horrendous losses while the United States had the only nuclear weapons in the world. We never challenged them then. Although it sounds coldhearted or cold-blooded to make this statement, it is difficult to argue that the existence of Communist governments in Eastern Europe had a significant effect on American security or on U.S. prosperity between 1945 and 1989.

Regarding China, it is going to be difficult for the United States to challenge a more assertive China in East Asia. Moreover, it is highly unlikely that either an assertive China or a more assertive Russia will emerge as an ideological threat. They will clearly emerge as political and military entities, but they will be more like traditional great powers that simply jockey for increased power and wealth on the world stage. They will not blaze with the ideological determination to transform the world or to bring the world under their thumbs, as most people thought Russia and China did when they were under Communist rule. These are judgment calls that American leaders will have to make. If we propose to confront Russia in Eastern Europe or China in East Asia, the size of the U.S. military will have to increase at least to the levels of the 1950s and the 1960s, levels near 8 or 10 percent of the gross national product. I cannot imagine that happening any time soon, short of all-out war. In my view, it will not happen because we have decided, although not explicitly, that these regions are not vital security interests.

QUESTION: Given your recent return from Oxford, what impression did you get as to the real underlying reasons that Britain, France, and Germany have not taken a more decisive or aggressive position with regard to the Serbian fiasco?

MR. TONELSON: As the conference was held in the United Kingdom, the British delegation was both large and high ranking. In attendance were people from the undersecretary and assistant secretary levels of the British foreign office and the British defense ministry. They were all experienced in transatlantic security affairs. The one single message that they were clearly determined to convey to everyone else—a message shared only slightly less intensely by the Germans—was that a more flexible NATO, a NATO in which the United States is free to opt out of military operations when its own security interests are not at stake, would be an ineffective NATO. In their view, such a NATO would not be relevant to Europe's current pressing security concerns, and that is a message the United States should take seriously.

An underlying message conveyed at the conference was their objection to the U.S. insistence on controlling all of NATO's military operations while at the same time refusing to commit forces when other NATO countries feel that significant, though perhaps not vital, interests are at stake. They feel that if the United States does not believe that places like Bosnia represent American vital interests, then it should not be actively trying to prevent the Europeans from dealing with these problems on their own. They make a strong point. At the same time, however, if they are going to deal with these problems on their own, they need military assets. Again, the West Europeans are not very willing to increase military spending significantly at the present time.

The very pointed question that they kept asking was, what if the British and the French decide to withdraw their forces from the Balkans, but the locals do not want them to go, and resist? Will the United States help them out? The response from a senior American at the meeting, who is a prominent politician from this state and experienced in U.S. military policy, was, "Don't count on it." The British and French then asked, "How could you possibly tell us that?" Many of us responded, "How could you expose your own forces and men to that kind of military danger without giving them the means to protect themselves?" And their answer was, "We are just peacekeeping; we are just there to save lives, and we have saved lives." Nevertheless, they were obviously uncomfortable with the possibility that their forces might have to be in the Balkans, exposed and vulnerable, in order to sustain that mission of saving lives.

QUESTION: If the nuclear umbrella over Japan is now practically more myth than reality, how does that affect Japan's perceived need? Their constitution now forbids the development of a nuclear capability. What is likely to happen, given U.S. military retrenchment?

MR. TONELSON: Were I a Japanese leader, I would begin to seriously examine a nuclear weapons option. For obvious historic reasons, the Japanese are loath to talk about it. The Japanese are unlikely to build a standing nuclear arsenal. A more likely Japanese strategy would be to let people know that they could put together

173

a large number of nuclear weapons and nuclear delivery systems in very short order—say, 25 minutes. In fact, I think that such a strategy accounts for Japan's continued interest in building those kinds of nuclear reactors that produce enriched uranium and weapons-grade material. I am not happy about the prospect of a nuclear-armed Japan or a nuclear-armed Germany, but the United States is unlikely to take the steps that would be needed to prevent that.

If the North Koreans do show themselves to possess not only nuclear weapons but also guided missiles that can reach Japan, it is doubtful that the United States would attack North Korea and eliminate those weapons. In fact, all the countries of East Asia and most of the countries of Western Europe have told us not to do anything militarily with regard to North Korea. The last thing the United States wants is a war. The best strategy is to try to draw the North Koreans back into the international economic system and basically give them what they want.

The word *appeasement* was mentioned a few minutes ago. I do not have any major problems with applying that word to North Korea, but I would caution against applying value judgments to it. I would urge people to recognize that the United States is doing much the same thing with one other large nuclear state that is in serious economic trouble—Ukraine. The United States has essentially said, "If you will discontinue building these things or if in a few years you hand them over, we will give you billions in aid."

It has been U.S. policy to require the implementation of some serious economic reforms before much aid is given to former Soviet republics. Ukraine may have just taken its first steps down that road. Its new president seems to be more receptive to the idea of reform than his predecessor was, yet although there is a long way to go, Ukraine is getting the money anyway. Moreover, it is not only receiving American money; it is receiving money from the World Bank as well. The World Bank has been given orders to give Ukraine a great deal of money, hoping it will hand over its fairly significant stock of nuclear weapons. In short, for better or worse, we are not pursuing this policy solely with North Korea.

QUESTION: Could you elaborate about the differences between American and European capitalism on the one hand and the East Asian version on the other? Are the differences matters of law and policy that could be easily changed, or are they deeply rooted in culture and likely to persist?

MR. TONELSON: I think it is mainly law and policy, although I don't deny that Japanese trade policy and corporate structures to some extent reflect the fact that Japan is a homogeneous island nation that really does not think much of the rest of the world. Culturally, the Japanese closed themselves off for hundreds of years. They do not naturally think in truly internationalist terms. I am not denying the role of culture; nevertheless, the Japanese economic system and the structures and policies that emerged after the end of World War II are in my view mainly matters of policy and law. Japan's postwar leaders put into effect a conscious plan to achieve economic recovery, and they were, in fact, fully aware that their approach was not going to be the American neoclassical economic approach. In fact, a senior Japanese bureaucrat who became a vice minister of the Ministry of International Trade and Industry (MITI) and who was one of the principal architects of the postwar Japanese miracle, was fond of saying over and over again, "We broke all the rules and made up our own rules as we went along."

The role of the consumer illustrates how East Asian capitalism differs from Western capitalism. Unlike the consumer in the United States and Western Europe, the consumer in East Asia is not king. There are no tax breaks for mortgages on second homes. There was no credit card interest deduction until the 1980s. The producer is king. These are countries that believe they are more likely to produce their way to wealth than to consume their way to wealth.

A friend of mine puts it quite well. Pat Choate says that the aim of U.S. economic policy is to give consumers the widest possible range of products at the lowest possible prices. The aim of Japanese, and to a slightly lesser extent German, economic policy, is to make their consumers so tremendously wealthy that they can afford anything. There is a great deal of truth to that theory. In terms of corporate structures, since the early 20th century

175

Americans have felt that all other factors being relatively equal, corporate bigness is bad. Americans do not want power concentrated in the hands of a small number of corporations. The Japanese love big business—the bigger, the better.

To be sure, Japan does have a fair trade commission with an antitrust division, but it does not do much. It has a small staff. Although changing currency values will put some strain on it, the keiretsu system of buying products and components only from one's own affiliate companies is alive and well in Japan and is being transplanted into Southeast Asia and possibly China. Many of these production-oriented, corporatist economic policies exist in Western Europe also. The big difference between the West Europeans and the Japanese and the rest of East Asia is that the Western Europeans also seem to be committed to both raising and maintaining living standards for the great bulk of their country's populations through various transfer payments. The idea of a social safety net is not well developed in the United States, but nevertheless, America has one. It is more developed in Western Europe. In East Asia, it is almost nonexistent.

NARRATOR: Isn't this isolationism you are proposing?

MR. TONELSON: No, because doing less doesn't mean doing nothing. In fact, I would not be opposed to a small or modest American military presence in both Western Europe and the Far East, principally for handholding and symbolic reasons. The countries of these regions seem to attach some value to this type of support. It would not cost us that much, and it would be worthwhile.

My big problem with American military deployments in these parts of the world is not their actual size but the fact that the main purpose of these deployments has been to deny the United States freedom of action regarding decisions of war and peace. A country should never give up the freedom to decide whether it will go to war, because it will never face a more important decision. In short, I would favor modest U.S. forces deployed in ways that would permit it to opt out of various conflicts and peacekeeping missions if it chose to do so.

176

NARRATOR: Thank you for sharing your insights on East Asia and Japan involving the United States and other countries. You have inspired us to think more along the lines of a strategic approach to American economic and trade relations around the world.

IV.

THE FUTURE
OF NATO

CHAPTER TEN

The Future of NATO*

DAVID C. ACHESON

NARRATOR: David Acheson has had a distinguished career in law and in public service. Born in Washington, he is now president of the Atlantic Council of the United States in Washington, D.C. He received his bachelor's degree from Yale and his bachelor of laws degree from Harvard. After being admitted to the Bar in the District of Columbia, Pennsylvania, and the United States Supreme Court, he joined the firm of Covington and Burling and has been a partner of it and several other distinguished law firms.

Mr. Acheson's public service has included U.S. attorney for the District of Columbia and special assistant to the secretary of the treasury (who was, incidentally, Henry Fowler, a member of the Miller Center Council) from 1965 to 1967. He was vice president, senior vice president, and general counsel for the Communications Satellite Corporation, and then a member of the presidential commission on the *Challenger* space shuttle accident.

David Acheson's publications include *Effective Washington Representation*; *A More Effective Civil Space Program* (co-author); and, with David McClellan, *Among Friends*. He was also the editor

---

Presented in a Forum at the Miller Center of Public Affairs on 21 February 1994.

of his father's essays entitled *This Vast External Realm,* and author of *Acheson Country: A Memoir by David Acheson.*

In the past, we have had the benefit of the wisdom of others at the Atlantic Council, notably General Andrew Goodpaster. We are especially pleased to resume that relationship with David Acheson, who will speak to us about the North Atlantic Treaty Organization (NATO), the Partnership for Peace, and the future.

MR. ACHESON: The newest development in the structure of NATO is one that has occasioned many questions, innumerable press articles, and quite a bit of confusion. I hope I can clarify rather than add to that confusion. My focus is the evolution of NATO or the recent outreach of NATO toward Central and Eastern Europe.

As agreed upon at the 11 January 1994 NATO summit, this initiative has been called "Partnership for Peace" by the Clinton administration. I don't like bumper sticker slogans particularly, and to me that seems like a glib phrase. One hopes it is for peace, but one can't be sure. I'm not sure it's a partnership in the sense with which I, as a lawyer, am familiar, wherein there are more or less co-equal partners. This Partnership for Peace of NATO is a much more diverse kind of relationship, with the influence of smaller countries a factor of, say, 10 and the larger powers a factor of 70. Nevertheless, a partnership is what it is called. Right now it is a plan approved by NATO but not yet given life by the participation of the former Warsaw Pact.

This is an important topic because NATO is turning distinctly to Central and Eastern Europe. In my view, it is turning to that region not to look for a new mission that would assure its institutional survival, but rather because the threat that NATO now has to address is one that exists within Central and Eastern Europe.

Why does NATO have to address it? you may ask. Who cares about Central and Eastern Europe? First of all, the Europeans care. The Western Europeans care because that region is the source of disorder and ethnic hostility, which is bound to spill over into the NATO region. The United States and Canada should care about this region because, historically, we have never succeeded in isolating ourselves from the security threats to Europe. Sooner or later they spill over and become major preoccupations for the United States. One need not go into all the reasons, but it is historically true. If you count Europe as a single economic entity, it is our largest trading partner. Given the history of World War II, the late 1930s, and World War I, it would be dangerous to assume that America will be detached from the security concerns of Europe in the future.

Many people have proposed in op-ed articles, letters to the editor, and in books that with the Cold War over and the Soviet Union having disintegrated, the role of NATO should end as well. Why should we concern ourselves any longer with committing troops and financial resources to support a true presence in the NATO area? NATO's basic mission, to which we as a country are pledged under the NATO Treaty, does not say anything about protecting Europe from attack by the Soviet Union. It speaks of the security of Europe, and the core commitment of NATO is to treat an attack upon one as an attack upon all under Article V. Although there probably won't be an overt attack across borders, ethnic hostility is certain to erode security on the edge of the NATO area. When refugees flow out of the hostile areas, arms usually flow in the other direction. It becomes a concern for both sides of the border when there is ethnic hostility. NATO now realistically sees this as the most likely threat, though not necessarily involving an attack. The question is, how can NATO deal with such a threat without making a pledge that will probably not be kept. The taxpayers and the voters of the NATO member countries have absolutely no wish to go to war to defend a country that is not in the NATO area.

Before asking what NATO can do for those countries, we must first clarify which countries we are discussing. Not all of the former Soviet Union should be of concern to NATO. What happens in Tajikistan is perhaps important, but is not a NATO concern. What happens in Georgia may be of NATO concern. What happens in Ukraine and the Baltics is certainly of NATO concern. We have a graduation in levels of direct consequence for NATO. Perhaps NATO's concern should be focused on European regions of the former Warsaw Pact such as the Baltics, Poland, Russia, Ukraine, the Balkans, the Czech Republic, Slovakia, and Hungary.

From this perspective, consider the dissolution of the Soviet Union and the disablement of the Soviet army. The Russian army, which in effect comprises the core of the former Soviet army, now actually has more officers than troops. If you look at the Soviet army as what it has always been—a full employment program—it is evident that the demobilization had to occur in the least politically sensitive sector of the Russian army where it would incur the least protest and resentment. For that reason, the officer corps was left largely intact, while at least half of the enlisted troops are now unemployed and without housing. They are a liability to the state that has to support them. The officer corps is left with little to do; there is no training underway, and their units are ill-equipped. Arms are often sold for the officers' personal gain. Demoralization is high; and it would seem, as far as anyone can judge, that the Russian army is in no position to attack anyone.

The countries of the former Warsaw Pact are saying to themselves, "Our former sponsor has evaporated and is no longer an ally and a support to us. It is a threat. It is a large neighbor with a still-large military force, a demoralized civil government, and a demoralized military—it is a source of nothing but potential trouble. What are we going to do, we little countries on the edge of Russia?"

What they have said they want, publicly and on many occasions, is an affiliation with the West. This link with the West could be built upon so that it eventually becomes a source of security and protection, possibly even a military alliance. At the very least, this link would give them someone to look to for comfort, support, mediation, and maybe eventually military support.

What entity would provide that link? There is only one: NATO. There is no other entity west of Russia with an organized military force and an organized cohesion under political agreements to whom these countries can look. The CSCE has no forces and is primarily a forum for "jawbone" mediation.

NATO has not been slow to recognize the need of the former Warsaw Pact countries and their own opportunity. For two years the NATO senior officers corps has been conducting programs with their military counterparts from the former Warsaw Pact area, even extending as far east as Rumania. Officers in the Supreme

Headquarters Allied Powers Europe (SHAPE) staff have been visiting the capitals of those countries, meeting with their military leaders, and basically conducting seminars on how the military works with a civilian government in a democracy—a phenomenon about which no one in that region knows anything.

Incidentally, SHAPE was formed by General Eisenhower. General Andrew Goodpaster, chairman of the Atlantic Council, was one of the supreme commanders. He is personally much engaged in this process of trying to mediate the education of the leadership of the former Warsaw Pact area.

In May of last year, I was in Brussels talking with the SHAPE staff. I asked them what the most important aspect of this educational process was, from their point of view. The answer was: military budgets. Military budgets are important because, first, they must be reasonably proportioned to the GNP of the country to ensure a military force that is reasonable in size and purpose. As far as these regions are concerned, that implies a defensively structured force—not one that might join in an attack on Germany.

Second, it is important that military budgets be transparent; that is, the public should know exactly what they entail. They should be reported in newspapers, and they should be the subject of hearings before the legislature. They should become public knowledge so the public will be in a position to register support or resistance to military programs. Voters in the Warsaw Pact region have not had this kind of information since the beginning of World War II, and in some countries such as Hungary, not for a generation prior to that. Transparency and proportion in military budgets is vital.

It is also vital that the military forces not be seen as instruments to solve political differences with neighboring countries. Virtually all these countries have compatriots living outside their borders as minorities, and they are also hosting minorities from other nations. Military forces must not be used to intimidate a bordering country into giving favored treatment to those emigrants and minorities. For example, there are many people of Hungarian descent who live in Rumania but still think of themselves as Hungarians. They are treated by the Rumanians as a Hungarian minority, thereby denying them certain fundamental rights of

185

Rumanian citizenship, at least in their view. The defense minister of Hungary visited the Atlantic Council about three weeks ago, and he said one of the most important aspects of military training is that the Hungarian military forces should not see themselves as an instrument to settle the dispute with Rumania over minority treatment, or vice versa, because Rumanians live in Hungary as well. Thus, the ideas promoted by the SHAPE officer corps—smaller, well-proportioned, and transparent military budgets and also the detachment of military forces from political objectives—may be having an effect.

Another essential aspect of military structure to consider is what the forces are organized, trained, and equipped to do. The Warsaw Pact forces had previously been designed, organized, and equipped for nothing less than an attack upon what was then West Germany. Their military establishment was totally out of scale with their GNP. Their equipment was mostly attack equipment and their training and doctrine was in attack maneuvers. It is now important that they be re-equipped, retrained, and reindoctrinated for defense and peacekeeping. The SHAPE officer corps is carrying that message.

A final aspect of reorganizing the military forces of the former Warsaw Pact countries is to develop within the defense ministries a corps of civilian leaders that is familiar with the military. They need to know how to handle military issues before the parliament, while engaging the loyalty and trust of the senior officer corps. Such civilian expertise has never existed in the Warsaw Pact area in the memory of anyone now in command. There is only a small corps of those who are just learning about military affairs. The defense minister of Hungary, for example, cheerfully acknowledges that he is a politician who was appointed to this job with great misgiving. He said, "The close question is whether the misgiving is more on my side than on the side of my military colleagues." He notes that he had to earn their trust, and he had to persuade them to earn his.

In Russia, defense ministers have been made out of generals; in some of the other Warsaw Pact countries, the person filling the role of defense minister is actually a general wearing a civilian suit. That does not mean he thinks like a civilian, however; he still thinks like a general. Yet, as they say at SHAPE, one of the things you have to learn is not to overthrow the government if they fail to appropriate the budget requested. Leadership by civilians in defense matters is a major priority.

The Partnership for Peace is basically designed to continue and extend the work with the Warsaw Pact countries that NATO has already been doing through the SHAPE officer corps, giving this work institutional depth under structured agreements. The Partnership for Peace evolved as an idea to engage the countries of the former Warsaw Pact, but in a way that would not yet pledge us to go to war in their defense under Article V of the NATO Treaty. The agreement would, however, pledge us to consult with them under Article IV on all matters of their security, giving them whatever help we could. This could involve joint maneuvers with NATO forces, either in NATO territory or in their own territory.

The NATO summit communique that extended this invitation to the countries of the former Soviet Union and the former Warsaw Pact in effect said, "NATO is ready to help you reorient your military and to help you with your security problems. Here is what we can do for you. . . ." It went on to describe a program of counseling, training, joint maneuvers, and other aspects of cooperation. Then it said, "Here is what we require of you . . ." with the requirements being that first, they renounce force as a way to solve disputes with their neighbors. Second, they must renounce any territorial claims beyond their present boundaries. Third, they must restructure their military force levels and budgets to a more reasonable proportion of their GNP and in accord with defense requirements. Fourth, they must adopt transparent, publicly accessible military budgets. There are various other secondary provisions, but those four are the keys.

The invitation also said, "If you will meet these undertakings, we would be glad to sign an agreement with you—that is, a bilateral agreement, with NATO on one side and each individual country that had belonged to the Warsaw Pact on the other—that will pledge us to do these things we have described and will exact of you those things we have described."

Rumania was the first country that actually answered the invitation in writing and asked to sign up. Poland, having always wished to be a full NATO member, has now seized upon the opportunity to join the Partnership for Peace. Hungary is similarly eager, and the Czech Republic and Slovakia have both signed up as well. Some of the countries that have taken up the invitation stretch credulity a bit, such as Albania, Rumania, and Bulgaria. Bulgaria, interestingly, had the first Atlantic Council of any country in the Warsaw Pact area and seemingly has a rather spirited, if small, body of citizenry moving in that direction.

After a country responds in writing to NATO's invitation, it must then submit a written proposal, which NATO will then amend or alter. If NATO's counterproposal is then agreed upon, both will sign it and that country becomes a member of the Partnership for Peace.

What the countries of the Warsaw Pact area are seeking is a feeling of comfort through kinship with the West, which they have never before had. Their 20th-century and earlier history has been wrapped in a feeling of inadequacy and vulnerability as small nations being surrounded and swallowed up by the great powers—Russia and Germany. They want a structured agreement with commitments and obligations from an organized entity of the West. The only one to answer that description is NATO. While this will probably not make their security apprehensions go away, at least they will become much less acute and therefore much less of an issue in their rather unstable domestic political affairs.

Inevitably, some countries will not be able to keep the commitments they make, while other countries will not even bother to offer any commitments at all. It's probably not helpful that Russia, perhaps the source of the greatest instability of the whole region, may be in the worst position of any of these countries to fulfill obligations of that kind. Even making such commitments may become a destabilizing political factor in Russian politics. I think these agreements will succeed in stabilizing at least some of the regions in Central and Eastern Europe formerly allied with the Soviet Union, if not Russia itself.

No one would say that the value of this project depends upon the certainty of its success. If you took that position, you would never begin. The success of NATO was an uncertain prospect back in 1949. NATO is the only entity that can deal with this problem,

188

and the Eastern Europeans want this relationship. The philosophy behind Partnership for Peace is, "Let's try it out. It will work in some places, but not in others; in any event, it can't help but improve the situation to a considerable extent."

QUESTION: Could you explain to us what, if any, connection this Partnership for Peace has with the U.N. General Assembly and the U.N. Security Council?

MR. ACHESON: In 1949, the North Atlantic Treaty was regarded by the signatory governments and by the United Nations as a regional pact, something that was explicitly foreseen and allowed under the U.N. Charter. The modification of NATO structure to extend this limited membership to Central and Eastern Europe would be regarded as consistent with the U.N. charter and with the NATO Treaty under article IV. In fact, some of the Partnership countries envision that their forces would be used in NATO peacekeeping operations under a U.N. mandate.

QUESTION: Why have these partners in the Partnership for Peace failed so miserably in the former Yugoslavia? Do you consider this the first real test since the breakup of the Soviet Union? It contributes nothing to a united Europe, so is it really something for the U.S. citizens to take seriously?

MR. ACHESON: First, the Partnership for Peace has nothing to do with Yugoslavia. Yugoslavia was never a member of the Warsaw Pact, and it was never a part of the Soviet Union. In other words, it is not part of the territories that are being invited to join the Partnership for Peace. I do agree that the Bosnian crisis and the earlier Croatian crisis represented what the questioner called "a miserable failure," but that was on the part of NATO, not on the Partnership for Peace.

It is worth explaining why the Yugoslav case has been what I have to call a qualified failure, because we may be looking at a partial retrieval of that failure presently. Certainly the water gone under the bridge does represent a failure. Contrary to what many people think, NATO is not a free-standing, corporate entity that can take independent action with its own private army. It is not like the East India Company in the 18th and 19th centuries, which interestingly had the largest organized army in the world.

For decision-making purposes, NATO is the Council of Foreign Ministers. At the time the Croatian crisis broke out, there were three features of the situation that made it difficult for NATO. First, every member government of NATO was weak, not necessarily in terms of military forces, but in the sense that it had a risk-averse government. Each faced a delicate situation with its parliament, and each was operating under the assumption, prevalent at the time, that NATO should not operate in such matters without a mandate from the United Nations. These conditions applied equally to the United States government, which is and was weak in the sense of being risk-averse, was having difficult relations with Congress, and faced a general shortage of resources. All these conditions continue.

We kept thinking of the United Nations as the place to go for a mandate. This became a circular exercise because the United Nations was not prepared to give a mandate unless the only available forces—the NATO forces—would declare their willingness to be used under a U.N. mandate; that is, the United Nations was not prepared to declare an empty mandate. Furthermore, it was not at all certain there would not be a veto in the U.N. Security Council. A veto would have killed a U.N. mandate, of course, since unanimity among the five permanent members is a precondition.

The third factor was that NATO had never actually fought a war. Although NATO had prepared to defend the Fulda Gap against the Red army, offensive action had never been planned, and NATO had never been in a combat engagement. The notion that NATO countries would be called upon to put their countrymen at risk in a place outside, strictly speaking, the NATO area caused a myriad of political problems, and the foreign ministers comprising the NATO Council were simply not prepared to take the risk of making a firm decision. They instead looked first for a U.N. mandate, while the United Nations was looking at the same time for NATO readiness and willingness to execute that mandate. The result was a circular delay.

I remember ruefully reflecting that in 1949 the foreign ministers were the impetus and backbone of NATO and took the necessary political risks. Today, it appears that the Council of Foreign Ministers is a group of friendly, distinguished members of a discussion society and are not prepared to take actions that carry political risks. That is the reason NATO didn't act.

To be honest, the Croatian problem appeared small enough to be solved without the use of a major armed intervention. The irony of history is always the same. Force can be used without risk to deal with matters when they are small, but precisely because they are small they don't appear to require the use of force. It is only when problems get big and almost unmanageable that political will rises to the occasion. By then you have maximum expense and maximum difficulty in solving the problem, however.

QUESTION: Is there a possibility that joint maneuvers with these countries will promote or preserve in them a sense of militarism? Also, you have mentioned several times "respond in writing." Are the governments and leaders of these countries that NATO is dealing with sufficiently stable to honor such a commitment?

MR. ACHESON: It is generally believed that the likelihood of promoting militarism in these countries is small because they have a common desire to demote militarism and use their resources for peaceful purposes. The goal of joint maneuvers is to give their military forces the capability to handle a military situation, but it is not believed this will cause them to exaggerate the role of the military in their countries' political systems.

The second question is sort of a chicken-and-egg question. There is instability in many of the countries of that region, although in some such as the Czech Republic, that risk is sharply diminishing. While some would say that Poland recently took a step backward, it was not a move toward instability; it was more a matter of using previous instruments of authority in a way we don't like. Hungary is a country well on its way to establishing itself as a major factor in the commercial and economic life of Europe, and it has put behind it any pretense of military ambition. In fact, Hitler was reported to have complained that despite its wartime alliance with Germany, Hungary had no military ambition.

On the other hand, one of the sources of instability in these countries is apprehension about their security. A relationship with NATO that was clearly evidenced through joint maneuvers would seemingly diminish that source of instability. If you sought 100-percent stability before taking the first step with these countries, however, then you would never take that step. The idea is that stability and the NATO relationship will progressively reinforce each other over time.

QUESTION: From the beginning, the supreme commander of NATO has been an American officer. Should this continue indefinitely, and if so, why?

MR. ACHESON: I'm sure you are aware of the demand in some quarters that there be a European commander at some point, and some say soon. This demand has most often come from the French, who ironically have been the least active in military cooperation. If American forces and participation are reduced to a certain level, a European commander would then make sense and would be politically inevitable. Yet this should not depend strictly on a count of troops on the ground because we supply the vast majority of air-lift operation, logistics, communications, intelligence, and encryption. These are the crucial aspects that make modern warfare possible. Without them there would probably be a sharp disablement of NATO. That factor, plus the need for continued commitment by the Congress, argues for continued American leadership, even though the U.S. troop count may greatly diminish.

If you are looking for a test of European capability to lead NATO, you have to realize that people who have fought most recently are likely to be the most highly qualified. Several European commanders have either fought or been on the edges of fighting in NATO peacekeeping operations, and they are high on the list in terms of military capability. From what I have read of Sir Michael Rose, he would certainly be a candidate.

QUESTION: Isn't there also a domestic American consideration?

MR. ACHESON: Absolutely! How long will Congress provide the resources for any form of American participation if the NATO leadership goes to another country? It is a situation full of risk, but it is nevertheless something we cannot decide unilaterally.

QUESTION: Has a resolution of the situation in Yugoslavia been delayed and drawn out because many people anticipate a Russian veto against any proposed U.N. action?

MR. ACHESON: Strictly speaking, I think not. We are acting under a broad U.N. mandate that has already been given to peacekeeping forces in Yugoslavia. The theory is that the U.N. peacekeeping forces and the NATO forces are not in competing roles, but that NATO is operating under the U.N. mandate. But a few days ago, Boutros Boutros-Ghali said that he would be the one to decide when air strikes should be made, and the U.N. Security Council said *it* would decide. The fact of the matter is, the air forces that would conduct these strikes are NATO forces.

We don't have to go back for a new U.N. mandate as long as we are dealing with pacifying the war within Bosnia. If violence spills over to Macedonia or some other region, however, then we would likely have to go back to the United Nations. In that case, we would face not only the likely threat of a Russian veto, but perhaps also the threat of a Chinese veto. China takes a stern view of interference in the domestic affairs of any country. It also has an expanded view of what is a purely domestic affair, so the threat of a veto by China would perhaps be as great as one by Russia. If Slavs were not involved in the next issue to arise, I don't think Russia would feel quite as sensitive about it. It is the ancient Slavic kinship with the Serbs that makes the situation so sensitive for Russia.

QUESTION: I was fascinated by your description of the requirements that NATO puts on the former Warsaw Pact countries, such as proportionally sized military budgets, transparency, civilian control, and so forth. With the SHAPE educational effort geared toward the military leadership, is there also a parallel effort geared toward informing the voters of those countries? It seems that would be important because they have no more knowledge of how a democratic system works than the military does.

.

MR. ACHESON: Education of the voters is indeed important. But it must come from the local government. Eventually the taxpayers of those countries will be asked to pay for whatever the military establishment is doing, and they may not give their consent unless it has been adequately explained to them. Under these circumstances, there seems to be a guarantee of public transparency and awareness. I have to laugh when I think of the first Ukrainian "democratic" military appropriation bill to be made public. It was a single line item with one number. Of course it was explained to them that this was not exactly how the West does it.

QUESTION: The circumstances that gave rise to NATO have drastically changed. If NATO were to be created today, what would be done differently, in light of the challenges or opportunities the future may hold?

MR. ACHESON: I have grave doubt that NATO *could* be created today. I have grave doubt that a threat would be seen as sharp enough or immediate enough by all the countries involved, including the United States, to go forward with such a scheme. I have doubt that the Western European governments and our own could muster the political will and the resources.

In that respect, the North Atlantic Treaty is remarkably foresighted and flexible in its provisions. The last article makes it possible for new countries to join as long as it is prepared to keep the obligations of the treaty. Also, Article IV allows any country that is a member of NATO, or is affiliated with it, to consult with the other members in matters of concern for its own security. This provision doesn't commit anyone to anything specifically, but it does open the door to arrangements like the Partnership for Peace. For this reason it was thought wise to use an already existing institution with open-ended provisions.

QUESTION: Has Russia applied for membership in NATO? Will it be denied?

MR. ACHESON: Russia has not yet applied but probably will eventually. There is a good reason why it was not among the first to apply. Up until the last minute, Russia denied the need for the Partnership for Peace and regarded any affiliation of NATO with the Warsaw Pact region as an act of hostility. The Russians need time to regroup, rationalize their change of position, and adapt to new circumstances. Russia probably will apply, but it won't be accepted unless it agrees to meet the requirements.

QUESTION: It seems the economies of these new countries are an important factor not only for the military, but also in the education of the people. What role will trade play in the development of these countries and in their admission to the Partnership for Peace?

MR. ACHESON: I think trade, investment, and employment will have a large effect, but there isn't much NATO can do in this area. NATO is not an economic organization. Certainly trade, as a way to build economic strength, is handicapped in these regions right now because of three powerful factors. First, their economies have been severely slowed by rising energy prices. Previously, Russian oil was sold to them at deeply discounted concessionary prices as a way of cementing the Warsaw Pact relationship. Now, with the dissolution of the Soviet Union and the Warsaw Pact, those concessionary terms have disappeared and they are buying all of their oil at world market prices. This is a great strain on their economies. Their whole energy infrastructure has suddenly been drastically repriced, making it extremely difficult to produce goods for export at competitive prices and therefore build their economy.

The second inhibiting factor is the European Union. The European Union's terms of trade under the common market are quite discriminatory toward Central and Eastern Europe. Unless countries in these regions join the European Union (EU), which many would like to do, they will not get the same terms of trade that other members of the European Union are getting. It means that their goods will be subject to higher tariffs, and other impediments such as inspection and safety rules that don't apply to Western European goods.

The third restrictive factor is that none of these countries have freely convertible currencies with the West. The countries of Central and Eastern Europe must therefore look to other regions for a market to sell their goods, which is a severe handicap. Russia and Ukraine have broken economies and thus cannot serve as useful trading partners. They have no hard currency with which to buy goods. Scandinavia and the European Free Trade Association is a possibility, but it is a much smaller market than the EU market. Furthermore, if these regions wish to trade with the United States, they still have to be competitive with the EU, which is difficult for them. They could possibly look to the Far East and South America, but nonetheless they face a long, hard road.

QUESTION: What is the likely timetable for the transition from Partnership for Peace membership to full NATO membership? What conditions would the candidate countries have to meet?

MR. ACHESON: It will take a different length of time for each country involved—not because NATO wishes to treat them differently, but because each country of that region will have to decide for itself what commitments can be made and kept. Its performance will be a highly individual affair. How long it will take Poland, for example, to negotiate its terms of entry may be quite different from that of the Czech Republic. Considering the Czech Republic's economy, the stable nature of its political system, and its disavowal of any military problems, it might be in the best position to go first into full NATO membership. Until the recent election, I would have said Poland might be first. The op-ed commentators in this country have been calling the election a step back because so many former Communists have been named to head the ministries in the government. The problem is there are very few people with experience who are qualified to lead a ministry who were not in the previous government. Nevertheless, Poland may still be the first to join NATO—we may be reading too much into the election.

QUESTION: Earlier you pointed out the central aspect of NATO is that an attack against one member is considered an attack against all. I was involved with the birth of NATO. The basic foundation of NATO's military strength was the possibility of a nuclear response, which is an awesome responsibility. It underlies all of NATO's military strategy.

I am worried that we may have had to compromise on the Partnership for Peace because of the threat Russia poses to these former Warsaw Pact nations. If Russia ever agrees to enter NATO under NATO's terms, what would that mean for "an attack against one is an attack against all," given Russia's sensitivity? These pieces don't seem to fit together yet.

MR. ACHESON: You are absolutely correct. The irony is that the alliance member you would most like to have is the one you are least likely to get, for the very reasons you most need him. You also put your finger on the reason we did not wish to admit the Warsaw Pact countries to Article V obligations. No parliament in the West, including our Congress, would have agreed to use nuclear weapons or any form of open warfare to defend countries that so recently had been our adversaries. This stepping stone—the Partnership for Peace—was politically necessary and makes a great deal of sense.

NARRATOR: We wish to thank you for a very insightful and informative discussion of a crucial policy issue.

CHAPTER ELEVEN

NATO's Prospects[*]

JOHN WOODWORTH

NARRATOR: John Woodworth is executive-in-residence and senior faculty member at the Federal Executive Institute, where he also teaches courses in global trends and issues in international security. He served at NATO headquarters in Brussels for five years as a nuclear policy adviser with the U.S. Mission and was a visiting fellow at the National Defense University for two years. He served as ambassador and deputy negotiator for INF (Intermediate-range Nuclear Forces) at the Nuclear and Space Talks with the Soviet Union from 1985 to 1987. Mr. Woodworth was deputy assistant secretary of defense for European and NATO policy from 1988 to 1989. His educational background includes a bachelor's degree from Duke University, a master's degree from Georgetown University, and a position as a fellow in public affairs at Princeton University.

Mr. Woodworth considers the question of how it is that the most successful international security organization in history is widely speculated to have no role to play in the future. Yet at the same time, questions are raised about the expansion of NATO membership and NATO's responsibilities outside of Western

---

[*]*Presented in a Forum at the Miller Center of Public Affairs on 28 August 1995.*

Europe. Another debate surrounds NATO's future leadership. Is NATO's leadership passing from American to Western European hands? In discussing NATO's future prospects, John Woodworth confronts these and other important questions about this remarkably successful alliance.

MR. WOODWORTH: This is a particularly useful time to take stock of the NATO Alliance. Much has happened in recent months in Europe and beyond. With events and the international environment changing rapidly, it would be impossible for NATO to remain unaffected.

At the same time, a temptation exists to take the measure of NATO by daily headlines and punditry. NATO then becomes rather like the stock market, with its current value rising and falling, depending on daily changes in the political scene. Current events certainly matter, but Americans need to try to understand the more enduring trends and interests at play to help guide them in judging what place NATO has in the world, how it serves U.S. and Western security, and what its prospects really are. I want to get at the root of the United States's core interests in a continuing and strong NATO Alliance.

Nevertheless, no one can dismiss the impact of critical current events like Bosnia. The turmoil in the Balkans has tested NATO in ways that it has rarely been tested before. This crisis has been a rude welcoming to the new world disorder for NATO. All of the alarms raised about NATO's future recently, as events have gone from bad to worse in the Balkans, are not of an altogether new kind. Many people forget that throughout much of its history the refrain "NATO in crisis" was common. This semi-hysterical label was often a product of attempts to make headlines and, in academic circles, gain attention. After all, things going smoothly rarely make a good story. What is striking, however, is the remarkable resilience that NATO displayed as it wrestled its way through the challenges of the Cold War. Without underestimating the stress that events in Bosnia have put on NATO, it can be salutary to recall trials that NATO has overcome in the past.

In this discussion, I want first to put NATO in a larger perspective because its prospects should be judged in a global context. Second, I will discuss what are now the two major defining issues for NATO's future—its need to successfully redefine its role in the post-Cold War period and NATO enlargement. Both issues are interrelated, and both are sharply affected by the dramatic changes since the end of the Cold War.

The lack of defining features in the post-Cold War world that would help the United States align its policy compass can induce a touch of nostalgia for the past. People forget, though, that the East-West confrontation that dominated the international stage for nearly 50 years was never quite as simple as many often recall it. How to meet the Soviet challenge was hotly debated. Moreover, many of the broad trends shaping the world today had momentum well before the fall of the Berlin Wall. The long struggle of the Cold War nevertheless made setting priorities easier.

The world is much more complex today. One principal consequence is that NATO, an offspring of the Cold War, will not hold as prominent a place on the world stage nor in U.S. policy as it enjoyed in the past. Instead, the demands on America's priorities, attention, and resources will be strongly affected by new preoccupations.

One important issue in this changing world is global economics. The emergence of an increasingly integrated global economy driven by information age technology will do more to shape the world into the next century than any other force. This statement does not intend to predict, as some savants did prior to 1914, that the threads of commerce and finance uniting the major powers would make conflict between them inconceivable. Security concerns remain capable of overwhelming all others. Economics is, however, likely to have a far greater impact on the world balance than at any other time in the past. The triumph of capitalism in the world today—one of the truly distinctive features of the modern age—has bred unprecedented interdependence and prosperity. Policies of autarky, which some countries may still be foolish enough to pursue, are now broadly discredited. Governments will be preoccupied with becoming or remaining big players in the global economic sweepstakes, or at least being important niche players. The incentives for stability are immense, and the consequences of alternative conditions are dire.

Related to this point is the growth of Asian economic strength. The world is in the midst of a shift in global wealth to Asia that is of historic proportions. The story here not only concerns China, which will emerge early in the next century as the world's largest economy, barring internal or external cataclysms. Other countries in East and South Asia will also assume increasingly prominent places on the economic scene. Europe will remain an important center of economic power in the world, but it will not loom as large as it has in the past. This change will drive American policy toward a wider focus than the Eurocentric tendencies of the past. Europe will also need to assume a similarly wider outlook if it intends to be a heavy player in the global economy.

The rise of China as a major power is the next important change. China will constitute one of the most important variables in the strategic landscape of the 21st century. Adjusting to this change will be difficult. The course of change will be determined fundamentally by internal developments in China, especially the nature of its government. If China pursues the role of regional hegemon by force, it will be countered, but with unforeseeable consequences. China may also decide to assume its place as a major power through cooperation. The future of the region will turn heavily on the path China chooses.

The gap between rich and poor is another important subject. The question of winners and losers will be a major issue for the next century. Some nations will share in global economic growth but others will not, particularly those whose human capital is already desperately behind the curve. These countries will not lose gracefully. Moral sensitivities will be tested in the developed world. Dealing with this problem will become a major global preoccupation. Part of the drama will emerge in how global capitalism, now the system of choice, deals with the growing gap between rich and poor not only between countries but within them as well, including the industrialized countries.

Lastly, Russia's future remains a key variable. The range of alternatives is large in Russia, and the outcomes are unpredictable. Russia is and will be an important country and will remain a large nuclear power for a long time to come. Combining the main indices of power which will determine the ordering of nations in the next century—economic prowess being first among others—Russia is, however, apt to be in the middle ranks with perhaps a dozen countries having larger economies. In short, Russia may not have the potential to be the kind of unsettling factor the Soviet Union represented in the past.

These trends and issues point toward a world where NATO will not command the attention it has in the past. Many of the high-priority issues that will preoccupy the United States and other countries will not be ones to which NATO can contribute solutions. This does not mean that NATO can be expected to fade away, as some have suggested. To the contrary, Europe will remain vital to U.S. interests for the foreseeable future. Those who foresee a "Pacific Century" ahead are wide of the mark in my view. The future will not allow the United States to pick and choose between major areas in such a manner. A better phrase will be the "Global Century." In this sense, Europe and NATO will remain important but share a much more crowded stage of global priorities.

In addition to its place on the global stage, NATO's future depends on how it sustains existing strengths and adapts to meet the real security challenges of today. It would be fruitless as well as wasteful for U.S. policy to aim only at maintaining the NATO of old.

The two issues that will be pivotal in shaping NATO's future prospects—its role in a changing world and the problem of enlargement—do not comprise the whole of NATO's agenda but their implications are far-reaching. In addition, they encompass a host of other key issues, including consensus building, public support, out-of-area challenges, and relations with Russia and other countries of the former Soviet bloc.

As for NATO's purpose, it is useful to trace the ups and downs of NATO since the fall of the Berlin Wall. The collapse of communism and dissolution of the Warsaw Pact during these difficult and surprising times lent justification and reward to decades of struggle. The immediate visceral reaction in NATO was that its days were numbered. After all, with a new world dawning, the security structures of the past hardly seemed appropriate. Sober second thoughts soon took hold, however, as the realization sunk in that the world was moving into a major period of transition that would be fraught with risks. The United States and other countries rapidly swung to strong support of NATO.

Beginning in 1990, NATO went through a process of transformation that was remarkable for its pace in a consensus-based organization often best known for its ponderousness. Some questioned the seriousness and depth of these changes, seeing them as desperate acts of bureaucratic self-preservation. They were wrong. In fact, NATO displayed a remarkable adaptability. It moved to the center of efforts to transform East-West relations. It more than held its own in the institutional jostling that occurred between the CSCE (Conference on Security and Cooperation in Europe), the Western European Union (WEU), the European Union (EU), and other bodies. Moreover, the clamor of Central European states to join NATO only enhanced its standing.

This period of transformation produced three main changes. First, the political conflict between East and West was declared over, and policies and mechanisms were established to begin building a relationship based on cooperation and partnership. Second, the NATO military strategy was revamped from its orientation eastward to a more flexible and multi-purpose strategy and force posture. Third, the Alliance struggled to reconcile out-of-area challenges to the security of NATO members, reaching a tenuous consensus at least in principle to take action in selected cases.

Despite the transformation of NATO in the last six years, the question of the purpose of the organization continues to hang over it with unsettling effects. This situation was inevitable as the singular and manifest threat from the East was replaced by the messy instabilities of today. These challenges may threaten important security interests of NATO members but not the vital security interest of territorial integrity. Are these new challenges sufficient to promote cohesion and justify common action? My answer to this question is yes, but it will be difficult.

Critical to understanding the essence of the problem is the evolution of NATO from the time of its founding in 1949. Animated by the Soviet threat, the original members were energized by the practical demands of military defense planning, but their ultimate purpose was the establishment of a framework of security in which the political and economic development of free societies in Europe could occur. This goal included the integration of West Germany into the Western community and the transcending of authoritarian vestiges from both the Left and Right in Italy, Turkey, Greece, Portugal, and Spain.

NATO was remarkably successful in this endeavor. What also happened on the way to this happy result was a profound maturing of habits of cooperation that became the hallmark of the West's strength. This maturation was found in the denationalization of defense, military transparency among NATO members, development of skills of consensus building, and an attachment to collective over unilateral action. The habits of cooperation that developed in NATO, in combination with a variety of other institutions linking Western countries, became and remains the foundation for the zone of peace that now prevails in the Atlantic community of democracies. In effect, what began as a threat-based organization has today become a value-based organization. The zone of peace among the Western democracies and the habits of cooperation that underwrite it have become ends in themselves.

These developments go to the heart of the current debate. The NATO allies uniformly want to preserve what has been gained, and particularly in security matters they want to keep the U.S.-Atlantic connection intact. For the United States, it certainly remains vastly in its national interest to sustain those gains and to continue to play a leading role in European security matters. All of the Allies agree on the value of NATO for its own sake to underwrite the Atlantic zone of peace. The question is whether this shared view, which is necessary to sustain the Alliance, is also sufficient. Are manifest threats a functional necessity to give NATO adequate purpose to remain relevant and cohesive and to maintain the habits of cooperation built up over the period of the Cold War?

This question is not trivial. Any organization needs purpose, and when the surrounding environment changes, its purpose needs to be adjusted accordingly. The starting point for NATO today must be to keep the security community intact. The dilemma, however, is that the contemporary threats of disorder and instability which now preoccupy NATO will not have the galvanizing effect that the Warsaw Pact used to provide, and may divide and weaken the very security community which has become the core NATO purpose.

The West can regret with good reason that the first major test for the Atlantic Alliance in the post-Cold War era came in the Balkans. Few issues could have been more confounding. However, contrary to a general impression of NATO's shortcomings in the Balkans, this first test of NATO out-of-area operations—and in fact the first test of actual combat operations by the NATO Alliance in its history—have been well planned and executed. The failure, if it is such, has been in the inability of Western leadership to agree on what should be done. The means have been available. The political will and consensus for action has not.

Other challenges that add to NATO's purpose extend beyond the regional instabilities from ethnic and religious conflict. First, proliferation is a vital security concern to which NATO has already given substantial attention and will do more. NATO's role, however, is only part of a much larger endeavor on this subject.

Second, Islamic countries represent a rising challenge, but the issue here is largely political. Islamic countries can be a security bother but not a serious military threat. NATO can and has begun to play a role in the dialogue between the Islamic world and the West, but this process is something that must occur at multiple levels.

Third, NATO has already played a leading role in construction of new forms of cooperation and transparency in the whole of Europe. This step began with the establishment of the North Atlantic Cooperation Council (NACC) in 1991 and has continued through the formation of the Partnership for Peace (PFP) program in 1994, now comprising some 40 members engaged in promoting new areas of military cooperation, information exchange, and advancement of democratic norms in civil-military relations.

This array of activities is impressive. It is nevertheless still necessary to ask what should remain of the historical core purpose of the Atlantic Alliance of defending against the threat of attack by a major power, which can only mean Russia. Many have suggested that the unspoken but real purpose of NATO is to be held in trust to respond if necessary to a resurgent Russia bent on imperial restoration. This perception will not diminish as an extended and profound revolution in Russia continues, the ultimate outcome of which is uncertain and may not be benign.

However, the dilemma and reality is that NATO cannot center its activities around collective defense against a future potential aggression from the East and at the same time make an effective contribution to overcoming the divisions of Europe. Indeed, pressing this residual role of NATO could stimulate the very outcome of an isolated, paranoid, and nationalistic Russia that it is overwhelmingly in NATO's interest to avoid. NATO has rightfully stood down major components of its military forces that could be used to defend against large external threats. There should be more than adequate warning time—measurable in years—to restore these capabilities if circumstances warrant. The West is much better placed to respond to such circumstances than it was 40 years ago, provided its leadership and peoples have not lost their bearings completely. The West need not be reticent in acknowledging this potential to its Russian colleagues. Indeed, they must understand that the West will watch for and react to aggressive moves against other sovereign states, Russian disregard of arms control and other agreements around which security is now built, and the emergence of nondemocratic government there.

In short, NATO can deal with a threatening Russia successfully. Moreover, a Russia that returns to imperial ambitions will be headed down a dead-end road that ultimately will only add to the decline and despair of that country and its people. The real challenge for NATO is whether it can achieve and maintain a sense of purpose and direction in circumstances which may never involve the threat of external aggression of the kind that would invoke the all-for-one provisions of the North Atlantic Treaty. Thus, the main issue will be whether the Atlantic Alliance can sustain democratic cooperation on security—the remaining most important function of NATO—while dealing with a disparate range of security issues where interests will vary among members. That will demand choice and prioritization, and that may divide as well as unite.

Turning to the problem of enlargement, this issue has been on the formal NATO agenda only for the past year, although the notion was born with the fall of the Berlin Wall in 1989. The majority of traditional NATO specialists were initially horrified by the idea. Enlargement has since gained a life of its own. Over the past year, the debate has been widespread, but a broad consensus among at least the foreign policy establishment does not yet exist. Among the public at large, it has barely appeared on the screen.

What is interesting is the perplexing spread of viewpoints on the issue. There is no general direction in the debate from left or right, liberals or conservatives, or positions in between. The Clinton administration is on record in favor of enlargement, although its ardor on the issue seems to have cooled. Democratic Senator Sam Nunn has decided he is against it. The "Contract-with-America" Republicans support early admission of new members, while others such as Republican Pat Buchanan think it is a bad idea.

The issue cannot turn simply on the sum of pro-and-con arguments. Most or all are now on the table, unless events add new ones. The issue really boils down to a matter of judgment about our country's core interests and what makes strategic sense. What NATO does and how it does it will heavily shape its prospects well into the future.

Without dismissing the wide range of arguments that have been made on both sides of the debate, two issues are really at the heart of the matter: Russia and the nature of the Atlantic Alliance. With respect to Russia, although essentially all commentators have agreed that NATO should not give Russia a veto over enlargement, opponents have fundamentally built their case around estimates of the Russian response. Like it or not, the West is in the thrall of Russian influence on this issue. It is fair to say, though, that if one does not have a solution to the Russian problem, one does not have a solution to enlargement.

Many Russian interlocutors have been alarmist, even apocalyptic, at the idea of NATO expanding eastward. In their view, whether NATO intends the step as an anti-Russian one or not, it will be seen as such by many who still harbor a Cold War image of NATO. Russian democrats fear that their nationalist, authoritarian opponents would exploit NATO enlargement, evoking images of new Western threats to a weakened Russia trying to regain its rightful place in the world. The democratic forces in Russia, they argue, would be unable to withstand the emotional impact and the boost this controversy would give to the Zhirinovskys of today and tomorrow.

This argument contains an air of unreality. Objectively, there are no plausible permutations of NATO in the future, whether at 16 members or some larger number, that would constitute a military threat to Russia, except in a case of self-defense. Still, Russians profess a paranoia about being threatened by outsiders, and they cite their tortured history to explain these feelings. Paranoias may be divorced from fact, but they can be no less real in determining human responses.

The problem the West faces is whether it makes sense to let Russian sensitivities that are divorced from the objective realities involved determine ultimate decisions on NATO enlargement. Certainly, if enlargement led Russia to scuttle any hope of democratic and economic reform, end cooperation on critical security interests like nonproliferation, and promote a resurgence of Russian regional imperialism, then a good and clear reason to draw back from this issue would exist.

Do such dire consequences, however, need to arise inevitably from a decision to move forward on enlargement? If there is a good side to this problem, it is that the sensitivities Russians profess and Westerners fear may be susceptible to political therapy and solution. If true objective threats to Russia existed, finding a solution would be quite another matter.

What are the trade-offs here? To get to the heart of this question, it is necessary to consider why NATO should add new members and whether and how this enlargement serves U.S. vital interests. These questions bring back the central question of the purpose of NATO in the post-Cold War era.

The clamor by Central and Eastern European states to join NATO no doubt reflects in the minds of some people at least a grasp for protection from a risk of Russian return to old imperial habits. If this notion became the real reason for admitting new members, it could not be hidden and would be seen by Russia as directed against itself. The result would be the hardening of lines across Europe that the West has declared it does not want.

The other reason for these countries seeking to join NATO and the more compelling reason to contemplate enlargement as a goal is less a fear of an external threat from Russia than a desire to get inside and be a beneficiary of the zone of peace that the NATO area has come to represent. Admission is seen as a validation of progress along the road of reform and the security foundation for the building of democracy and market economies. If NATO's political victory in the Cold War has any meaning, it must include the possibility of embracing like-minded states in the region who want to join and can increase the value of collective defense and the democratic security community in Europe. To refuse to contemplate enlargement would set in motion uncertain but potentially adverse trends that probably could not be contained solely through other forums like the Partnership for Peace, the Western European Union, or other bodies.

At the same time, NATO has every reason to be demanding in its expectations, deliberate in its approach, and discriminate in its admission of new members. Haste is unnecessary to assuage the impatient as long as the line-of-march is clear. Moreover, the European allies must pursue parallel openness in the further evolution of the European Union and the Western European Union. Movement in tandem should occur in all of these multilateral institutions and not just in NATO. Moreover, new members must bring a capacity to contribute a fair share to the security tasks undertaken by NATO. Assuming a continuing absence of major external threats, those tasks will center on the out-of-area threats to stability that the West can expect to bedevil NATO and persistently test consensus building. Finally, aspirant countries must not import security problems in the form of unsolved ethnic strife or irredentist claims on the territory of other states.

NATO's ongoing examination of the conditions for admission of new members is useful. It buys time and allows the issue to ferment, as it should. Ultimate decisions, though, should be based not on rigid criteria, but on political judgment.

As for Russia, the United States must recognize that while the West's influence may work at the margins, the course of events there will fundamentally unfold according to internal dynamics. Nonetheless, with respect to the issue of NATO enlargement, the United States and other allies should make sure that they keep choices open for Russia and work hard at areas of continuing cooperation. The Russia question needs to be addressed on a number of levels. First, the Alliance should not exclude Russia in principle from NATO membership. Second, the dialogue that has begun on a more formal security linkage between Russia and NATO should be pressed forward. Third, PFP cooperation should be intense. In addition, no troops or nuclear weapons should be stationed on any new Central European member's territory. Finally, the United States and other allies should work steadily and patiently on many levels in explaining to Russia the nonthreatening nature of NATO enlargement. None of these measures will be easy. Time, however, should prove a helpful ally. It will allow for the amelioration of suspicions, more opportunity to gauge the depth of reform in the Central European countries that are likely to be the earliest candidates for membership, and a clearer picture of the direction of change in Russia.

In conclusion, NATO must remain a collective defense organization in contrast to a collective security organization, but it also must become more than that sort of institution. Its prospects depend on how and how well it serves as the underwriter of a continuing democratic security community. Its function will no longer rest simply on providing for a collective response to external aggression. Its challenge now will be to sustain the habits of cooperation and the skills of consensus building on more difficult issues. NATO has already made impressive strides, but the agonies of the Balkans crisis reveal how hard the future may be. These are the real issues of the day, and NATO cannot remove itself from them if it wants to remain relevant, influential and capable of serving Western security interests. All of these tasks will be more difficult than in the past. At the same time, NATO should not back away from enlargement, but the pace of change in this area and the selection of new members should be evolutionary and conditioned by hard-headed calculations of self-interest.

QUESTION: What do you think of the possibility of converting NATO into a global security organization without geographic requirements, but with the requirement that countries have to have kept their treaty obligations for the past five or possibly 10 years?

MR. WOODWORTH: Your question provokes one of the interesting issues about enlargement. If NATO begins to enlarge, where does it stop enlargement? The question goes even a step further. Should it become a global phenomenon?

My reaction is that it should not. NATO is and ought to remain a regional organization; that is, centered in Europe and the Atlantic community. By staying centered in Europe, it draws in, as it did from the beginning, the United States and Canada. In that sense, the United States is a European power and part of Europe. If NATO were to try to move its scope beyond that region, it would truly lose its focus and cohesion and be unable to carry out the essential functions that it needs to do in Europe. By Europe, I mean Europe extended, including the Eurasian landmass—at least its Russian and the formerly Soviet parts. Nations in other parts of the globe can turn to other regional organizations, or perhaps new regional organizations can be created. For example, Asia is a region where steps are moving forward on that idea. Asians, however, have a long way to go before they can duplicate in Asia what NATO did in Europe. But they can at least begin to channel security issues in a more constructive direction than they might otherwise go.

QUESTION: The United Nations was formed 50 years ago to prevent precisely the problems currently discussed. Should the United Nations be a part of this whole process, and if so, how?

MR. WOODWORTH: In the larger sense one might see the United Nations as a collective security organization with nonaggression rules. What it lacks that a collective defense organization has is a consistent capacity to arrive at consensus for action.

What the world needs is a whole spectrum of possibilities, structures, organizations, and approaches to deal with security issues across the board. At one level, the world needs the United Nations, despite its shortcomings in recent situations such as Bosnia. If the world did not have the United Nations, it would have to invent one. Everyone, however, cannot rely on that organization to deal with *the* most critical security issues that have to be confronted. In other words, the United Nations cannot provide for the kind of security that NATO provided in the Cold War.

COMMENT: NATO certainly has not been unanimous in its decisions on the issues involving Bosnia.

MR. WOODWORTH: No, it hasn't. It is interesting that people are now going through a phase of U.N.-bashing and to some degree NATO-bashing because of their perceived failures in Bosnia. It is nevertheless significant to remember that the decisions being made in the United Nations and NATO are all being made by the same countries. The problem here has centered on the lack of agreement among the principal governments and in particular the Western governments about what to do. Is this lack of consensus a failure of NATO as such, or is it a failure of the United Nations? I am uncertain about the answer to that question. If nothing else, this lack of consensus is a testament to the agonizing difficulty of the problem. Maybe there are problems for which there are no good solutions. Some nuts are hard to crack, and Bosnia could well be one of them.

I do not mean to suggest that NATO and the United Nations could not have done better in the Balkans. It must have been possible to do better than they have thus far, even though this situation was not an easy one to resolve.

QUESTION: Has there been resistance on the part of any of the NATO members to becoming a military arm of the United Nations?

MR. WOODWORTH: No. One of the features of the Bosnian situation was a decision by NATO to carry out certain limited functions. This situation, however, is the first time that NATO as an organization has taken actions outside of the immediate treaty area, in other words, the territories of the member countries. NATO has undertaken two tasks in the Balkans. It has contributed to the embargo, mainly the maritime side of that embargo, and it has monitored the no-fly zone over Bosnia. These are the only two limited functions that NATO agreed it would do at the request of the United Nations. NATO as an organization is not involved in the situation on the ground in Bosnia, although NATO countries are involved in that area. NATO did make the decision that it would carry out certain activities on behalf of the United Nations. The problem was and continues to be the degree of mandate that was given to NATO.

The Gulf War was a U.N. action. The United Nations decided in the Security Council that Iraq's aggression against Kuwait had to be reversed. It decided to take all measures to do so, and it gave a mandate to an ad hoc group of countries to carry out that decision. After that point the United Nations was uninvolved, and the ad hoc group of countries pursued its mission unimpeded by U.N. interference. In many ways, this path is really the more efficient, effective way for the United Nations to operate in an important military crisis of this kind—to give a mandate to a group of countries for a solution to the problem and not get directly involved. The problem in Bosnia is that while NATO agreed to undertake certain tasks, the United Nations has remained in political charge of the operation instead of giving NATO a mandate to deal with the situation. That arrangement has complicated the command structure and introduced a whole different level of politics that has made it remarkably more difficult to deal with the crisis.

NARRATOR: In charge and yet not in charge—can you explain this dual key approach that the Clinton administration is apparently now rejecting?

MR. WOODWORTH: In effect, the mandates from the U.N. Security Council kept responsibility in the hands of the United Nations to conduct the operations in Bosnia. The international military forces deployed in Bosnia, Croatia, and in other operations that are part of the Balkan issue are all responsible to and appointed by the U.N. political authority. The Bosnia operation may now be shifting into the alternative model where NATO may be given a broader mandate to do certain things in support of the U.N.'s objectives. If this political change takes effect, NATO will then need no further reference to the United Nations to pursue those objectives. Impediments to this change are found in the Security Council, which has critics (Russia and maybe others) of

NATO's sympathetic stance toward the Muslim and Croat side who can complicate the problem by arguing that the existing Security Council mandate on Bosnia is being exceeded.

QUESTION: It seems that the strongest proponents of a more unified Europe must be looking at the Western European Union as a potential military force in the future. Is this statement accurate, and if so, would it complicate the debate about NATO enlargement and NATO's future role?

MR. WOODWORTH: One of the important issues in Europe today is how far Europe will move in terms of its own defense and security identity and in establishing its own military capability within the European Union. The Western European Union is the body that currently represents that effort, functioning as the security arm of the European Union. Next year Europeans will discuss how far they might be able to go in arriving at what is called a common foreign and security policy. For Europe the tricky issue is satisfying both its desire to advance the cause of European unity, including in the defense and security area, without undercutting NATO, which despite aspirations for stronger European unity, the European Alliance members still want to keep. The Atlantic connection remains important to the interests of all Europeans. My own view is that they will not take actions to achieve aspirations for a stronger European security arm that will undercut NATO. They will instead try to walk a line where they can move forward on steps related to their own security cooperation but keep those moves consistent within a larger Atlantic community. I think this is possible.

QUESTION: Wouldn't that strategy work against any enlargement eastward?

MR. WOODWORTH: Not necessarily. In addition to the interest that the Central European countries have in joining NATO, those same countries are also deeply interested in joining other European structures, including the European Union, the Western European

Union, and other bodies. Indeed, they are already in some of these structures at differing levels of association.

In many ways, a range of things all will proceed in tandem—some at the economic level, some at the political level, and some at the security military level. That multilevel approach is certainly the way Western Europe should deal with the enlargement issue.

QUESTION: Is Russia, as an unstable, unpredictable, potential threat, now a kind of catalyst for a security organization that would have to be invented if it did not exist? Is the West actually fortunate to have Russia around to keep NATO going by preventing it from disintegrating?

MR. WOODWORTH: Does the West need a threat to galvanize a collective defense organization, or is that threat likely to be a real one? As I mentioned earlier, the peculiar thing with Russia is that if it goes in directions that threatens the security of the NATO Alliance and its members, that direction will also bring the seeds of further serious Russian decline. Russia cannot build a competitive global economy by moving in a direction of nationalistic xenophobia.

The question has now become, Who can threaten NATO? Other threats give purpose to the organization. The secretary general of NATO, Willy Claes, said earlier this year that the Islamic threat has replaced the Communist threat of the past. That prospect is wildly exaggerated, and it seems to me imprudent to make that statement. The Islamic world will never be able to join together to comprise a serious military threat to the West. Rogue nations in the Islamic world might get missiles, and the West will have to deal with those situations, but Islamic countries do not pose a major military threat.

The Islamic world is engaged in a serious internal struggle of self-definition. What is more interesting about the Islamic world's relations with the West is its condition internally and how it is trying to reconcile its traditions with a modern and changing world. Muslims will attempt to resolve that situation in a variety of ways—including instances of terrorism and political repression in that part of the world. The West needs to be concerned about those possibilities, and NATO can have a role in the dialogue that should take place to promote moderation and reconciliation. The bottom line, therefore, is that the West does face a problem, but there is not a basic threat similar to the Soviet Union that galvanized NATO in the past.

QUESTION: The United States is just as uncertain of NATO in many ways as Russia is. American leadership is needed in this area. What is the United States going to do about NATO?

MR. WOODWORTH: For 40 years NATO functioned successfully very much under the leadership of the United States. During NATO's history, however, the image that the United States dominated the organization and simply did whatever it wanted to do is incorrect. It was never that simple. There was always a lot of give and take in NATO decision making. Having give-and-take is the way it should be. Today, I doubt that the United States can exercise the same sort of dominant role that it played during the Cold War. Leadership will not be as easy as before.

On Bosnia, the United States chose in 1990 and 1991 to hold back and let the Europeans take the lead on the issue. There has and will be a great deal of debate in retrospect about what went wrong and what the United States should have done in Bosnia. In my view, to the extent that one regards a security community as something where all of the members pull together to solve problems, the United States should not have taken a backseat. Had the United States played a stronger role early in that issue, it may have helped in galvanizing more cohesive and effective Western action. It may also have gotten the United States more heavily involved on the ground. The United States will need to pay more attention to how it exercises its leadership.

QUESTION: If NATO is expanded, the prospects for conflicts increase. How does one attain a consensus for action with such a big, broad base of countries?

MR. WOODWORTH: This point is one of the most persistent objections to NATO expansion and a fair one that has to be addressed. It is easier to reach an agreement with five countries than with 15. The question is whether the current members are willing to accept the tradeoffs. Are they willing to accept complications for the sake of gains in other areas? My answer to that question is that yes, new members should be accepted, but NATO should nevertheless be careful about which countries it lets in and the circumstances under which admission is granted. One major criterion is not to bring in new problems such as unresolved ethnic conflicts or other issues.

NATO has lived with the unresolved tensions between Greece and Turkey for 40 years. No one wants more of those types of problems. What is so frustrating about the Greek-Turkish dispute is its persistence and the difficulty that the Greeks and Turks have had in overcoming their animosities, quite apart from the practical issues they struggle over in the Aegean. NATO aspirants with similar problems are not ripe for membership.

QUESTION: One of the great strengths of NATO has been its ability to coordinate foreign policy. Many people talk nostalgically about the simplicity and clarity of Western foreign policy during the Cold War, but it was not that simple. NATO members had great disputes over the nature of the Communist regime and the nature of the threats it presented in various parts of Europe and the territories involved. What happened, though, was that NATO members built instruments, both military and political, to coordinate their policies. The danger now is that the ability to coordinate policy will be lost. Will NATO have to add another layer, namely, formal coordination of foreign policy among members?

MR. WOODWORTH: I fully agree. In fact, one of the most distinctive features of the Atlantic Alliance was not only its military success in terms of constructing an effective defense organization but also its political dimension. One of the great achievements of the past 46 years in the NATO Alliance was the ability of its members to align their foreign policies.

Will they be able to achieve that goal in the future? That issue is really the one I pose in this discussion. The capacity to link interests is something of high value that the West must make every effort to preserve, and that is why preserving the security community which accomplishes this feat is important.

NARRATOR: We thank Mr. Woodworth for putting the future of NATO in perspective for us and for his in-depth discussion of the problems and challenges facing NATO in the future.

CHAPTER TWELVE

The Future of NATO[*]

ANDREW J. PIERRE

NARRATOR: Andrew Pierre received his undergraduate degree from Amherst College. He continued his studies and earned a doctorate degree in political science from Columbia and also a degree from the Institut d'Etudes Politiques in Paris. He is now a senior associate of the Carnegie Endowment for International Peace. From 1991-92, he was director of the Face-to-Face Program of meetings on international issues at the Carnegie Endowment. He is also affiliated with the Carnegie Endowment's Moscow Center for Russian and Eurasian Programs.

Dr. Pierre previously was director general of the Atlantic Institute for International Affairs in Paris. For 18 years, he was senior fellow at the Council on Foreign Relations in New York, spending part of that time as director of the Project on European-American Relations.

In addition to these and other important positions he has held, Dr. Pierre has published widely in the field. In particular, he has done a great deal of writing, speaking, and counseling on arms proliferation. One of his most recent and important books is *The Global Politics of Arms Sales* (1982). Other books he has written

---

[*]*Presented in a Forum at the Miller Center of Public Affairs on 3 October 1994.*

was prepared to support. The Maastricht Treaty ran into rather strong opposition in a number of European countries to the point where the next phase of European political evolution is more likely to be what Charles de Gaulle called the "Europe of States," rather than the "United States of Europe" that Jean Monnet would have liked.

During this same time period, the Eastern Europeans have been clamoring to be fully admitted to the Western institutions of NATO and the European Union. We cannot fault them for pursuing the national interests of their countries, though they have had mixed success in this regard. Russia has gone through enormous turmoil but remains today somewhat ambivalent about its own identity. Is Russia a European power, or is it a power that goes beyond Europe? Do Russia's primary interests lie in being locked into European economic, political, or security structures, or do its interests lie in reintegrating the parts of the former Soviet Union, reinvigorating the Commonwealth of Independent States (which includes the parts of the former Soviet Union), and delineating a certain sphere of influence around what the Russians call their "near abroad" (again, the former states of the Soviet Union). This type of influence makes many Western countries uncomfortable in that it raises the question, "To what extent are Russia's perceived security interests compatible with NATO's interests?"

Given the discussion of recent years, the point also needs to be made that European security in the classic sense of that phrase is unlikely to be threatened by military force. Western Europe isn't going to be subject to an invasion from the East—though a more nationalistic, resurgent Russia is certainly not an impossibility. At the same time, however, the main problems for Europe in the security field are going to be of a different nature than in the past. They are going to involve ethnic conflict, political instability, mass migration, and a disruption of oil flow—problems that arise from outside of Europe and could hinder European interests. Think at this point of the Iraq War and the European interest in supporting the United States in this war. Terrorism is also a concern, especially in France, given the possibility of a fundamentalist Islamic government coming into power in Algeria. The whole Maghreb could become more radical, which is of particular concern to France, Italy, and Spain. Nuclear proliferation is an issue that the Europeans see in somewhat less global terms than the United States does, but they are nevertheless concerned about the threat of ballistic missiles originating in the Middle East and North Africa. As a result, some Europeans have been talking about the need to develop a tactical ballistic missile defense against a possible future nuclear threat to Europe.

Discussion of these issues has mostly revolved around the future of institutions, institution-building, or their transformation. In an age in which the power of individual states has diminished and broad political and economic forces sweep across states, this institutional orientation seems to be quite natural. With these points in mind, I would like to talk about NATO and the institutions competing with NATO.

The first issue that should be addressed in thinking about the institutional structure of a new Europe is the Conference on Security and Cooperation in Europe—CSCE, recently renamed the Organization for Security and Cooperation in Europe (OSCE). The origin of CSCE goes back to the early 1960s as a Soviet proposal for what they then called a European security conference. The United States did not like the proposal because it excluded the United States from membership. The CSCE then became part of the Helsinki Accords. The West transformed the proposal by emphasizing human rights within the Helsinki framework. The CSCE developed four baskets: an economic basket, a political basket, a security basket, and the human dimension basket. The United States and Western Europe used the CSCE as a vehicle to assist democratic forces, such as dissidents in the Soviet Union and especially Eastern Europe, by giving such forces an international forum in which to state their aims and claims. People like Vaclav Havel of Czechoslovakia and his group, Charter 77, were closely linked to the CSCE-Helsinki process in Czechoslovakia. In general, the Eastern Europeans liked the CSCE because it gave them an identity in the international field that was separate from the Warsaw Pact and the Soviet Union.

A great advantage of the OSCE today is that it applies to a Europe that extends from Vancouver to Vladivostok. At last count its membership totalled 53 countries. Nevertheless, in the past the OSCE has also had significant disadvantages. For example, the OSCE's decision making is consensual, but achieving a consensus among 53 countries is very difficult. Member countries of the OSCE are diverse and have few common interests, other than the lowest common denominator. The OSCE lacks structure. The United States in particular has been reluctant to endow the CSCE with a secretariat (which now does exist in a modest form), an international civil service, and any real power because the United States saw it as deflecting attention away from NATO, which traditionally has been the prime institution to which the United States gave its strong support. The Eastern Europeans wanted the OSCE developed further, but they have been somewhat locked in a battle on this not only with the United States, but also with some of the other larger NATO countries.

Nevertheless, the OSCE does have the advantage of including all of Europe. In the period from 1990-92, quite a bit was heard about the promise of the OSCE as the framework for a new European architecture, but since then this prospect has fallen off the main screen. The principal reason for this is the war in the former Yugoslavia. Clearly, the OSCE has not been relevant in any way in the Yugoslav tragedy. I think, however, that blaming the OSCE is unfair. After all, as in all international institutions, it is the member-states that must make the decisions, and the member-states of the OSCE simply weren't prepared to support OSCE involvement. The OSCE has no peacekeeping capability at this time. Nevertheless, the inability of the OSCE to play any significant role in the former Yugoslavia has engendered skepticism—even if such skepticism is not warranted.

One would have thought that NATO would not survive the end of the Cold War. It is, after all, an institution that was created as a result of the Cold War. The *raison d'être* of the NATO alliance had been to keep the Cold War "cold," not "hot." NATO, however, has survived and has even done remarkably well during the past five years—better than one would have supposed in 1990 or 1991. There are three basic reasons for its survival. First, it is the only effective military alliance capable of taking organized action by integrating the military forces of a number of significant states. It does not

226

have any competition in that regard. Second, NATO has adapted to changed circumstances in a relatively imaginative way. Third, credit must be given to Manfred Wörner, who was the secretary general of NATO during this period of time, because as secretary general he staked out an agenda for NATO (which at times was ahead of the agendas of individual governments) and pursued it vigorously. Manfred Wörner passed away on 13 August 1994. His replacement, the former foreign minister of Belgium, Willy Claes, is a man who is not very well known in the international field, nor does he have any significant experience in political-security issues. That does not mean he will not succeed or that he will fail to rise to the occasion. There is no way of knowing the quality of his tenure. Yet if NATO is to continue its evolution successfully, it will need the same type of energetic leadership that Manfred Wörner gave it.

There are several components to the adaptation of NATO to changing circumstances. The first component is the North Atlantic Cooperation Council; second, the Combined Joint Task Forces; and third, the Partnership for Peace.

The North Atlantic Cooperation Council (NACC) was conceived in 1991 as a way to bring together the former Warsaw Pact countries and the NATO countries. The NACC was seen as a way to open and develop a dialogue between these two sets of approximately 18 countries. Over a period of time, the representatives of Poland, Hungary, Czechoslovakia, Rumania, Russia, and several other countries have come to Brussels (where NACC is located) for regular political discussions. The countries exchange military officers and hold seminars on issues such as defense strategy and arms control. These meetings are attempts to bring the militaries of these countries into the kind of international strategic dialogue that we have had in the West for several decades. Discussions have also been held on problems specific to the Eastern European countries, such as defense conversion and civil-military relations. The basic aim of the NACC has been to find a way to involve Eastern European countries in the affairs of NATO, to make them feel like a part of NATO rather than the enemies of NATO, as they were for several years.

The Combined Joint Task Forces (CJTF), which is less well known and is still very much embryonic, came into existence as a result of a meeting between the heads of NATO states in January 1994. The CJTF is a concept designed to deal with the fact that if and when NATO undertakes military action, the engagement is far more likely to take place outside of Europe than within Europe—in places like the Middle East or Africa. Given that assumption, consensus for joint military action outside of Europe will be far more difficult to achieve now that the Soviet threat—or any comparable monolithic threat—no longer exists. Therefore, countries that are part of and contribute to the NATO infrastructure and plan to take collective action in a "coalition of the willing" in response to specific incidents need to be brought together. This flexibility will give NATO the political ability to bring together an ad hoc group of NATO countries to accomplish certain goals—for example, peacekeeping in Rwanda—by using NATO experience and parts of the NATO command structure, but in such a way that those who want to participate can, and those who do not can stay out of it. The creation of the Combined Joint Task Force emphasizes the need for flexibility in the post-Cold War environment. Though it is still in the conceptual stage and is still being fleshed out in Brussels, the CJTF it is still a step in the right direction.

The Partnership for Peace (PFP) program is the product and resulting compromise of a grand debate between 1992 and 1993 over the question of which states should be included in the expansion of NATO. At this point, the success of this compromise is far from clear, although government spokesmen will be quick to tout its many attributes. The compromise reflects two views or poles of thought. On the one end are those who want to admit Eastern Europe—particularly Poland, Hungary, the Czech Republic, and Slovakia—into NATO immediately or as soon as possible. People and governments who take this view are primarily motivated by the need to assure those countries (and in time, perhaps, other potential members of NATO) that they will be supported in terms of security. They argue that including these countries into NATO is important, especially now, given the great uncertainty within Russia and the former Soviet Union, the growing nationalism in

Moscow, and the increasing talk about Russian spheres of influence, not only with regard to the Russian near abroad, but also potentially with regard to parts of the former Warsaw Pact.

At the other end of the spectrum are those motivated by the sense that although there is some need to eventually bring these countries into NATO, the urgency is not as great as has been depicted. Their second reason for delay is their belief that the West, or NATO, should not undertake steps that would be seen by the Russian political and military class as highly offensive. I have made three trips to Moscow in the past year. Most Russians with whom I have come in contact (with the exception of some international academics attending Western conferences) are quite negative about expanding NATO to include the Eastern European countries. NATO is, after all, the institution which the Russian public was taught and trained to think of as the enemy. What the Russians say is, "Why is it important to bring Poland, Hungary, and other countries into NATO? Is this move going to create an alliance against us?" The irony is that Russia is currently a member of the Partnership for Peace. Russia's membership in it raises the question of what the purpose of expanding NATO is. Is its purpose to give assurances against Russia, or to bring Russia into the European arena? A rather fundamental contradiction exists. Is Russia a friendly power, or a power we are ready to fight? This contradiction hasn't been resolved.

It is my belief that NATO's expansion should be slow for an additional reason beyond the question of Russian sensibilities. NATO is based on Article V of the North Atlantic Treaty, which provides for the automatic defense of NATO territory. An attack on one member of NATO is an attack on all. I am not sure that we have carefully thought through the implications of that provision. Is the United States prepared to guarantee the security of Bucharest and Bratislavia? The nuclear dimension of an expanded NATO in particular is a significant factor that needs to be carefully considered.

The Partnership for Peace is now doing a great deal of practical work in joint planning, joint military exercises, and so on. In some ways it does duplicate the North Atlantic Cooperation Council, but it is actually creating joint military activities in a way that the NACC did not. One may ask why are Polish-German joint maneuvers or American-Russian joint maneuvers necessary if they are never going to fight a war together. The answer is that these maneuvers represent a process of acculturation. The close military-to-military contacts that occur when they are in the field together are part of a process through which participants come to know each other better, trust each other more, and dispel the belief that they are targeting each other. Engagement in such joint maneuvers is especially important with regard to the Russian army because the impact of the Russian army on Russian politics should never be discounted. Meanwhile, the PFP countries are laying the groundwork and taking the steps that full acceptance into NATO would require.

Not surprisingly, a certain amount of disagreement exists within the West as to who should be admitted into NATO and with what speed. The major Western country that most favors early admittance of the Eastern European countries to NATO is Germany, and its support has been very consistent. Great Britain, on the other hand, is very reluctant and France and the United States lie somewhere in between the British and German positions. Even within the United States government, a wide variety of views exists. It has been reported that the incoming assistant secretary of state for European and Canadian affairs, Richard Holbrooke, who for the past nine months or so has been ambassador to Germany, is pushing hard for American support of full membership in NATO for some Eastern European countries. The U.S. Department of Defense, which looks at some of the practical aspects of this question, is more reluctant. Strobe Talbott, the deputy secretary of state, is very experienced in Russian affairs and is also lukewarm about bringing the Eastern European states immediately into NATO. Ultimately, the future of the Partnership for Peace and most related issues will depend upon what happens in Russia.

The third European institution that merits consideration is the Western European Union (WEU). Its future, surprisingly enough, may be more promising than that of NATO. By the future, I mean the next millennium, which is only about seven years away. Created in the 1950s, the WEU was a moribund organization for a long time, but it has been revived in the past three or four years. It is a West European security institution that has now become the defense arm of the European Union. It is basically a paper organization. There are no WEU armed forces. The military units that the WEU might use are the same military forces the British, French, Germans, and Italians have committed to NATO. To use the language of the day, these troops are "double-hatted"—they have two potential command structures. The WEU, however, does present a way by which the Europeans can take action and follow their interests independently of the United States, which is not possible within NATO. Although the WEU doesn't have any military forces, it has already conducted some activities. For example, the naval capabilities of the European countries in the Adriatic, which have been used to support some NATO and U.N. activities in the former Yugoslavia, have been orchestrated out of Brussels by the WEU.

The WEU is important because it embodies the notion of a European security and defense identity. It has a future not only because of that identity, but also because the United States is no longer posing an obstacle to the WEU. One of the unheralded but important changes that the Clinton administration has made with respect to European policy has been to "lift" the U.S. veto and encourage the development of an effective WEU. As one looks at the crystal ball beyond the year 2000, we are seeing the development of the twin pillar framework that John F. Kennedy foresaw in the early 1960s—the twin pillars being the United States and Europe linked by a loose NATO within which the Western Europeans have coalesced among themselves, and the United States is no longer the dominant or, as the French would say, hegemonic power in Europe.

In conclusion, we will have a melange of perhaps overlapping institutions. I am not particularly bothered by this state of affairs. At a time of transition and adaptation after 45 years of a fairly rigid Cold War situation, growth and accommodation are natural and to be expected. The WEU will gain a European identity that will be stronger than it is today or has been in the past. A sense of European identity will be politically important in symbolic terms. Ironically, the WEU as a military institution will not have much to do in Europe. Its effectiveness and presence will be felt primarily outside of Europe, which raises the question of whether the Europeans can develop a common foreign policy for dealing with matters outside Europe that are of interest to the European countries. They have had difficulty in this area thus far, but if Europe is going to develop politically and economically, it also must evolve in terms of a common foreign policy and a common security policy. Europeans must be prepared to undertake some joint activities either among themselves, with the United States, or with other countries, as particular situations arise. This notion is farfetched, but if a situation like Haiti should arise 10 or 15 years from now, WEU involvement along with the United States is conceivable, provided that the WEU countries supported American notions about the purpose of the intervention.

I see the future American role in NATO as being vastly different from what it is today. I believe NATO will become more Europeanized, but will continue to exist because it is the institutional framework that brings Europe and the United States together. One should not lose sight of the fact that the Russians—perhaps even the Ukrainians—will still have nuclear weapons in the thousands. There is real cause for concern with regard to the command and control of these systems and fissile materials. As long as that is the case, the Europeans will want the United States involved, and the United States will have an interest in Europe through NATO. Nevertheless, the OSCE will be the institution that could have the greatest growth. Barring resurging concern about Russia, the principal threats to European security will be ethnic conflict and antagonisms, civil strife, and disintegration, primarily within Eastern Europe and also parts of the former Soviet Union. In dealing with this type of situation, classic military force like NATO will be less relevant than activities that diplomats and peacekeepers can do best: conflict prevention, arbitration, mediation, conciliation, and fact-finding. Modalities of this type need to be developed further by the international community and are more applicable to the world of the future than they have been in the past. The OSCE is the institution that can achieve the most in these areas and is in fact very quietly gaining experience. The OSCE has had missions in Nagorno-Karabakh (the so-called Minsk Group, which has attempted to develop negotiations between the differing parties), Macedonia, Moldova, and elsewhere. The secretariat of the OSCE has now been brought together in Vienna, and a secretary general of the OSCE, Dr. Wilhelm Höynck, was appointed in June 1993.

Thus, the European security architecture, which already looks different today than it did five years ago, will look more different five years from now and probably even more different ten years from now. The United States will be relevant to Europe, but it will no longer be the leader that it was in the past. It will be a necessary and wanted participant and will play a role, but this situation will return the United States to its normal place rather than the dominant role that it has had in Europe since World War II.

QUESTION: What if, for example, eight members reach a consensus on pursuing a particular action, but the other eight members were either opposed or simply didn't want to participate? Could these other eight members veto the entire action? With that possibility in mind, how could any important action in a structure such as the WEU be taken without virtual consensus?

MR. PIERRE: The Combined Joint Task Force, to which you refer, is based on the idea that a lack of consensus should no longer impede joint action by those countries that are willing to act. For example, let's say a reason arises for some countries such as France, Italy, and Spain—but not Great Britain, the United States, Canada, or other members of NATO—to get involved in North Africa. The Combined Joint Task Force concept allows those countries that favor action to do something without requiring any involvement from those opposed. Such a situation does therefore point in the direction of moving away from the consensus ideal. The question is whether action would proceed if there were strong opposition in the North Atlantic Council. That possibility has not yet been tested. By allowing greater flexibility than in the past, the Combined Joint Task Force concept may represent a historic change.

The notion of consensus, to which NATO became so accustomed, was based on the assumption that the only threat that would prompt NATO action would be a Russian or Soviet threat;

therefore, all of the members of NATO had a common interest. Today, however, the situation has changed considerably. With the Cold War over, NATO countries face new threats—for example, the upheaval in Maghreb—upon which there may be no agreement. If NATO expands to 20 or 25 countries, consensus will be even harder to reach. The expansion of NATO (to the extent that it occurs) can work numerically against the notion of consensus, which would therefore be one reasons to develop a more flexible approach.

QUESTION: One of the two main reasons for forming NATO was to integrate Germany into a Western European or North Atlantic defense arrangement. That goal was accomplished in the 1950s. The Cold War is now over, but Germany is the strongest power in Europe. How will the West proceed as far as Germany is concerned?

MR. PIERRE: The big issue in Germany is still the integration of its two parts. Keeping in mind that I have never been to the eastern part of Germany except when it was still Communist, my perception is that its sense of "Easterness" has remained strong and perhaps has even increased in some ways in the last year or two. This sense is significant because it has many implications in terms of how Germans vote, how they look at their role in Europe with respect to both the East and the West, and how they think of themselves as Germans. The West Germans, and what I would call the Bonn political class, remain committed to the integration of Germany as a bulwark of Western institutions. Whether Germany will be the kind of psychological anchor of Western Europe in the future that it has been in the past is somewhat uncertain. This is one reason the French ought to fear the Germans less. In the early 1990s, during the debate about the future of the European Community, there was a great deal of concern—particularly in France, but to some extent elsewhere—that Germany was going to become the great Leviathan in Europe and therefore dominate the entire continent. Instead, what has happened is that Germany has become one of the greatest supporters of European integration. Germany may have acquired 17 million additional people and a 30-percent increase in territory, but it has also acquired many problems

234

and economic and social tasks that will direct its focus domestically while maintaining good relations with the East. It is not surprising that the Germans have been the greatest proponents of expanding NATO or that they are very open to augmenting Eastern European access to the European Union markets. I am not worried about Germany becoming militaristic, nationalistic, or fascist.

Another question is whether the Germans, being the Germans or being in many ways the most significant and important nation in Europe, will now be prepared to undertake the international role that the United States would like them to take. Will they become members of the U.N. Security Council? The German Constitutional Court recently ruled that Germany could take part in international peacekeeping activities, but beyond that ruling, I haven't seen much evidence of their being ready to participate in peacekeeping. A great deal depends on the younger generation in Germany.

QUESTION: One of the surprising things that I found was that the tendency toward pacifism is much greater than the tendency toward militarism among young intelligent Germans. That trend is also found in Japan. We have to remember that Germany was a completely defeated country. These young people grew up not really feeling any responsibility for the Hitler period, but at the same time they say, "We never want to entrust our destiny to the military and that gang of people again." I agree that Germany isn't going to be a military power in its own right, but my question is what will Germany see as its national interest in Eastern Europe in the context of this new Europe? Will Germany's national interests come at the expense of the Russians?

MR. PIERRE: As best as can be foreseen at this time, German expansion eastward will be constructive economic expansion. Germany continues to be an extremely important and interesting place to keep watch, but at this point the United States should not think of it as a vast disturber of European stability.

NARRATOR: We thank Mr. Pierre for his very wise and thoughtful discussion on the future of NATO.